Chapter One

Introduction

In 2014, the Judicial Committee of the Highwood Congregation of Jeho-vah's Witnesses in Calgary, Alberta, "disfellowshipped" Randy Wall. The committee determined Wall had failed to be "sufficiently repentant" for the sinful behaviour of drunkenness and verbally abusing his wife (Bronskill 2018). Wall, a real estate agent, was prohibited from speak-ing to other members of the congregation about non-spiritual matters. This hurt his business, as the bulk of his clients were his co-religionists. Wall sought to have his disfellowship overturned through the congrega-tion's own appeal processes. Ultimately unsuccessful in this pursuit, Wall turned to the courts to pursue judicial review.

Essentially, the courts were being asked to adjudicate the private dis-ciplinary actions of a church. Wall's case eventually went all the way to the Supreme Court of Canada, where he argued that the decision of the congregation's Judicial Committee was inconsistent with the prin-ciples of natural justice and the duty of fairness. Writing for a unanimous Supreme Court, Justice Rowe declined to overturn the committee's decision and quashed the original application for judicial review (*High-wood Congregation of Jehovah's Witnesses v. Wall* 2018). The Court found that judicial review was not available to Wall because there was no pub-lic activity (or "state action"), as Wall's congregation was a civil-society group without any statutory basis (paras. 3, 12). Justice Rowe held that "issues of theology are not justiciable," reminding Wall that "private par-ties cannot seek judicial review to solve disputes that may arise between them; rather, their claims must be founded on a valid cause of action" (paras. 12–13). In addressing the relevance of the Canadian Charter of Rights and Freedoms, Justice Rowe reiterated the Court's long-standing approach to the Charter's role in private legal disputes:

> As this Court held in *RWDSU v. Dolphin Delivery* [1986] ... the *Charter* does not apply to private litigation. Section 32 specifies that the *Charter* applies

to the legislative, executive and administrative branches of government ...
The *Charter* does not directly apply to this dispute as no state action is being
challenged, although the *Charter* may inform the development of the common law ... In the end, religious groups are free to determine their own
membership and rules; courts will not intervene in such matters save where
it is necessary to resolve an underlying legal dispute (*Highwood Congregation
of Jehovah's Witnesses v. Wall* 2018, para. 39).

The Court's framing of the Charter's relationship to the private sphere –
that it only applies directly to state action rather than private disputes –
is emblematic of the traditional liberal approach to constitutionalism,
which strives to preserve the distinction between public and private
spheres. Yet the Court has not always been so clear as to where this line
should be drawn. Its decision in *Wall*, and the difficulty with which it and
other high courts in the Commonwealth have policed the line between
public and private, raises several questions addressed in this book. What
is the proper scope of a constitution? Should the Charter be relevant to
private disputes? Once an issue becomes judicialized, can it be reversed?
And if everything becomes judicialized, what are the implications for the
relationship between courts and legislatures? Each of these matters are
areas currently in flux as part of an ongoing clash of constitutionalisms
in Canada and around the Commonwealth.

This book contributes to a debate within the tradition of liberal-democratic constitutionalism about how best to protect rights. One side of
that debate (contemporarily identified as "political constitutionalism")
holds that rights are best protected through "political" channels, such as
the elected offices of government. The competing view ("legal constitutionalism") holds that rights are best conceived as legal categories under
the primary care and supervision of the judiciary. This "clash of constitutionalisms" has many facets, some of which deserve more attention
than they have thus far received. One aim of this study is to shed light
on some of the debate's still shaded nooks and crannies. Another aim is
to provide a novel integration of many of the debate's dimensions. Both
aims are fostered by a comparative approach to the issues, with a particular focus on the quarrels between political and legal constitutionalism in
Canada, New Zealand, and the United Kingdom.

Political and legal constitutionalism provide differing institutional and
normative accounts of constitutional democracy, each informed by ideational priors about rights protection. From the political-constitutional
perspective, rights ought to be debated, defined, and reconsidered
through a battery of democratic and non-judicial checks and balances
such as bicameralism, federalism, parliamentary politics, and electoral
accountability (Bellamy 2007; Tomkins 2005; Waldron 2016). Political

constitutionalism is more than simple majoritarianism or populism. It holds that rights conflicts are about reasonable disagreements and that democratic processes possess more legitimacy and are more effective than the judiciary at resolving these disagreements. As such, political constitutionalists believe in both the capacity and the superiority of legislative institutions to articulate and define limits on rights (Ajzenstat 1997; Waldron 1999), and as a result possess a skepticism about judicial decision makers.[1] By contrast, legal constitutionalists hold that limits on government power, particularly limits relating to rights and freedoms, are best determined by the judiciary (Allan 1993; Dworkin 1996; Waluchow 2007). Because of security of tenure and judicial independence, judges are institutionally best suited to define the constitution. Certain matters (particularly matters related to rights) should not be left to ordinary law, but should instead be based on higher law that is both difficult to change and subject to judicial review. Legal constitutionalism thus provides a theoretical basis for the necessity of both a constitutional bill of rights and judicial interpretative supremacy.

Political constitutionalism was the prevalent view at the American founding,[2] where the initial 1789 Constitution lacked an explicit bill of rights. During the ratification debates, Alexander Hamilton maintained that no such bill was needed because the rest of the Constitution – i.e., the structural constitution, with its checks and balances – was "in every rational sense, and to every purpose ... a bill of rights" (Hamilton et al. [1788] 2003, 421). This was a classic statement of what we now call political constitutionalism (Bellamy 2007; Ceaser 2012; Gee and Webber 2010; Tomkins 2005).[3]

It is important to note that Hamilton was not opposed to legal constitutionalism in all respects. Indeed, in *Federalist No. 78*, he justifies judicial power with respect to the structural constitution. Hamilton stresses the

---

1 This skepticism is reinforced by studies showing how judicial attitudes and ideology influence high courts' constitutional decision making (Segal and Spaeth 1993; Ostberg and Wetstein 2007). In contrast to the attitudinal approach favoured by some political scientists, legal constitutionalists are more likely to believe that law and doctrine have independent force, and less likely to view judicial decisions as the reflection of personal policy preferences.

2 In *Federalist No. 57*, Madison states that the "aim" of a "political Constitution" places "effectual precautions" (i.e., institutional checks and balances) on rulers who will pursue the common good for society (Hamilton et al. [1788] 2003, 277).

3 Gardbaum notes that the "proto-argument for both legal and political constitutionalism can be found in the *Federalist Papers*." He recommends a comparison of "Madison's reliance on structural/political limits on governmental power in Nos. 10 and 51 with Hamilton's arguments for legal constitutionalism and judicial review in No. 78" ([1788] 2013, 22n7).

judiciary would be the "weakest branch" – a significant statement about the nature of judicial power. Hamilton recognizes that circumstances will necessitate the judiciary invalidating unconstitutional behaviour by the executive or the legislature (Banfield and Knopff 2009, 15). But Hamilton's conception of judicial invalidation is quite limited. He thought the judiciary would only be called on to void "acts contrary to the manifest tenor of the constitution" ([1788] 2003, 379). Hamilton simply saw no need to extend this kind of legal constitutionalism into the realm of rights protection.[4]

As is well known, Hamilton soon lost this argument when the United States Bill of Rights, in the form of the first ten amendments to the Constitution, came into effect in 1791. True, judicial enforcement of the Bill of Rights did not play a substantive role for a considerable period,[5] but it eventually became a significant dimension of American political life. Today, strong judicial supervision and enforcement of the US Bill of Rights is the example par excellence of legal constitutionalism in the realm of rights protection (Tushnet 2016).

The bill-of-rights skepticism of political constitutionalism persisted much longer elsewhere, including in Westminster parliamentary democracies such as the United Kingdom, Canada, and New Zealand, which until recently lacked formal bills of rights (Erdos 2010). Canada enacted a statutory bill of rights in 1960, but it had relatively little effect (Hiebert 2004, 1969), and the now prominent Canadian Charter of Rights and Freedoms was adopted in 1982, nearly two centuries after the US Bill of Rights. New Zealand followed with its Bill of Rights Act (NZBORA) in 1990, and the United Kingdom adopted the Human Rights Act (HRA) in 1998.

---

4 Peter Russell (1983b) makes a similar distinction with respect to the judicial role in the Charter era. Russell predicted that courts would not be called upon to deal with *prima facie* violations of "core rights" (i.e., religious toleration, political freedoms) but rather asked to weigh in on peripheral questions stemming from core rights (e.g., hate speech laws). These secondary issues are really matters of reasonable disagreement rather than actions against the "manifest tenor" of the Constitution, to use Hamilton's language. The contestability of these issues is why the elected branches ought to be able to participate in shaping them, according to political constitutionalists (Bellamy 2011, 90–3).

5 The US Supreme Court's prominence is a relatively recent development. It was not until the Bill of Rights was "incorporated" and began to apply to both state as well as federal law that judicial power began to expand. Blockbuster decisions of the Warren Court, such as *Brown v. Board of Education* (1954) (desegregating public schools) and *Roe v. Wade* (1973) (overturning state restrictions on abortion) are not representative of the Court's more historically restrained role.

The rights documents in Canada, New Zealand, and the United Kingdom were part of a broader proliferation of such documents in the latter half of the twentieth century (Epp 1998; Hirschl 2004), a proliferation so extensive that the Diceyan tradition of parliamentary supremacy (Ajzenstat 1997) without a bill of rights exists almost nowhere. Australia now stands out as the major exception in the liberal-democratic world because it lacks a bill of rights, except in two subnational jurisdictions, the state of Victoria and the Australian Capital Territory (ACT), which have enacted statutory bills of rights.

In one way of thinking, the kinds of bills of rights adopted by New Zealand, the United Kingdom, Victoria, and the ACT do not merit the label "constitutional," both because they are ordinary statutes subject to legally easy repeal, rather than documents entrenched by difficult amendment procedures, and because they can be ignored by legislatures. Others, emphasizing the moral difficulty of repealing or ignoring rights documents, consider them at least quasi-constitutional (Masterman and Leigh 2013, 1–2; Smillie 2006, 183), and often include them in discussions of constitutionalism.[6] Stephen Gardbaum (2013), for example, entitles his book on Commonwealth bills of rights *The New Commonwealth Model of Constitutionalism*. The present study will follow Gardbaum's usage, not least because the concepts of political and legal constitutionalism can be more readily (and appropriately) used to illuminate and compare the different kinds of rights documents.

The constitutional status of the United Kingdom's HRA is reinforced by its relationship to the European Convention on Human Rights (ECHR). The HRA was adopted to incorporate the ECHR (an international treaty signed by the British government in 1950) more explicitly into the United Kingdom's domestic law,[7] thus enabling British citizens to pursue rights-based litigation in their own courts for the first time, though they can appeal to the European Court on Human Rights (ECtHR) in Strasbourg, which formally has the "final say" on matters

---

6 Many scholars consider these statutory bills of rights as having "constitutional status" (Hirschl 2004, 26; Kavanagh 2009, 1), even though it is formally much easier to repeal or modify these acts than it is to amend the Canadian Charter or the American Bill of Rights. The NZBORA and the HRA can be viewed as "organic statutes" – that is, statutes codifying constitutional rules (Malcolmson et al. 2016, 18). Traditional organic statutes include the United Kingdom's Reform Act (1832), Parliament Act (1911), and, up until recently, the 1875 Canadian Supreme Court Act (see *Reference Re Supreme Court Act ss 5 and 6* 2014).

7 The HRA's first provision recognizes the "Convention rights" (i.e., the rights and freedoms) of the ECHR and then cites a schedule in the act reproducing verbatim the ECHR articles 2–12 and 14.

related to Convention rights. However, while section 2 of the HRA states that UK courts ought to consider ECtHR rulings in their own jurisprudence, it does not say they are bound by them (Gardbaum 2013, 157).

Does the modern expansion of bills of rights represent the victory of legal constitutionalism? Not if one adopts Gardbaum's definition of legal constitutionalism as involving "the power of courts to disapply acts" (2013, 22). This judicial power to "disapply" or "invalidate" – the central feature of what Mark Tushnet (2002, 2784) calls "strong-form" judicial review – is famously exercised by American judges under the US Constitution, but is not available to their New Zealand or British counterparts under the statutory bills of rights in those countries. The latter documents give courts only the "weak-form" power (Tushnet 2002, 2786) to interpret legislation in accordance with relevant rights document *when possible*; if a rights-friendly interpretation is not possible, the United Kingdom's HRA gives courts the authority to explicitly "declare" the "incompatibility" between the statute and protected rights. New Zealand's NZBORA does not explicitly provide for such declarations of incompatibility or inconsistency, but they have been found to be implicit. In such cases of clear conflict, however, the rights-infringing statute remains in force, unless the legislature *chooses* to change it in response to the judicial ruling. This weak-form strategy obviously preserves more parliamentary supremacy than exists under strong-form systems. In other words, the fact that legal constitutionalists have won the main battle – whether or not to have a documentary bill of rights – does not mean the defeat of political constitutionalism (Tushnet 2002, 89). The debate now concerns the best *kind* of rights document.

For completeness, it is worth mentioning that there are similarly strong and weak forms of the common-law constitutionalism – i.e., unwritten constitutionalism (Goldsworthy 2008, 289, 293).[8] According to Robert Leckey (2015, 35), "weak common-law constitutionalists emphasize the judiciary's reference to common-law values and presumptions when

---

8 Some legal constitutionalists argue courts have the authority to protect certain deep rights, which cannot be infringed even by so-called supreme parliaments in regimes with unwritten constitutions, even in the absence of formal rights documents (Gardbaum 2013, 23–5). This is known as "common-law constitutionalism" because the non-documentary rights are embedded in the historical case-by-case development of judge-made common law (Allan 1993; Poole 2003; Waluchow 2007). Although common-law constitutionalism is a fascinating (and controversial) version of legal constitutionalism – one that will appear occasionally in these pages – this study will emphasize the more prevalent (indeed, dominant) version of legal constitutionalism, in which judges derive their rights-protecting authority from an explicitly legal rights document.

construing statutes, although conceding that sufficiently clear legislation may effectively override fundamental values." Ordinary legislation, in other words, can trump weak-form common-law rights just as they can trump weak-form bills of rights. By contrast, "strong common-law constitutionalists, tracing even parliamentary sovereignty to the common law, see judges as refusing to enforce purported legislation that overrides common-law rights or fundamental values" (Leckey 2015, 35). In this version of common-law constitutionalism, judges possess the kind of power to "disapply" or invalidate legislation enjoyed by judges under entrenched documents like the US Constitution. Leckey's "strong common-law constitutionalists" are what Gardbaum (2013, 23–4) identifies with "legal constitutionalism."

For Gardbaum, documents like New Zealand's NZBORA or the United Kingdom's HRA "offer a third institutional form of constitutionalism in between" political constitutionalism defined as legislative supremacy, and legal constitutionalism defined as constitutionally based judicial supremacy (2013, 25). Australian scholar Julie Debeljak (2002, 324) likewise favours "constitutional and legislative structures that encourage and respect an inter-institutional dialogue" over structures that privilege either legislative or judicial monopolies on rights definition. Canada's Charter of Rights and Freedoms falls within this "third option" because, although it gives courts a US-style invalidation mandate, it also allows legislatures to reverse such invalidations by employing a so-called notwithstanding clause. The existence of Gardbaum's "third option," or "new model" of constitutionalism, means that legal constitutionalism – again, defined in judicial supremacist terms – has not won a complete victory.[9]

Rejection of "the full veto power of judicial supremacy" is not the only way in which Gardbaum's third-option regimes preserve a role for the political branches in defining and protecting rights. They do so also by mandating "pre-enactment political rights review" (2013, 25–6). Under section 7 of New Zealand's NZBORA, for example, the attorney general must alert the legislature to any way in which a proposed bill "appears to be inconsistent" with NZBORA rights. Section 19 of the UK's HRA imposes a similar duty on the minister shepherding a bill through either house of Parliament. There is no explicit provision of this kind in the Canadian Charter of Rights and Freedoms, but the federal minister of justice is legislatively required to examine bills for consistency with the Charter, and

---

9 It is odd, then, to find Gardbaum asserting at one point – though in a footnote – that "as a practical matter, the real world debate has been decisively won by legal constitutionalism" (2013, 24n14).

to report any inconsistencies to the House of Commons. In addition to pre-enactment political rights review, Gardbaum's third-option regimes also provide kinds of post-litigation rights review by the legislature that do not exist in fully strong-form regimes. The Canadian notwithstanding clause is one example; the ability of the New Zealand and UK legislatures to ignore judicial rulings of rights incompatibility is another.

While all of these features of Gardbaum's new Commonwealth model generate debate between political and legal constitutionalists, this study will not address the matter of pre-enactment political review. Others have shed valuable light on this corner of the debate within the Canadian context (Hiebert 2002; Kelly 2005, 2009), and more recently in the other parliamentary systems under consideration (Hiebert and Kelly 2015). I will focus instead on the debates between political and legal constitutionalists, both on and off the bench, about judicial review and post-litigation political review in Canada, New Zealand, and the United Kingdom. As is already apparent, comparative reference to the strong-form United States cannot be avoided, and American examples and debates will thus be brought into the analysis where appropriate. Australia will also provide occasional comparative context. The primary focus, however, is on debates generated by the Canadian Charter of Rights and Freedoms, New Zealand's Bill of Rights Act, and the UK Human Rights Act – all three examples of Gardbaum's "new Commonwealth model."

Gardbaum's new Commonwealth model surely enhances legally based judicial power as compared to the simple parliamentary supremacy of traditional political constitutionalism. At the same time, of course, it preserves more legislative authority (hence political constitutionalism) with respect to rights issues than do systems of strong-form judicial review. For this reason, I prefer to think of the modern Commonwealth systems less as a stand-alone "third option" between political constitutionalism and legal constitutionalism than as an attempt to blend political and legal constitutionalism. Mark Elliott (2012, online) comes to a similar conclusion,[10] arguing that "the question is not whether [a regime] has a political or legal constitution, but the appropriate balance between political and legal forces and constraints in any particular context and the wider lessons to be drawn for our understanding of the constitution."

The Commonwealth model, in other words, falls into the category of what James Ceaser calls "compound regimes," which blend competing

---

10 As does Kent Roach in the revised edition of his book *The Supreme Court on Trial* when he observes that a "dialogical or interactional approach to judicial review draws on the virtues of both political and legal constitutionalism" (2016, 407).

principles (1990, 8). For Ceaser, liberal democracy as a whole is a "compound" of "liberalism" (involving limited government in the name of rights protection) and democracy (involving majoritarian decision making). What is true of the larger compound of liberal democracy is also true of its rights-protecting component, inasmuch as bills of rights reflect a compound of political and legal constitutionalism.

Thinking of institutions in this way naturally focuses attention on the tensions between the opposing dimensions of any particular blend or compound – between liberal democracy's democratic majoritarianism and its liberal rights protection, for example. Because the "guiding expectations" of compound institutions are ambiguous, they will "always be subject to interpretation, debate, and contestation" (Mahoney and Thelen 2009, 11). One should, in short, expect an ongoing politics of interpretation in which the partisans of an institution's opposing dimensions continue their struggle, perhaps shifting the balance over time in one direction or the other.[11]

How does this politics of interpretation affect the middle-ground blend of political and legal constitutionalism embodied in Gardbaum's Commonwealth model of rights protection? Is Tushnet right (2003b, 824) in thinking that weak-form systems might escalate over time into the more pronounced legal constitutionalism of strong-form systems? Or, to turn the coin over, can one discern the continuing, though perhaps rearguard, resistance of political constitutionalism in the jurisprudence of a strong-form system? How, in short, does the interpretive battle between the perspectives of political and legal constitutionalism play out in practice under the different kinds of rights documents that have emerged in recent decades? That is an animating question of this study. To answer it, this book takes a cross-national interdisciplinary approach, drawing from legal studies, political science, and constitutional theory. This project involves a qualitative comparison of high court decisions from Canada, New Zealand, and the United Kingdom, three Commonwealth states chosen because they adopted rights documents in the late twentieth century. It focuses on leading judicial decisions related to constitutional application and inter-institutional dialogue by the highest courts in these countries. It then situates these decisions within the debates between political and legal constitutionalists, paying particular attention to how "constitutional

---

11 Robert Schertzer describes a similar process in the conflicts around competing perspectives of federalism: "As a result of this mobilization by groups and the associated belief of their particular perspective, the Canadian federation has developed in such a way that the subscribers of each model can point to elements of the legal and institutional structure of the state to support their perspective" (2016, 11).

culture" affects how these disagreements play out in each country (Palmer 2007). David Erdos observes how "cultural self-conceptions of the judiciary have proved critical in determining ... the legal impact" of bills of rights (2009, 96). This approach stresses that a nation's legal or constitutional "culture," in terms of its commitment to parliamentary sovereignty, can temper the expansion of judicial power in some contexts (Geddis and Fenton 2008; Hunt 1999; LaSelva 2018). In doing so, it builds on research from historical institutional scholars of law and politics to consider how "broader structural and institutional factors" such as "norms, values, and ideas" influence judicial decisions (Macfarlane 2013b, 31; see also Smith 2008). Such norms include the constitutional culture within each case country, and this helps contextualize how the disagreements of each side in the clash of constitutionalisms take place.

Assessing how rights documents have shaped the battle between political and legal constitutionalism also requires interrogating the aforementioned distinction between strong-form and weak-form judicial review. Political constitutionalism clearly animated the choice of weak-form Commonwealth bills of rights. While legal constitutionalists were successful in securing judicially interpreted rights documents through their very adoption, political constitutionalism was present in the design stage of each document, as shown by the ambivalence towards judicial power expressed by the framers (Erdos 2010, 94, 101, 121–2; Dodek 2018, 341). In Canada, New Zealand, and the United Kingdom, constitutional framers rejected the strong-form invalidation mandate of American judicial review because it gave too much policymaking power to judges (Leane 2004, 153; Rishworth 2004, 255). They were certainly prepared to enhance judicial power to some extent, but they retained enough political constitutionalism to want a more robust interaction – or "dialogue" – between the judicial and political branches of government than seemed possible with an unconstrained invalidation mandate (Geddis and Fenton 2008, 735; Jackson 2007, 93). In Canada's Charter of Rights and Freedoms, that political-constitutionalist desire expressed itself in two main ways. First, the Charter explicitly invites governments to justify a statutory infringement of rights as the kind of "reasonable limit" that "can be demonstrably justified in a free and democratic society" (section 1). Second, legislatures can reverse some rights-based judicial invalidations by invoking the notwithstanding clause (section 33) of the Charter. New Zealand replicated Canada's "reasonable limits" clause in section 5 of its rights document, but the drafters of both New Zealand's NZBORA and the UK's HRA considered the Canadian notwithstanding provision to be a largely ineffective counterbalance to legal constitutionalism. Both documents thus went further in the weak-form direction, restricting judges to an interpretive mandate with no power of invalidation. These debates about what I call "constitutional strength" are explored in chapter 2.

Political and legal constitutionalists disagree not only about issues of constitutional strength but also about what I will call "constitutional reach." Just how much of human activity is covered by the relevant rights document, whatever its strength? How far does it reach? Political constitutionalists generally want to restrict reach, thus preserving constitution-free zones in which political actors can operate without judicial interference. The Supreme Court of Canada's decision in *Wall*, which found private religious disputes beyond the scope of Charter review, is an example of limited constitutional reach. For their part, legal constitutionalists want to extend the reach of judicially applicable constitutional documents, including, in some circumstances, to private religious disputes. The scope of reach itself raises two distinct questions: First, how much of the public sector (or "state action") is covered by the relevant document? Second, how much of the private sector is covered? These questions are explored in chapters 3 and 4, respectively.

The question of constitutional reach into the private sphere is especially intriguing. While everyone agrees that rights documents apply directly to the executive and legislative activities of the state as it interacts with private individuals, the extent to which (and the ways by which) they might apply to the actions of private actors with each other involves a second clash of constitutionalisms, the clash between "liberal constitutionalism," which sees constitutions mainly as limiting the state in order to protect private liberty, and "post-liberal constitutionalism," which wants constitutions to require government regulation of the private sphere in the name of equality and a differently understood liberty (Bateman 2015, 2018; Mix-Ross 2009; Tushnet 2008b). The identification of the interaction between liberal and post-liberal constitutionalism, on the one hand, and political and legal constitutionalism, on the other, is a significant contribution of this study. Chapter 4 shows that in general – though not always – post-liberal constitutionalists favour greater constitutional reach than do liberal constitutionalists.

As both chapters 3 and 4 demonstrate, expansive interpretation of the relevant rights document is a prominent way of extending constitutional reach. Judges of a legal-constitutionalist bent have maintained, for example, that a document explicitly protecting certain dimensions of privacy – for example, the prohibition of "unreasonable search and seizure" – implies the broader protection of privacy as such, and thus reaches such unwritten matters as personal privacy (see *Hosking v. Runting* 2004). Political constitutionalists, including judges of that persuasion, dissent from this approach, arguing that stretching legal language too far involves creating new rights rather than applying existing ones. What legal constitutionalists see as the appropriate interpretation of a rights documents appears as dangerously "strained interpretation" to political constitutionalists.

Regarding the private sector, no one doubts that rights documents apply to statutes that govern "private" interactions (e.g., statutes governing marriage and divorce); such statutes are clearly forms of state action and thus belong to the issue of public-sector reach. But what about the considerable realm of private action that is not subject to statutes? There are, to be sure, completely private actions – say, the choice of friends – that are altogether beyond legal control, but much of the private sector is not this kind of lawless place. Some ostensibly private issues (e.g., marriage and divorce) are governed by statute; others may not be governed by statute but are governed by non-statutory judge-made "common law" (e.g., tort and contract law). Do rights documents reach such "private" common law to the same extent, and in much the same way, as they reach public statutes? This question about private common law is one of the neglected nooks and crannies of the debate between political and legal constitutionalism illuminated by this study. It turns out to be a difficult question – difficult enough that in Canada, for example, courts have avoided taking a clear stance, seeking instead to bring "private common law" within the reach of Charter *influence* without subjecting it to the full weight of Charter *application*. Similar doctrinal developments have occurred in New Zealand and the United Kingdom. These controversies about private common law lie at the heart of chapter 4.

Common law affects not only private action but also public or state action. Important areas of "public law" – the law governing state institutions and the interaction between the state and individuals (e.g., criminal law) – continue to be governed by judge-made common law (e.g., the *mens rea* and *actus reus* requirements in criminal cases). Common law as whole, in both its public and private dimensions, poses additional understudied issues in the debate between political and legal constitutionalism, issues addressed in chapter 5.

Chapter 5 shows how considerations of legal hierarchy affect debates about constitutional reach over both public and private common law. Contrary to strong-form common-law constitutionalism, the orthodox view holds that supremacy of Parliament trumps conflicting common law of both kinds (Hausegger, Hennigar, and Riddell 2015, 11). In other words, statutes enacted by representative legislatures are "hierarchically superior to the common law" (Reichman 2002, 340) and can displace judicially produced common-law rules. This is not always easy because of the "staying power" (from a legislative perspective) of a policy status quo, including a judicially changed status quo (Flanagan 1997; Manfredi 2007; Morton 2001), but it arguably becomes even more difficult if the judicial common-law innovation purports to implement the norms embodied in rights documents (Reichman 2002, 329–30; Tushnet 1995, 259).

In the weak-form systems of New Zealand and the United Kingdom, a determined legislature can certainly enact a statute reversing a rights-based common-law innovation, with that statute then being open to interpretation and findings of inconsistency in subsequent litigation. Such back-and-forth between the judicial and legislative branches arguably counts as the kind of inter-institutional dialogue that leads political constitutionalists to prefer weak-form judicial review.

But what happens when courts base common-law innovation on strong-form constitutional documents with an invalidation mandate? This question is particularly interesting in the Canadian context, where it involves the circumstances under which the Charter's section 33 notwithstanding clause should (or must) be used to reverse a common-law innovation. Political constitutionalists point out that government does not always get to mount a "reasonable limits" defence of the pre-innovation common law as it generally does with impugned statutes, and that no litigation involving a reasonable limits defence will occur about legislation with a notwithstanding clause. Objecting to the loss of "reasonable limits" dialogue, they argue for the intermediate possibility of legislatively reversing a rights-based common-law innovation without a notwithstanding clause, allowing governments to mount a reasonable limits defence in a subsequent challenge to the statute (Baker and Knopff 2002; Knopff et al. 2017). Legal constitutionalists, on the other hand, tend to deplore this intermediate option and insist on a notwithstanding clause as the only legitimate way of reversing a rights-based common-law innovation (Roach 2016). This debate is taken up in chapter 5.

Chapters 6 and 7 turn to the debate between political and legal constitutionalists about rights-based statutory interpretation. This debate is prominent in such weak-form regimes as New Zealand and the United Kingdom, where the rights documents give judges mainly an interpretive mandate with respect to statutes, but it also occurs in regimes like Canada's, where judges enjoy an invalidation mandate. Recall that the NZBORA and HRA emphasize that judges should interpret legislation to conform to the bill of rights if possible. Extending the reach of the bill of rights through expansive interpretation of its provisions (the subject of chapters 3 and 4) means more standards that legislation should be interpreted to respect. But if legislation is clearly inconsistent or incompatible with the rights document, whatever its reach, that legislation remains in place and fully applicable. At this point, legal authority ends and the political process takes over. It is up to the political branches to decide whether or how to respond to a judicial finding of inconsistency. Indeed, in the UK case, an official "declaration of incompatibility" is designed to trigger political consideration and response. Moreover, leaving in place what judges find incompatible is a legitimate outcome – at least to the political-constitutionalist mind.

Leaving in place what judges consider a rights-infringing law does not sit nearly as well with legal constitutionalists, however. Rather than risk this outcome, judges of the legal-constitutionalist persuasion some-times work extra hard to come up with a rights-friendly interpretation of a statute rather than finding it inconsistent with the rights document. Here, we re-encounter the concept of "strained interpretation." In other words, as with expansive interpretation of the rights document, debates arise about whether the judicial interpretation stretches statutory lan-guage beyond reasonable bounds. What legal constitutionalists persuade themselves is a plausible interpretation of ambiguous statutory language sometimes appears to political constitutionalists as the illegitimately "strained interpretation" of the statute. True, the legislature could respond by re-enacting what disturbed the judges in even clearer terms. Insofar as it is more difficult to actively reverse the judicial construction of a statute than to passively ignore a judicial finding of inconsistency, however, judges in the legal-constitutionalist camp may have a strategic preference for "strained" statutory interpretation. That, at least, is what worries political constitutionalists.

Interestingly, the issue of strained statutory interpretation also arises in regimes like Canada, where judges enjoy the stronger invalidation mandate. The existence of the invalidation option does not mean the absence of a statutory interpretation option, although the interpretive option is less explicit in strong-form documents than in weak-form ones (Leckey 2015, 94). Judges working in a strong-form context, in other words, sometimes prefer a rights-compatible statutory interpretation that allows them to uphold an impugned statute to a rights-infringing interpretation that would require them to strike it down. Here, too, debates about strained interpretation arise, though with some additional complications that will be explored in chapter 7.

What follows is a study of political thought, or, more precisely, of con-stitutional thought as a form of political thought. It is not an exercise in constitutional law. Although the raw materials for this study are often legal texts, judicial decisions, and legal commentary, no attempt is made to comprehensively canvass the evolution or current state of case law for any constitutional issue. The goal, rather, is to select and analyze

illustrative examples of the positions taken by legal and political constitutionalists in their disagreements about how best to balance powers
exercised by the judiciary and the other branches of government. How
much of life and policy to legalize and judicialize is ultimately a *political* question, even when it is brought to light through careful analysis
of selected judicial opinions and legal literature. This book is thus an
application of what Jeremy Waldron (2016, 6) calls "*political* political theory" – the examination of political institutions through political theory
by considering "the way our political institutions house and frame our
disagreements about social ideals." As a study of multiple countries, it is
also relevant to comparative constitutional studies (see Glendon 1987;
Hirschl 2004; Jacobsohn 2010).

Finally, by comparing rights protection in three countries, this study
contributes to comparative political science, particularly with respect to
institutional design. Constitutional politics, argues Christopher Manfredi, "can be conceptualized as a competitive game of institutional
design" (1997, 113). That game consists of "macro" and "micro" constitutional changes. Macro-changes are formal amendments – like the
decision to add a bill of rights – whereas micro-changes can take place
through the interpretative application and disagreement about formal
rules (114). By exploring institutional design and rights adjudication,
this study explores the effect of macro and micro constitutional changes
over time. On the macro side, the battles of political and legal constitutionalism point to different institutional designs, which are reflected in
the different rights documents in Canada, New Zealand, and the United
Kingdom. I examine those designs mainly as a way of clarifying the political thought involved in the contemporary "clash of constitutionalisms";
they are among the illustrative examples chosen to illustrate the disagreements in this clash. Far from ending with the original institutional
design of the different rights documents, of course, the struggle continues in an ongoing "micro" politics of interpretation in which each side
seeks to read its preferences into the different documents. The institutional design and interpretive struggles explored throughout this study
amount to a *political* clash of competing lines of constitutional thought,
which are illuminated through comparative investigation. My aim is not
to resolve the issues in this clash but to clarify the competing lines of
thinking about these issues by identifying their respective ideational
foundations. This is, in other words, a study *of* constitutional thought,
not a work of *my* constitutional thought.

Although political and legal constitutionalism are relatively modern
concepts, this book shows that they can help to frame and contextualize a variety of long-standing debates, both on and off the bench.

These include debates about how strongly judicial interpretations of the different rights documents can withstand the more obviously political branches (constitutional strength), and debates about the scope of public and private activity captured by the judicial application of rights documents (constitutional reach). I argue that this distinction between strength and reach provides a logic that captures how constitutional politics are interpretatively fought over in Canada, New Zealand, and the United Kingdom. In particular, assessing the strength and reach of rights documents helps to foreground disagreements between political and legal constitutionalists over subtle forms of judicial policymaking through revision of common-law rules and strained statutory interpretation. Although much of the law-and-politics subfield has focused on the invalidation of government action, this book shows how interpretively fixing a law can attract controversy, and how this development, too, is made intelligible through the clash of constitutionalisms. Very few studies address the phenomena of judicial actors interpretively fixing laws (Gardbaum 2013; Geddis and Fenton 2008; Roach 2005), and even fewer emphasize the impact bills of rights have on the common law (Harding and Knopff 2013; Leckey 2015). Integrating these and other manifestations of the ongoing struggle between political and legal constitutionalists into a single, systematic analysis is this study's chief contribution.

Constitutional Strength and Bills of Rights

How strongly should legal rights documents and (especially) their judicial interpretations withstand the more obviously political branches? This is the first and perhaps most prominent of the disagreements between legal and political constitutionalists explored in this study. Legal constitutionalists typically favour what legal scholar Mark Tushnet has called "strong-form" judicial review, while political constitutionalists prefer what he calls "weak-form" review. Both approaches allow some degree of dialogue between courts and legislatures, with legal constitutionalists preferring judicially constructed outputs while political constitutionalists want elected branches to have more room to resolve rights issues. But there is tension between formal capacity and actual outputs. Both strong- and weak-form systems are unstable, and that generates flexibility in the character of dialogue. That instability is shaped by how judges choose to use their rights document and whether legislatures are willing to respond to court rulings. For instance, the formal distinction between weaker and stronger forms of judicial review becomes less important if courts rewrite laws under the auspices of the bill of rights and legislatures rarely respond.

Strong-Form and Weak-Form Judicial Review

Strong-form judicial review is exemplified in the United States, where the courts possess an "invalidation mandate" allowing them to strike down laws that conflict with their interpretation of constitutional rights, and where the judicial interpretation is considered to be binding on the other branches of government (Tushnet 2002, 2784); courts armed with such an invalidation mandate are considered to be interpretively supreme.[1] Judicial decisions can be appealed, of course, but once the highest court has interpreted a rights issue, it is very difficult for the elected branches of government to displace that interpretation. The other branches have three ways of responding to judicial input under strong-form review. The first response is "court packing," which is the practice or threat of changing the composition of the bench in hope of generating different jurisprudential outcomes. A second and related response is to wait for the "judges to retire or die and replace them with judges who hold the better view of what the Constitution means" (Tushnet 2008b, 22). The final option is to pursue a constitutional amendment to overturn the Court's opinion.

Weak-form judicial review, in contrast, allows for ordinary legislative majorities to displace judicial interpretation of a constitution in the short term (Tushnet 2002, 2786). In other words, legislatures can (at least formally) disagree more easily and fully with a judicial interpretation. In Canada, this is made possible by section 33 of the Canadian Charter of Rights and Freedoms.[2] As in the United States, Canada's judiciary possesses an invalidation mandate. That is, it can invalidate legislation enacted by the federal or provincial legislatures that it finds to be inconsistent with the substantive provisions of the Charter. If the law has been invalidated under any of sections 2 and 7–15 of the Charter, however, the legislature can reverse the judiciary's decision through the use of section 33.[3] This provision of the Constitution allows for legislatures to insulate legislation from judicial rulings for renewable five-year periods. It is in many ways the most explicit ode to political constitutionalism in the Charter, as its political-philosophical origins drew from a concern about protecting Canada's tradition of parliamentary-based rights protection (Newman 2019).[4] Section 33 maintains the more explicit

---

1 There are some scholars who question the framing of the United States as a regime based on judicial interpretive supremacy (Baker 2010, 4–5; see also Clinton 1989; Fisher 1988).

2 Section 33(1) reads in part, "Parliament or the legislature of a province may expressly declare in an Act of Parliament or of the legislature, as the case may be, that the Act or a provision thereof shall operate notwithstanding a provision included in section 2 or sections 7 to 15."

3 Legislatures can also pre-emptively insulate laws from constitutional challenge under section 33 by inserting a notwithstanding clause prior to any courtroom challenge, thereby preventing such challenges.

4 "The dominant story of the notwithstanding clause," writes Dwight Newman, "is that it was not based on any theoretical vision and was simply a last-minute concession by Prime Minister Pierre Trudeau to get recalcitrant premiers on board with the Charter" (2019, 214; see also Hiebert 2009). But Newman shows how that dominant story underplays how the clause "built upon historical antecedents and deep thought by premiers of varying ideologies concerning the very nature of parliamentary

parliamentary (and politically constitutionalist-oriented) approach inso-far as the legislature merely needs to declare that the legislation shall operate "notwithstanding" the Charter as the law makes its way through the normal legislative process. There is no need to resort to court pack-ing or constitutional amendment. In principle at least, section 33 gives Canada a weaker form of judicial review than the United States. Indeed, for Tushnet (2002, 2785) and others (see Gardbaum 2001, 719, 724), section 33 pioneered the phenomenon of weak-form judicial review in the Commonwealth regimes.

Section 33 pays homage to Canada's tradition as a regime based on parliamentary supremacy (Russell 2007). However, section 33 has never been invoked by the federal Parliament and has been used in relatively few instances by provincial legislatures until recently (Kahana 2001). The limited use of section 33, combined with Canadian legislatures' def-erence to court rulings, has led some to conclude that Canada has esca-lated from a weak-form system of judicial review into a strong-form one (Geddis and Fenton 2008, 739; see also Tushnet 2003a, 100; Huscroft 2009; Hiebert 2006). Others maintain that Canada's can still be consid-ered a weak-form system (Roach 2019, 285; see also Hogg, Thornton, and Wright 2007; Kelly and Hennigar 2012).

The view that the notwithstanding clause has become a "paper tiger ... available in theory, but not used in practice" (Leeson 2001, 322) may need to be revisited given recent events. Since 2018, four provinces have introduced six pieces of legislation invoking the notwithstanding clause: Saskatchewan, in response to a lower court ruling[5] concerning student access to publicly funded Catholic education; Ontario, in response to two lower court decisions invalidating laws that reduced the number of coun-cillors on Toronto City Council and restricted campaign finance rules;[6]

---

democracy" (2019, 214). Indeed, many of the provincial leaders who were advocates of the notwithstanding clause also testified at the Special Joint Committee on the Constitution and raised concerns about impact of the Charter on legislatures' ability to define rights and freedoms (Dodek 2018, 340–1).

5 The School Choice Protection Act c. 39 (2018) was enacted by Saskatchewan legislature in response to *Good Spirit School Division No. 204 v. Christ the Teacher Roman Catholic Separate School Division No. 212* (2017).

6 In 2018, the Efficient Local Government Act (Bill 31) was introduced by the Ontario legislature, but did not receive royal assent. The bill was a response to *City of Toronto et al. v. Ontario (Attorney General)* (2018). The bill was removed from the order paper after the Ontario Court of Appeal stayed the original court's decision in *Toronto (City) v. Ontario (Attorney General)* (2019). In June 2021, the Ontario legislature re-enacted the Election Finances Act with the notwithstanding clause. This was a legislative response to *Working Families Ontario v. Ontario* (2021), which invalidated aspects of the previous law's restrictions around third-party campaign spending.

Quebec, as part of its law[7] barring government officials from wearing religious coverings and a bill to strengthen the French language; and New Brunswick, in a bill preventing parents from receiving non-medical exemptions from vaccinating their children in public schools.[8] All six invocations of the notwithstanding clause were controversial, spurring a renewed scholarly debate[9] over the merits of section 33 of the Charter, but as of this writing, only three – Saskatchewan on school choice, Ontario on election financing, and Quebec on religious coverings – actually passed into law. Whether this constitutes a temporary blip or a full revival of the clause remains to be seen.

Even with the notwithstanding clause, Canada seemed too strong-form to the Commonwealth jurisdictions – e.g., New Zealand and Britain – that subsequently enacted rights documents, as their more parliamentary-oriented constitutional cultures[10] made them resistant to giving courts too much power (Geddis and Fenton 2008, 770). These regimes, aware of the Canadian example, chose to institutionalize weak-form judicial review not by allowing legislation to operate "notwithstanding" a judicial invalidation, but by altogether denying judges the "invalidation mandate" that exists in both the United States and Canada. When New Zealanders were considering the 1990 NZBORA, for example, they explicitly rejected a Canadian-style notwithstanding clause in favour of section 4 of the resulting act,[11] "a provision which expressly prohibited

---

7 Quebec's National Assembly passed the Bill 21, An Act respecting the laicity of the State, in 2019. At the time of writing, the Quebec government announced it would use the notwithstanding clause to strengthen Quebec's language laws in Bill 96, An Act respecting French, the official and common language of Quebec, in 2021.

8 New Brunswick's Bill 11, An Act Respecting Proof of Immunization, was introduced into the Legislative Assembly in 2019. The government removed the notwithstanding clause, but the bill was still defeated via a free vote (Poitras 2020).

9 To canvass some of this renewed debate, see Webber, Mendelsohn, and Leckey 2019; Sirota 2019; Mancini and Sigalet 2020.

10 In New Zealand, "a strong conception of parliamentary democracy made the achievement of a fully constitutional (i.e. supreme and entrenched) bill of rights impossible," and this led "reformers towards the more limited statutory and interpretive model eventually enacted as NZBORA" (Erdos 2010, 94). Similarly, in the United Kingdom, drafters of the HRA wanted to ensure that it did not "detract from the democratic involvement of the people through Parliament." That concern, David Erdos argues, was "a product both of a political culture which prioritized resolving disputes through Parliament and a diffuse fear about the 'reactionary' nature of parts of the British judiciary" (2010, 114–15).

11 "No court shall, in relation to any enactment (whether passed or made before or after the commencement of this Bill of Rights), – (a) Hold any provision of the enactment to be impliedly repealed or revoked, or to be in any way invalid or ineffective; or

the courts from invalidating legislation that was inconsistent with the Bill of Rights" (Dodek 2007, 331). Section 4 has been called an "anti-supremacy clause," telling the courts "what they are not to do" both by subordinating the NZBORA to other enactments and by denying the courts the power of invalidation (Rishworth 2004, 258–9).

Nor did the British adopt a notwithstanding clause as part of the 1998 HRA. Instead, the rights documents in New Zealand and the United Kingdom limit judges to only (or mainly) an "interpretive mandate," instructing them to interpret laws in a manner consistent with the rights document whenever possible. This can involve using the rights document as a guide both in evolving judge-made common law and in interpreting legislation. In the case of legislation, judges must continue applying inconsistent laws. In other words, when a rights-consistent interpretation of legislation is not possible – i.e., when a statute clearly and unambiguously infringes the rights document – judges cannot invalidate or "strike down" the law in a "strong-form" manner. Instead, the incompatible statute remains in place and must continue to be applied by the courts. This is, on its face, clearly a weaker form of judicial review than exists in either Canada or the United States.

When a court in the kind of weak-form system represented by New Zealand or Britain *does* find it possible to give a statute a rights-compatible interpretation, ordinary legislative majorities can use the normal legislative process to change or reverse the judicial ruling. Legislative majorities can similarly enact statutes reversing a rights-based alteration of judge-made common law. Not only is there no need for court packing or constitutional amendment to disagree with a court, there is no need to resort to a notwithstanding clause as provided in Canada's section 33. A simple legislative enactment, like any other, will suffice.

New Zealand's NZBORA is the classic example of this kind of weak-form system because (formally) it establishes *only* this kind of interpretive mandate. For Tushnet, the NZBORA mandates a "pure interpretive requirement," which is "the weakest form of judicial review one can devise" (2008b, 214), short of having no rights document at all. Indeed, New Zealand judges and commentators sometimes suggest that nothing much has changed since the time when the country had no rights document at all. In this view, judges prior to the advent of the NZBORA enjoyed essentially the same interpretive mandate subsequently provided by that document. Far from inviting "a new and distinctive approach

---

(b) Decline to apply any provision of the enactment – by reason only that the provision is inconsistent with any provision of this Bill of Rights."

to statutory interpretation," in other words, the NZBORA was simply "a legislative manifestation of the established common-law principle that legislation is, where possible, to be interpreted consistently with fundamental rights recognized by the common law" (Geiringer 2008, 62–3). For example, in *R. v. Rangi* (1992), an early post-NZBORA ruling concerning a statute criminalizing the public possession of a knife, the New Zealand Court of Appeal interpreted the statute as requiring the Crown to prove criminal intent, rather than requiring the accused to prove possession for innocent purposes. The Court mentioned (almost in passing) that its ruling was supported by the NZBORA's section 25(c) right to be presumed innocent, but it relied just as strongly on the traditional common-law principle against reversing the Crown's traditional onus to prove guilt and requiring the accused to prove innocence. As Andrew Geddis notes, the Court found "the two sources of value (common-law and statutory) simultaneously to justify [its] conclusion that the relevant legislation should not be interpreted as reversing the onus of proof" (2008, 76). Moreover, both sources – the traditional common-law principle and its new statutory embodiment in the NZBORA – led to the same practical result – namely, that if the legislature wanted to establish a "reverse onus," it would have to give a more "clear indication of its intention" than could be found in the "plain language" of the statute under consideration (*R. v. Rangi* 1992, 388–9). Absent such a clear legislative statement, the Court would give the law a rights-consistent interpretation, as the NZBORA specifies, and as the common law had always required.

Ten years later, when the New Zealand Court of Appeal used the principle of "natural justice" to interpret a statute in *Drew v. Attorney-General* (2002), it similarly "found no need to refer to the guarantee" of that principle "in s.27 of the Bill of Rights." It was content to apply "natural justice" in its pre-existing common-law version, although it did concede that the NZBORA guarantee "affirm[ed] and strengthen[d] the appellant's case" (para. 67).[12] In effect, the courts in *Rangi* and *Drew* treated the NZBORA as legislatively institutionalizing the "weak common-law constitutionalism" mentioned in the previous chapter.

The British HRA has the same essential structure as the NZBORA – with one important exception. While courts in both countries must continue to apply statutes they consider clearly incompatible with the

---

12 *R. v. Rangi* (1992), *R. v. Pora* (2001), and *R. v. Poumako* (2000) also feature instances where the judiciary recognizes a common-law right that possesses a corresponding codified right in the NZBORA.

relevant rights document, under the HRA, judges are explicitly given the power to issue a formal "declaration of incompatibility,"[13] a power not explicitly set out in the NZBORA. This difference should not be overstated. After all, as Rishworth points out, when a New Zealand court "decides that it must apply" a rights-infringing enactment, it follows "by definition" that "a conclusion of inconsistency has at that point been reached," even if it has not been formally declared (2004, 259–60). In other words, while a finding of inconsistency or incompatibility is clearly and publicly "declared" by UK courts, it has traditionally remained implicit and unheralded in New Zealand (Gardbaum 2013, 140; Geiringer 2007, 405). It is worth noting, however, that although no power to declare inconsistency is explicit in New Zealand's NZBORA, the country's courts have gradually been formalizing the implied power. Thus *Moonen v. Film and Literature Board of Review* (2000, para. 17) suggested there could be instances where it could be appropriate to exercise a power to declare statutes incompatible with the Bill of Rights (Huscroft 2002, 120), though that power was not exercised in *Moonen* itself. Recently, the New Zealand Court of Appeal upheld a lower court decision that issued the first explicit declaration of inconsistency with respect to a statutory ban on prisoner voting (*Taylor v. Attorney-General* 2017). There has, in short, been some convergence between the two systems.

An important difference remains, however. After a declaration of incompatibility has been made under section 4 of the UK's HRA, section 10 of the act gives the relevant minister of the Crown the ability to fast-track a response through the legislative process, a power that is not provided by New Zealand's NZBORA. However, nothing in the HRA obliges the UK Parliament to respond to a judicial declaration of incompatibility. The same is true when a New Zealand court suggests or (more strongly) declares inconsistency with the NZBORA.

The ability to issue declarations of incompatibility is what Tushnet calls an "augmented interpretive mandate" (2008b, 27–9). This augmented mandate arguably makes a weak-form system somewhat stronger in the sense that an official declaration of incompatibility might shame and embarrass the government into amending or repealing the offending legislation in order to comply with the judicial view of rights compatibility (Jenkins 2009, 184; Tushnet 2008b, 29). It remains a weak-form system, however, insofar as the government can express its disagreement

---

13 Section 4 of the HRA reads in part: "If the court is satisfied that the provision is incompatible with a Convention right, it may make a declaration of that incompatibility."

with a judicial interpretation by simply ignoring the judicial ruling and leaving the existing legislation in place. In Canada, by contrast, a government cannot register and implement outright disagreement with the judicial invalidation of a statute by ignoring it.

Geoffrey Leane has arrayed the rights documents along a "continuum of rights protection," between a "legislative supremacy end," where rights "are still vulnerable to something very close to legally unlimited majoritarianism," and an end characterized by "fundamental rights protection entrenched in a constitution enabling judicial review" (by which he means the strong-form review preferred by legal constitutionalists). Although he does not use the terms, this is essentially a continuum running from political to legal constitutionalism. He places the NZBORA "at, or very close to, the legislative supremacy end" of the continuum, and "the UK Act ... a little closer to the judicial review end by virtue of its empowering the courts to make declarations of incompatibility." This difference has narrowed somewhat, as we have just seen. The Canadian Charter, in his view, "lies quite close to" the judicial review end of the continuum, especially because "the constraint of the Section 33 notwithstanding clause has (with the exception of Quebec) effectively lain dormant" (Leane 2004, 171; see also Roach 2007, 185). In other words, as already suggested, Canada has (at least as far as section 33 is concerned)[14] moved to the strong-form end of the continuum, with NZBORA and the HRA representing variants of weak-form review.

New Zealand and the United Kingdom rejected the strong-form invalidation mandate in favour of the weak-form interpretive (or augmented interpretive) mandate because they wanted "a 'richer and more balanced' constitutional *dialogue* between judicial and legislative institutions, a new 'collaborative enterprise'" (Joseph 2004 quoted in Leane 2004, 173, emphasis added; see also Hiebert 2006; Jackson 2007; Bellamy 2011; Hickford 2013). This concept of inter-institutional "dialogue" has become a key component of the debates about constitutional strength.

Dialogue in Strong-Form and Weak-Form Systems

The dialogue metaphor has been especially prominent in Canadian legal discourse,[15] but is referenced ubiquitously by scholars in other Common-

---

14 While Saskatchewan's and Quebec's 2018 use of the notwithstanding clause shows it is no longer "dormant," it nevertheless remains an outlier against the general practice of non-use.

15 Webber (2009, 446–7) notes the concept of "dialogue" actually began in the American legal context (e.g., Bickel 1986; Whittington 2002). However, Hogg and

wealth jurisdictions (Gardbaum 2013, 14–15, 111; see also Dixon 2009; Jackson 2007; Masterman 2009; Sigalet, Webber, and Dixon 2019; Young 2017), and even among policymakers (Hiebert 2006, 17). The debate between political and legal constitutionalists is in part a debate about what kind of rights document best promotes inter-institutional dialogue between courts and legislatures. Simply put, while legal constitutionalism prefers a strong-form invalidation mandate with its tendency towards judicial interpretive supremacy, political constitutionalism prefers the greater opportunities for inter-institutional "dialogue" afforded by weak-form systems.

Certainly, the political constitutionalists in New Zealand and the United Kingdom who founded, respectively, the NZBORA[16] and the HRA[17] saw inter-institutional "dialogue" as too "court-centric" in strong-form systems, which tend to be dominated by assumptions of judicial interpretive supremacy with respect to rights documents (Roach 2016, 61, 68, 70–2). Given the manifest difficulty of using section 33 in Canada, they rejected the option of a notwithstanding clause. But what about the other route to dialogue emphasized by most Canadian dialogue theorists – namely, the "reasonable limits" clause of the Canadian

---

Bushell's (1997) formulation has had the most currency in comparative parliamentary systems. As Alison Young notes, the concept of "democratic dialogue" has been used in many ways throughout the Commonwealth. For Young, this dialogue is best understood as a constitutional model including both empirical and normative aspects for evaluating how well a particular legal system achieves those standards (2019, 44).

16 Erdos (2010, 97–100) argues that it is impressive that any rights document was adopted in New Zealand, given its constitutional culture. Groups normally associated with advocacy for more judicialized politics (i.e., civil libertarians, equality-seeking groups, and legal elites) were hostile to adding a bill of rights. Even the proponents of the NZBORA within the Labour Party "expressed the traditional fears of a party of government that a bill of rights would be proved 'unduly restrictive of the freedom of the government to act nimbly' and 'could result in rights being ossified.'" These attitudes "pushed supporters towards the more limited statutory and interpretative model eventually enacted as NZBORA" (97). The opponents to the NZBORA at the parliamentary committee – whether associated with the political Left or Right – tended to echo views reflecting political constitutionalism: "these contributors were strongly committed to a democracy which placed its trust in the ability of discrete decisions made by a democratically elected Parliament to resolve all political disputes fairly" (100; see also Hiebert and Kelly 2015, 38–9).

17 The United Kingdom's advocates for the HRA faced similar resistance to those in New Zealand. The most prominent civil liberties group lobbied to ensure the language of the HRA would retain Parliament's upper hand in defining the meaning of rights (Erdos 2010, 114–15). Hiebert and Kelly (2015, 238–9) describe the aversion to the adoption of the HRA and how it is still a frequent partisan target for the UK Conservative Party (see also Young 2017, 296–8).

Charter? As noted in the previous chapter, section 5 of New Zealand's NZBORA replicated this clause. The United Kingdom's HRA does not feature a similar clause, but, as we shall see, aspects of "reasonable limits" analysis have emerged in UK jurisprudence.

When a Canadian court invalidates a statute under the Charter of Rights and Freedoms, it does so because it sees the law as *unreasonably* infringing a Charter provision. Section 1 of the Charter allows for such "reasonable limits as are demonstrably justified in a free and democratic society." The Canadian Supreme Court established a highly formalized and systematic framework for "reasonable limits" analysis in *R. v. Oakes* (1986), four years after the Charter came into force. Among other things, *Oakes* confirmed that the government bore the onus of "demonstrably justifying" a "reasonable limit" on protected rights. The rights claimant, who must establish a rights violation, does not also have to prove that it was an *un*reasonable violation. Instead, the government must demonstrably justify it as a reasonable limit in a "free and democratic society." This requires demonstrating that the impugned law has a "pressing and substantial" objective and that it employs "proportional" means to achieve that objective. The proportionality component of the *Oakes* test in turn has three parts. First, there must be a "rational connection" between the law's means and its objective. Second, there should be "minimal impairment" of protected rights. Third, the benefits of the law must outweigh the cost in lost rights.

"Reasonable limits" analysis under the NZBORA is less formalized (and often more perfunctory) than the comparable analysis in Canada. The issue of onus has not been clearly addressed in New Zealand (Hiebert and Kelly 2015, 145–6, 159), for example, and the criteria of reasonableness have been looser and more haphazard (Wilberg 2015). New Zealand judges are aware of *Oakes*, and sometimes cite it, but nothing as systematic as the *Oakes* test has emerged in New Zealand jurisprudence. Some of the same proportionality concepts (e.g., "rational connection") come into play, but usually in a more ad hoc fashion (Geiringer 2013, 126–7). Moreover, as Paul Rishworth reports, although reasonable limits analysis appears in rights-based jurisprudence "no case ... has really turned on the application of a s[ection] 5 test" (2007, 346; see also Geiringer 2013, 138). This stands in marked contrast to the situation in Canada, where Charter cases often turn mainly on section 1 reasonable limits analysis. In the United Kingdom – even in the absence of a limitations clause – courts have also noted and dabbled with *Oakes*-inspired proportionality analysis from time to time (*R (Daly) v. Secretary of State for the Home Department* 2001, para. 26), but again only "in a relatively ad hoc way" (Hickman 2007, 33). As in New Zealand, "the principle of proportionality" in the UK "remains unelaborated, uncertain and its application unstructured" (Hickman 2007, 33).

Returning to the Canadian situation, it is the minimal-impairment component of the *Oakes* test that most obviously allows room for dialogic responses that do not involve a section 33 notwithstanding clause. In concluding that a law is not saved by section 1, in other words, a court often indicates that a more "minimal impairment" of Charter rights would pass constitutional muster. Although there can be dialogic legislative sequels to judicial invalidations in Canada without the use of section 33, the prevailing orthodoxy holds that legislatures must work within the room for manoeuvre set by judicial rulings, especially with respect to the issue of "reasonable limits" on Charter rights. This means that the legislature cannot disagree with (and hence legislate outside of) the interpretive parameters established by the Court's minimal-impairment analysis. Indeed, most commentators believe that even cases using Charter principles to alter judge-made common law can be legislatively reversed only with a section 33 notwithstanding clause (Cameron 2001; Roach 2016). In this view, legislatures do not share interpretive authority with courts – i.e., they do not possess the power of so-called coordinate interpretation (Baker 2010) – and thus cannot legitimately disagree with authoritative judicial interpretations, at least not without using (the rarely available) section 33. As Hogg, Thornton, and Wright put it, "If 'genuine dialogue' can only occur where legislatures share coordinate authority with the courts to interpret the constitution, then by definition it cannot exist in Canada, where legislatures have no such authority" (2007, 31; see also Roach 2016, 385). Whether the legislature has stayed within its judicially assigned boundaries or illegitimately exceeded them without resort to section 33 is itself a question for determination by interpretively supreme judges in so-called second-look cases.[18] We see in this perspective the hallmarks of legal constitutionalism under modern rights documents – namely, the treatment of protected rights – including the matter of "reasonable limits" on those rights – as legal categories under the primary care and supervision of the judiciary.[19]

Not all Canadian theorists agree with this kind of "court centric" dialogue. Observing that under this version of the dialogue metaphor

---

18 The term "second-look cases" come from Hogg, Thornton, and Wright (2007, 19–24). They define these cases as those "where the Court reviews the validity of legislation enacted to replace a law struck down in a previous *Charter* decision" (19).

19 Political constitutionalists who see the "reasonable limits" clause as a leaning away from legal constitutionalism often see the establishment and evolution of the *Oakes* test as leaning in the direction of legal constitutionalism (Morton 2001, 113).

courts do most of the talking and legislatures do most of the listening (Morton 2001, 117), political constitutionalists see the metaphor as little more than a rationalization for judicial power (Huscroft 2009). In this view, meaningful inter-institutional dialogue requires "a legislative response which dissents, to some degree, from the court's ruling" (Hennigar 2004, 8; see also Baker and Knopff 2002; Hiebert 2002; Macfarlane 2013a; Manfredi and Kelly 1999). Legislative responses deviating from a judicial interpretation are rare but do occur from time to time: after the Supreme Court struck down Canada's prohibition on medically-assisted suicide in *Carter v. Canada (Attorney General)* (2015), Parliament's 2016 response in Bill C-14 did "depart in some measure from the policy laid down by the Court," and some parliamentarians invoked the dialogue metaphor in justifying the new legislation (Bateman and LeBlanc 2018, 389; see also Nicolaides and Hennigar 2018, 322–36). Statistically, however, meaningful dialogue is rare in Canada: in his study of legislative responses to Supreme Court of Canada decisions affecting legislation, Emmett Macfarlane found only 17.4 per cent of cases led to a "genuine" dialogic response, even when using a measure that "erred on the side of dialogue, so that any significant deviation from the Court ruling was taken into consideration" (2013a, 47). The infrequency of genuine dialogue, combined with an imprecise use in the literature, has led some scholars, like Macfarlane (2012), to question its utility. Despite these debates over the uses of dialogue, it "nevertheless ... remains entrenched in the literature, perhaps because of its attractive implication that constitutional law is best understood as the product of inter-institutional interactions" (Knopff et al. 2017, 610).

Those supportive of genuine dialogue deny the need for judicial interpretive supremacy, and insist that the more obviously political branches of government possess a "coordinate" authority to interpret rights documents – that legislatures "can and should participate" in constitutional interpretation, and can do so through ordinary legislation, as Parliament did with its response to *Carter* in Bill C-14 (Baker 2016, 1–2; see also Baker 2010; Peabody 1999; Webber 2009). However, this preference of "coordinate dialogue" to its "court centric" alternative – clearly the preference of political constitutionalists – is a minority view in Canada.[20]

---

20 Dennis Baker (2016, 3) justifies coordinate interpretation as a "parliamentary check" on judicial interpretive supremacy for three reasons: because judges make mistakes, because judges take sides in what constitutes a "reasonable disagreement," and because judges can render ambiguous rulings. For scholars such as Rainer Knopff (2003, 215), coordinate interpretation is preferable to "oracular judicial finality" when dealing with deeply moral and political questions about which reasonable people

While political constitutionalism is the minority view in Canada, however, it is precisely what animated the more clearly weak-form systems in New Zealand and Britain, where legislatures can more fully disagree with judicial interpretations through ordinary legislation (with no notwithstanding clause) or by ignoring findings of incompatibility or inconsistency. In New Zealand this means that the courts must try to interpret a law in a manner that does not *unreasonably* conflict with NZBORA provisions. If the legislature disagrees with such an interpretation, it can simply pass a new law that goes beyond boundaries of "reasonableness" established by the court. And if the court finds that a law is not a reasonable limit on the NZBORA, the law continues in effect, and the finding of unreasonable inconsistency can, in principle, be ignored. The UK Parliament can similarly ignore rulings that declare a "disproportional" rights infringement to be "incompatible" with the HRA.[21]

Not that it is always easy to ignore declarations of inconsistency or incompatibility. They can carry a certain moral weight. Thus, the New Zealand court in *Taylor* hoped that "pointed" declarations of inconsistency would foster inter-institutional "dialogue" because of "the reasonable expectation that other branches of government, respecting the judicial function, will respond by reappraising the legislation and making any changes that are thought appropriate" (2017, para. 151). The court's hope, in short, was that declarations of inconsistency would give a somewhat greater "legal constitutionalist" tilt to inter-institutional dialogue in New Zealand. Perhaps this will occur, but formally it will remain the case in New Zealand, as it is in the United Kingdom, that, in Kent Roach's words, "the legislature enjoys the burden of inertia" (2016, 70). It is the legislature, in other words, that "must enact corrective legislation if the rights declared by the courts are to be respected either prospectively or retroactively." If there is legislative inertia – i.e., if the legislature ignores the court – the judicial declaration of unreasonable inconsistency or incompatibility comes to nothing; the impugned law remains in force and fully applicable.

---

disagree. This is particularly true insofar as courts themselves are majoritarian – a 5–4 decision is just as legally determinative as 9–0 one. As Knopff notes, defenders of judicial power, including dialogue theorists, ultimately "prefer majoritarianism in the courtroom to majoritarianism in the electoral and legislative arena" (2003, 210).

21 In the Australian context, Julie Debeljak is critical of the lack of dialogue under Australia's statutory Charter of Human Rights and Responsibilities Act, passed in 2006. Debeljak argues that, while Victoria's Charter has increased attention to rights issues and provided a framework for debate, executive dominance prevails (2017, 407–8).

In Canada, by contrast, the rights claimant who has succeeded in having a law struck down as an unreasonable violation of the Charter enjoys "the burden of legislative inertia." The legislature cannot preserve what is judicially invalidated as an "unreasonable" limit on rights by ignoring the court's ruling; it must either re-enact the invalidated law with a notwithstanding clause or more finely tailor a new law within judicially established parameters of "minimal impairment." Reasonable limits analysis is much more consequential in Canada than it is in New Zealand. Might this help explain why "reasonable limits," or "proportionality" analysis, has been less systematically formalized in New Zealand and the United Kingdom? It arguably matters more in Canada, where it can help guide a legislative sequel that might restore some aspects of the invalidated law, than it does in New Zealand or the United Kingdom, where the legislature can maintain all of the "incompatible" law by doing nothing. There is, in other words, more room for political constitutionalism in the weak-form systems of New Zealand and the United Kingdom than in stronger-form Canada.

It is worth further unpacking how the different treatment of "the burden of inertia" in the rights documents under consideration reflects the opposing perspectives of legal and political constitutionalism. Roach prefers the Canadian situation, where "those who have their rights unreasonably violated by legislation enjoy the burden of legislative inertia" (2016, 70). Their rights will be respected unless the legislature proactively responds with new legislation that can be justified (before the courts) as a reasonable limit under section 1 or that explicitly includes a section 33 notwithstanding clause. As Grant Huscroft points out, however, this assumes judicial supremacy in determining whether rights really have been "unreasonably violated by legislation" (2002, 125). If one makes this legal-constitutionalist assumption of judicial supremacy, it naturally follows that the rights claimant who has been successful in court should enjoy "the burden of inertia." But what if, as political constitutionalists think, "the correctness of the courts' decisions" is often "the very thing in dispute" (Huscroft 2002, 125). In that case, one might well prefer the legislature to enjoy "the burden of inertia," as the framers of the UK and New Zealand rights documents clearly did. For Huscroft, who adopts the political-constitutionalist perspective, there are certainly "arguments that can be made against this sort of system, ... but arguments based on assumptions as to the inherent superiority of judicial review cannot count among them, since rejection of those assumptions underlies the decision to limit the power of the courts in the first place" (2002, 125). In other words, the New Zealand and UK rights documents give the legislature "the burden of inertia" precisely to allow for greater and easier disagreement, including interpretive disagreement, between courts and legislatures in order to establish "a more balanced parliamentary dialogue on rights and freedoms" (Kelly 2009, 87; see also Hiebert 2005) – i.e., precisely the kind of coordinate dialogue that Hogg and others reject for Canada.

Arguments for and against judicial supremacy in the interpretation of protected rights do not, however, exhaust the debate about whether interinstitutional dialogue is best served by weak-form or stronger-form systems. As Huscroft notes, there may be other "arguments that can be made against" weak-form systems (2002, 126). One such argument concerns the interpretation not of protected rights but of legislation subject to those rights. Both the New Zealand and the UK documents, as we have seen, give judges mainly an interpretive mandate, exhorting them to interpret legislation in a rights-compliant manner when possible. Only if it is not possible to do so should they find or declare incompatibility. But what if judges engage in "strained interpretation" of legislation that is more plausibly seen as incompatible with protected rights (Gardbaum 2013, 136; Geddis and Fenton 2008; Jackson 2007; Rishworth 2004)? We know that judicial actors often behave strategically (Baum 2006; Knopff, Baker, and LeRoy 2009; Manfredi 2002), and it is possible that judges might see strategic advantages in "strained" or "creative" interpretations. That is, knowing that a finding of inconsistency or incompatibility can be ignored by the legislature, judges might prefer to rewrite a clearly incompatible law to make it rights-compliant. Doing so essentially reverses the intended "burden of inertia." True, the legislature in such systems can respond by re-enacting, even more explicitly, its original legislative purpose, but given the "staying power" of a policy status quo (Flanagan 1997; Morton 2001), this might be more difficult than ignoring a finding of incompatibility. If, as F.L. Morton writes, "any half-clever judge can use procedural objections as a pretense to strike down legislation that he opposes for substantive reasons" (2001, 113), one could also imagine an equally "half-clever" UK judge using creative interpretative techniques to fix a law in the manner they prefer with perhaps little risk of legislative reversal.

Similar issues arise under the Canadian Charter. Despite the Charter's strong-form invalidation mandate, Canadian judges sometimes exercise an implied interpretive mandate. In *Butler* (1992), for example, Canada's Supreme Court upheld the Criminal Code censorship of obscenity by interpretively bringing it into line with the Charter. Conceding that the law had originally prohibited most explicit erotica on moralistic grounds, the Court found it possible to read it as now criminalizing only pornography that involved harm to women and children (1992, 493). Had it continued to prohibit most erotica, it could not be justified as a reasonable limit on freedom of expression. Having been given a narrower, harm-based reading, however, the law became justified as a reasonable limit.

The Court's *Butler* opinion insisted that it was not rewriting the law, but rather giving it a new but possible rights-compatible interpretation. Kent Roach disagreed. In his eyes, the case exemplified a growing and regrettable phenomenon "under the Charter to fix laws through creative and strained interpretations" (2005, 748–50). This "spurious technique of statutory interpretation" entailed the "fiction that the court is not departing from the words and intent of the legislature when it applies a presumption that the legislature intends to respect rights." The "fiction," in other words, is that the Court is not rewriting a statute when that is in fact what it is doing. As Macfarlane notes, there are also more open or transparent ways of judicially rewriting statutes, including " 'reading in,' 'reading down' or severing words in the legislation" (2013a: 43). As for Roach, he is clearly no friend of the UK- or New Zealand-style interpretive mandate, and he actively opposes the use by Canadian judges of interpretive strategies that "make the Charter more like the interpretative bills of rights" found in those countries (2005, 735).

As indicated above, there is reason to think that "strained interpretation" of statutes will be even more attractive to strategic judges in New Zealand and the United Kingdom than it is to Canadian judges. If New Zealand or UK judges find a law inconsistent or incompatible with their rights document, they essentially leave the law in effect and hope that the legislature will address the defects they have identified. Unlike their Canadian colleagues, they cannot invalidate the law. They might thus prefer to engage in strained interpretations, betting (not unreasonably) that the legislature will find it more difficult to actively reverse their ruling than it will to passively ignore or inadequately address a finding of incompatibility. Certainly, analysts of the weak-form jurisdictions have often expressed such concerns about "strained interpretations" under the interpretive mandate (Geddis and Fenton 2008; Jackson 2007; Rishworth 2004). According to Gardbaum,

> The enacted line between judicial interpretation or construction and judicial law-making is a fine one in practice. This issue inheres in all interpretative bills of rights, at least those without greater specification of the duty, and has been a major source of contention both in New Zealand and, even more, in the UK. It is also the source of the claim that – through radical use of the interpretative power to rewrite legislation – statutory bills of rights can, and indeed have, come to resemble fully constitutional ones in practice, leading to de facto judicial supremacy. (2013, 136)

In other words, if strained interpretations are common and if they turn out to be nearly as difficult to reverse as section 33 has become difficult to use in Canada, then the greater dialogic potential weak-form systems were intended to promote will have been subverted by the same assumptions of judicial interpretive supremacy that characterize strong-form systems (Allan 2000; Huscroft 2007). Similar questions can be raised about findings of incompatibility in weak-form systems. Might assumptions of judicial interpretive supremacy regarding rights issues be strong enough to force legislatures generally to amend the relevant legislation to bring it into line with judicial views? Tushnet (2002, 2008b) himself provides the framework for considering such issues when he argues that weak-form systems can "escalate" into strong-form systems.

Instability and Escalation

As already indicated, Tushnet and others (e.g., Huscroft 2007, 2009) acknowledge that Canada has escalated into a de facto strong-form system insofar as the notwithstanding clause has not been used at the federal level, which in turn is partially explained by the fact that the judiciary enjoys a privileged position when it comes to interpreting constitutional rights.

Tushnet also claims that strong-form review can "degenerate" into weak-form judicial review. There are even occasions in the Canadian context when, despite the overall escalation into a strong-form system, slippage into the weak-form direction sometimes occurs. Thus, although the Canadian Parliament resists ever using section 33 (evidence of strong-form escalation), it has on occasion passed legislative sequels that clearly enact what a Supreme Court majority has found to be unconstitutional without using section 33 (*R. v. Daviault* 1994; *R. v. O'Connor* 1995; *R. v. Mills* 1999), and on at least one occasion, the Supreme Court has deferred to such legislation in a second-look case (*R. v. Mills* 1999). These cases, which clearly challenge the strong-form assumption of judicial interpretive supremacy and point towards the more coordinate dialogic disagreement that weak-form systems were intended to facilitate, will be discussed in more detail in chapter 5. They show that Parliament can sometimes successfully disagree with, and legislatively reject, judicial interpretations. Such instances of "degeneration" in the weak-form direction are clearly exceptions to the rule in Canada, however.

What about the "escalation" thesis in the other weak-form systems? With respect to New Zealand, Tushnet reports that "there appears to be no strong sense ... that the legislature has some constitutional or even political obligation to rectify the constitutional defects once they have been pointed out" (2008a, 214). In other words, New Zealand exhibited no strongly developed sense of judicial interpretive supremacy at the time Tushnet wrote, at least not when a court "pointed out" defects that the legislature might wish to address. That is, the New Zealand legislature seemed willing to simply ignore decisions that found inconsistency between a statute and the NZBORA.

The empirical and normative commentary with respect to New Zealand is mixed. For instance, some observers claim that the NZBORA has produced a welcome balance between Parliament and the judiciary (Huscroft 2002; Joseph 2004; McLean 2001; Leane 2004). Other scholars lament the growth of judicial power associated with the NZBORA (Allan 2000, 2006; Smillie 2006). Still other scholars are concerned that the New Zealand model does not go far enough to protect rights and that more constraints need to be placed on Parliament (Kelly 2011; Hiebert and Kelly 2015). According to Gardbaum, "The political costs of legislative disagreement with the courts may be lower than in Canada (and the UK), and perhaps too low overall, but they are not zero – and the very fact that such inter-institutional disagreement over rights exists and is aired at all goes beyond what is typical of traditional parliamentary sovereignty" (2013, 150). Still, the political costs seem low enough to allow the legislature to ignore findings of inconsistency.

In the United Kingdom, there is little consensus concerning the impact of the HRA; instead, there is a "spectrum" of attitudes (Gardbaum 2010, 189–92) ranging from the HRA being too weak to claiming the HRA has ushered in judicial supremacy (Kavanagh 2009). In the United Kingdom, Parliament generally responds to declarations of incompatibility. By 2013, there had been twenty-seven declarations of incompatibility issued by the judiciary (Gardbaum 2013, 173). Parliament responded to each of these instances by either repealing offending legislation or amending it (Masterman 2009). In other words, in Britain there does seem to be a sense of some "obligation" to address "defects once they have been pointed out."

What about legislative responses to "strained interpretations" under the interpretive mandate in New Zealand and Britain? Does the New Zealand legislature find those as difficult to change as it appears to find the pointing out of defects easy to ignore? And how does the British Parliament respond to "strained interpretations"? Have assumptions of judicial interpretive supremacy, in combination with the "staying power of the status quo," created a de facto strong-form dynamic with respect to "strained interpretations" in either country? Tushnet (2008b) suggests it is possible for systems *formally* designed to foster inter-institutional perspectives to "escalate" along judicial-supremacist lines. However, he is not specific about how this process takes place.

For instance, Tushnet argues, "a nation's legal culture gradually accepts the proposition that judicial review takes a strong or a weak form" (2002, 2786). However, even more than institutional design, change can occur "not [only] by the constitution's designers themselves, but by the legislators and judges who implement the constitution" (2786). Yet one aspect of Tushnet's thought remains underdeveloped. On the one hand, he claims "courts in a weak-form system cannot themselves choose to exercise strong-form review," but on the other, he recognizes that judges can choose to be part of a "long-term process through which weak-form review is converted into strong-form review" (2787). Tushnet does not elaborate on what such a process would look like.[22] Part of Tushnet's "long-term process" can be thought of in terms of the ongoing philosophical battle between political and legal constitutionalists.

Conclusion

There is obviously much more to appreciate about the institution of judicial review than knowing whether a regime has a bill of rights or not. Simply adopting a rights document neither entrenches legal constitutionalism nor extinguishes political constitutionalism. Whether a regime has strong-form judicial review in the US mould or something closer to New Zealand (the "weakest form of judicial review one can devise," according to Tushnet 2008b), there persists a debate over the proper role between courts and legislatures in defining rights. Debate rages particularly over the potential for inter-institutional dialogue along the strong- to weak-form continuum of regimes. Political constitutionalists will press for greater legislatively determined policy outcomes, whereas legal constitutionalists will champion judicially interpreted ones. Even if the barriers for entry for one perspective are formally high, both legal and political constitutionalists find room to manoeuvre and press their cases.

All systems of judicial review are unstable. The formal mechanisms of rights protection matter, as do the participants (judges and legislatures), in shaping whether a system degenerates or escalates in Tushnet's sense.

---

22 For example, under the Canadian Constitution, the federal government still possesses the powers of disallowance and reservation. But over time and through a concerted effort by the opponents of these powers, they have been informally turned into dead letters (on the delegitimization of the disallowance power, see Cairns 1992, 617; Vipond 1991).

Ambitious judges inclined to legal constitutionalism – even in systems with formally weak rights documents – will emphasize judicial power in defining and implementing rights. Similarly, political constitutionalists in regimes under strong-form review will encourage legislatures to take advantage of the mechanisms available to them to participate in defining the meaning of rights. In short, conflicts over constitutional strength will not soon abate. Nor will the controversies over constitutional reach discussed in the next two chapters.

Constitutional Reach: Severe Limits or Constitutionalizing Everything?

In addition to debating the relative strength of constitutionally based judicial power, political and legal constitutionalists also clash over the appropriate *reach* of such power. Political constitutionalists want to limit the judicially applicable reach of rights documents, whereas legal constitutionalists want to expand that reach.

Stephen Gardbaum (2013, 37–40) provides a continuum that helps in thinking about the issues of constitutional reach. At one end of the continuum is "pure political constitutionalism," under which all "rights-relevant issues and conflicts in a society" should "be resolved politically, through ordinary, non-constitutional laws made and executed by political actors who remain fully accountable for them to the electorate." This is the kind of "strong legislative supremacy" that, as noted in the previous chapter, used to be common but is now rare in the liberal-democratic world. At the other end of the continuum is "pure legal constitutionalism," under which the judicially supervised constitution "decides or strongly influences virtually all rights-relevant issues and conflicts in a society," leaving "relatively little room for discretionary, autonomous political decision-making or law making." The "scope or reach of legal constitutionalism" (37) at this end of the continuum is so wide that it has come to be known as the "total constitution" (Kumm 2006) or "constitutional totalism" (Bateman 1998).

Between these two polar versions of political and legal constitutionalism, we find a middle ground in which the "higher law as construed and applied by the constitutional judiciary resolves some but not all of the rights-relevant issues and conflicts in a society" (Gardbaum 2013, 37–8). This middle ground, which arguably includes Canada, New Zealand, and the United Kingdom, entails the victory of legal constitutionalism over "pure political constitutionalism," but just as important, it resists the legal-constitutionalist pole of constitutional totalism. While giving the judiciary strong influence over "certain issues and narrow[ing] the range of permissible political options on others," the middle ground also preserves "space for politically accountable decision-making." In other words, while the middle ground represents legal constitutional-ism insofar as it "takes some issues off the political agenda," it represents political constitutionalism insofar as it "leaves others on it" (Gardbaum 2013, 38).

But just how much has been taken off the political agenda by legal constitutionalism, and how much room for continuing political constitu-tionalism remains? This turns out to be a matter of continuing struggle between legal and political constitutionalists. There is, in other words, no stable fixed point in Gardbaum's middle ground between the "pure" poles of legal and political constitutionalism. It is instead the site of an ongoing tug of war between the two perspectives.

W.R. Lederman has strongly outlined the political-constitutionalist position in this tug of war, arguing that constitutional reach should be strictly limited:

> If we characterize too many things as constitutional, we put too much of potential legal change to meet societal needs beyond the reach of the fle-xible statutory means of change ... The problem of limiting what is to be considered "constitutional" in this sense is very real. The limits have to be severe. You cannot constitutionalize the whole legal system. (1991, 119)

According to David Robertson, Lederman's side has been losing ground to legal constitutionalism. Robertson reports that around the world con-stitutional review by courts has increasingly become "a mechanism for permeating all regulated aspects of society with a set of values inherent in the constitutional agreement the society has accepted" (2010, 7; see also Elliott 2011, 607). Robertson, in other words, sees a shift towards the pole of "constitutional totalism."[1]

Robertson's assessment is correct. Even constitutional conventions, the paradigmatic preserve of political constitutionalism, seem more

---

1 Robertson's case countries come mostly from continental Europe and have civil law systems (Germany, France, the Czech Republic, Poland, and Hungary). But he also considers Canada, primarily a common-law jurisdiction, and South Africa, a mixed system. It can be argued that these European states' legal traditions make them more fertile ground for total constitutionalism (Kumm 2006). But as this chapter illustrates, common-law jurisdictions associated with limited constitutionalism have also been susceptible to expansive constitutional reach with assistance from judicial interpretation and their rights documents.

subject to judicial supervision than they used to be. And the idea that certain "political questions" arising under rights documents might lie beyond judicial purview has lost ground. Similarly, expansive judicial interpretation of rights documents by courts often overwhelms the space for "discretionary and autonomous political decision-making" that few and "narrowly defined" rights maintain (Gardbaum 2013, 37–8). Finally, courts have often moved towards constitutional totalism by reading rights documents to "reach into the private sphere" and to impose "affirmative duties on government" (Gardbaum 2013, 37–8).

The issue of "reach into the private sphere" brings us to an important distinction between two versions of constitutional totalism. The first, more limited version retains the classically liberal perspective that constitutions limit the *state*, not the private sector (Castiglione 1996, 422). This version holds that the constitution infuses all "state action" – i.e., all statutes, regulations, and executive action. This might be called the "state action" version of constitutional totalism. The second, more comprehensive (or "totalistic") version of constitutional totalism wants the constitution to reach more directly into the private sector. This has become known as "post-liberal" constitutionalism, in which "the personal becomes the constitutional" (Bateman 1998, 13).

There have been important advances towards both state-action and private-sector, post-liberal constitutionalism. Constitutional totalism has not won a total victory, however. Political constitutionalists, both on and off the bench, continue to dig in their heels. This and the following chapter explore the ongoing debates. The present chapter begins with a brief account of the state of play with respect to conventions and political questions. It then moves to the centrally important issue about how expansively to interpret legal rights, an issue that affects constitutional reach as it relates to both state action and the private sector. The next chapter focuses more comprehensively on questions of constitutional "reach into the private sector."

Judicial Supervision of Conventions and Executive Prerogative

Constitutional conventions are non-legal public-sector rules and principles of clear constitutional status and often of considerable importance, such as the conventions of responsible government. Being non-legal, they have traditionally been considered beyond the reach of judicial supervision and enforcement (Dicey [1885] 1962, 439; Haynes 1965, 11). Political actors were understood to form these conventions through political precedents, and the rules were enforced (and then reinforced) by the

actors feeling bound by them (Knopff, Baker, LeRoy 2009, 71; Malcolmson et al. 2016, 16–17). This emphasis on *political* actors in the formation
and enforcement of conventional rules places constitutional conventions in the category of political constitutionalism. It is possible to imagine entire constitutions being completely conventional in this sense.
Indeed, this was a traditional way of characterizing the British Constitution during the heyday of "parliamentary supremacy." In this sense, even
a "totalistic" constitution might be an entirely conventional "court-free"
zone, entirely free of "legal constitutionalism."

Yet legal constitutionalism has made inroads even with respect to constitutional conventions, gradually bringing them within judicial reach in
interesting (though ambiguous) ways. True, Canadian judges continue
to insist that they cannot "enforce" constitutional conventions (*Conacher
and Democracy Watch v. Canada* 2010, para. 12), but when called upon to
exercise what Peter Russell (1983a) has called "bold statescraft," they
have also engaged in what he terms the "questionable jurisprudence"[2]
of defining the very conventions they cannot enforce (and sometimes
defining them in novel and surprising ways).[3] A similar tension appeared
in the recent UK decision relating to the "Brexit" process of leaving the

---

2 In the Supreme Court of Canada's famous "Patriation Reference" (*Reference Re Resolution
   to Amend the Constitution* 1981), it pronounced that the power to amend the then British
   North America Act, 1867, required a "substantial degree" rather than unanimous
   consent of all ten provinces. In their submissions to the Court, only one province
   (Saskatchewan) requested substantial consent, whereas the rest of the "Gang of Eight"
   provinces pushed for the traditional requirement of unanimous consent. It has been
   argued that the result of this decision led to the break between Quebec and the
   other members of the Gang of Eight that eventually led to patriation of the Canadian
   Constitution (Romanow, Whyte, and Leeson 1984). Not long after, in the "Quebec
   Veto Reference" (*Reference Re Objection by Quebec to a Resolution to amend the Constitution*
   1982), the province of Quebec attempted to get the constitutional amendments of
   1982 reversed by arguing that the Supreme Court had sidestepped the widely accepted
   process of constitutional convention formulation described by Sir Ivor Jennings: "First:
   what are the precedents; secondly, did the actors in the precedents believe they were
   bound by a rule; and thirdly, is there a reason for the rule? A single precedent with
   a good reason may be enough to establish the rule" (quoted in Knopff, Baker, and
   LeRoy 2009, 71). On the "Quebec Veto Reference," Peter Russell remarked, "It was not
   the Supreme Court's most convincing performance ... It was a political response to a
   political challenge dressed up in judicial clothing" (2004, 129).
3 In New Zealand, several observers (Butler 2014, 8; Joseph 2004, 325) have noted that
   the judiciary has preserved the traditional understanding: constitutional conventions
   should not be within the purview of judicial construction (see *Shaw v. Commissioner of
   Inland Revenue* 1999, 158). In the United Kingdom, by contrast, there is an instance
   (*A.G. v Jonathan Cape Ltd.* 1976) where the High Court used one of the conventions
   of responsible government (cabinet solidarity) to inform its understanding of

European Union. On the one hand, judges were portrayed as "neither the parents nor the guardians of political conventions; they are merely observers." On the other hand, they could "recognise the operation of a political convention in the context of deciding a legal question" (*Miller* 2017, para. 146).

The ambiguity resulting from judges recognizing and defining what they will not attempt to enforce must be underscored. Judges have sometimes taken a role in *supervising* the evolution of conventional rules, as opposed to *applying* them in the manner of more obviously *legal* rules. Although legal constitutionalism has advanced in the realm of conventions, it has not secured a complete victory. The continuing reluctance of judges to enforce conventions in the way they enforce obviously legal rules demonstrates the persistence of some degree of political constitutionalism.

It has also been argued that highly contentious matters involving executive prerogative concerning foreign policy and international relations are "political questions" that, like conventions, lie beyond the reach of the judicially enforceable constitution and should be left to the exclusive determination of the non-judicial branches of government (Hausegger, Hennigar, and Riddell 2015, 71). In the United States, this "political questions" doctrine retains some vitality (O'Brien 1986, 172–4), but the Supreme Court of Canada has rejected the doctrine in Charter jurisprudence (*Operation Dismantle v. The Queen* 1985).[4] On political questions, it seems that the Canadian judiciary enjoys greater reach than its American counterpart – that legal constitutionalism has, in this respect, advanced farther north of the 49th parallel. Yet, here again, the Court obviously remains aware of the problems that support the "political questions" doctrine – namely, the difficulty of judges second-guessing highly sensitive international matters. Although constitutionally based judicial power may reach these issues, in practice the Court has been cautious about imposing too many constraints on executive discretion (see *Canada (Prime Minister) v. Khadr* 2010).[5]

---

confidentiality to prevent the publication of a cabinet minister's private writings (Jenkins 2009, 182–3).

4 This case concerned a section 7 Charter challenge brought against the government in an attempt to block the US government's testing of cruise missiles over Canadian soil.

5 In its unanimous ruling the Supreme Court ruled that Canadian officials had violated Omar Khadr's section 7 rights to liberty during his interrogation in Guantanamo Bay in a manner not in accordance with the principles of fundamental justice. Despite this finding, the Court did not impose a remedy, citing the need to respect the executive's ability to conduct foreign policy.

In the United Kingdom, the judiciary has historically recognized that a royal prerogative existed but refrained from ruling on the merits of its use in particular cases (Poole 2010, 148). Courts in the United Kingdom have ruled that Orders in Council enacted by the Crown should be treated as legislation subject to the HRA, but they have not treated prerogative powers generally in this way (*A. v. Secretary of State for the Home Department* 2004; *R. v. Secretary of State for Foreign and Commonwealth Affairs, ex p Bancoult (No 2)* 2008). In the *Miller* ("Brexit") decision mentioned above, the UK Supreme Court was asked whether triggering article 50 under the 1972 European Communities Act was a matter of Crown prerogative or whether Parliament needed to be consulted. The Supreme Court ruled that leaving the EU required consultation of Parliament. On its face, this decision might appear to be a victory for political constitutionalism's desire for greater legislative participation in such an important matter; however, several scholars with political-constitutionalist leanings were critical of the narrowing of the executive's discretion to enter and exit international treaties (see Elliott 2017; Finnis 2016).[6]

In New Zealand, the judiciary has acknowledged that the NZBORA applies to Crown prerogative and can affect executive action (*Burt v. Governor-General* 1992). But as in the United Kingdom and Canada, courts have been reticent to use the NZBORA to limit prerogative powers (Rishworth 2003, 88–9).[7] In New Zealand, too, political constitutionalism retains some life.

Underlying Constitutional Values

What about more mundane questions of domestic public policy? Here the question of judicially applicable constitutional reach concerns how narrowly or expansively to interpret explicit constitutional provisions. In Canada, for example, there has been a long-standing debate about whether, and if so, to what extent, labour law is governed by the Charter of Rights and Freedoms. Section 2(d) of the Charter guarantees

---

6 This dynamic repeated itself in a subsequent Brexit constitutional dispute. The so-called *Miller II* (2019) case concerned the justiciability of prorogation. The UK Supreme Court limited the scope of when it is lawful for a prime minister to request the Crown to prorogue Parliament. Here, too, political constitutionalists raised concerns about the further expansion of judicial supervision of executive prerogative (Ekins and Laws 2019; Finnis 2019).

7 There are some limits to what the New Zealand courts will supervise when it comes to Crown prerogative. In *Curtis v. Ministry of Defence* (2002) the Court said challenging a minister's decision to reduce the size of the air force was not justiciable (Joseph 2013, 127).

"freedom of association," but in an early Charter decision, *Reference Re Public Service Employee Relations Act (Alta)* (1987),[8] a majority of the Supreme Court determined that this was an individual rather than a collective right. That is, section 2(d) guaranteed the right of individuals to do in association what they were free to do as individuals, but it did not vest rights directly in such groups as unions. Thus, collective bargaining and the right to strike were not constitutionally mandated. However desirable these rights might be in principle, the Charter did not require all desirable things. As Justice McIntyre put it in the majority 1987 judgment, "while a liberal and not overly legalistic approach should be taken to constitutional interpretation, the *Charter* should not be regarded as an empty vessel to be filled with whatever meaning we might wish from time to time" (para. 151). From this perspective, the collective dimensions of labour law had been left to legislative discretion. As Christopher Hunter (2011) puts it, the Court's traditional jurisprudence "viewed the collective bargaining process as a creature of modern legislation, distinct from, and not protected by, the fundamental freedoms envisioned by the *Charter*." Simply put, it lay beyond the Charter's reach.

This reading of the Charter's section 2(d) "freedom of association" was controversial from the beginning. In *Reference Re Public Service*, it generated the vigorous dissent of Justices Dickson and Wilson, who insisted that both collective bargaining and the right to strike were protected by the Charter's guarantee of freedom of association. In subsequent cases, the perspectives of this dissent gradually chipped away at McIntyre's majority judgment, until the Supreme Court dramatically and explicitly reversed course in *Health Services* (2007).[9] Gone was the view of "the collective bargaining process as a creature of modern legislation, distinct from, and not protected by, the fundamental freedoms envisioned by the *Charter*" (Hunter 2011). The two-decade-long exclusion of collective bargaining from the Charter's ambit, said the Court's majority, could "not withstand principled scrutiny and should be rejected" (*Health Services* 2007, para. 22). The Court followed this up in *Saskatchewan Federation of*

---

8 *Reference Re Public Service Employee Relations Act* (1987) is one of the three *Labour Trilogy* Supreme Court decisions handed down on the same day in 1987; see also *PSAC v. Canada* (1987) and *RWDSU v. Saskatchewan* (1987). These three cases dealt, respectively, with the following three labour issues: provincial legislation prohibiting essential public-sector workers from striking, federal legislation altering public-sector wages outside of collective bargaining, and back-to-work legislation.

9 In an attempt to reduce growing health-care costs in British Columbia, the provincial government passed a law to overturn several collective agreements and loosen restrictions on contracting out work in provincial hospitals. The law was challenged and was eventually decided by the Supreme Court of Canada in *Health Services*.

Labour (2015, para. 3) by giving "constitutional benediction" to the right to strike, finding that it was "an indispensable component" of the right to meaningful collective bargaining.[10] Both of the features of labour law – collective bargaining and the right to strike – that had been beyond the Charter in 1987 had now been brought within its reach. The earlier, narrow interpretation of freedom of association had been replaced by a much broader reading.

Not everyone agreed with the Court's change of mind, however. Writing two years after *Health Services*, Peter Hogg affirmed the appropriateness of the earlier perspective, arguing that "without any clear prescription in the Charter, there is much to be said for leaving the regulation of labour relations to elected legislative bodies (and the sanction of the ballot box)" (quoted in *Fraser* 2011, para. 227). Quoting Hogg with approval in *Fraser* (2011), Justice Rothstein called for the reversal of *Health Services*, holding that the right to collective bargaining was "a stand-alone right created by the Court, not by the Charter" (*Fraser* 2011, para. 200). Legal scholar Dwight Newman (2015) later levelled the same charge against the Court's 2015 creation of a right to strike, noting that "Canada specifically contemplated such a right when the drafting process for the Charter was underway in 1982 and specifically excluded it." For these critics, the Charter did not explicitly reach important elements of labour relations, and the Court should not extend constitutional reach (and its own authority) by creating new rights.

Of course, the majority of judges in *Health Services* and *Saskatchewan Federation of Labour* did not see themselves as creating new rights. As they saw it, rights that were not explicit in the constitutional text were necessarily implicit in the principles or values underlying that text. According to *Health Services*, for example, collective bargaining must be constitutionally protected because it complements and promotes the "Charter values" of "human dignity, equality, liberty, respect for the autonomy of the person and the enhancement of democracy" (2007, paras. 81–5). Because the terms describing some of these underlying principles – e.g., "human dignity" or "autonomy" – appear nowhere in the relevant constitutional text, they are often also described as "unwritten principles" (McLachlin 2006, 151).

Justice Rothstein expressed serious doubts about the rigour of this underlying-principles approach: "Either the Charter requires something

---

10 The Saskatchewan government enacted several laws expanding the scope of public workers considered "essential" (therefore constraining the ability to strike) and increased the threshold employee support needed to form a union (therefore making it more difficult to collectively organize).

or it does not" (*Fraser* 2011, para. 252). The point of constitutional inter-pretation, Rothstein insisted, "is not to simply promote, as much as possi-ble, values that some subjectively think underpin the *Charter* in a general sense" (para. 252). These comments echo Justice McIntyre's warnings in *Reference Re Public Service* that "the *Charter* should not be regarded as an empty vessel to be filled with whatever meaning we might wish from time to time" (1987, para. 151).

Rothstein's concerns were rejected by his colleagues in the *Fraser* majority. Justices McLachlin and LeBel wrote, "We can only respond that a value-oriented approach to broadly worded guarantees of the *Charter* has been repeatedly endorsed by the *Charter* jurisprudence over the last quarter century" (*Fraser* 2011, para. 96). McLachlin and LeBel are right about the prevalence of the Charter values approach. Yet their dismissal of Rothstein's views was too quick and easy. The issues Rothstein raises are of enduring jurisprudential significance and interest. They bring us to what is nowadays perhaps the most important disagreement between legal and political constitutionalists with respect to constitutional reach – namely, their differing views of the relationship between explicit con-stitutional provisions and the broader principles or values underlying those provisions.

To avoid confusion, the constitutional values or principles of inter-est should be distinguished from the constitutional conventions consid-ered above. Although conventions – politically generated, extra-legal constitutional rules – are also generally described as "unwritten" parts of our Constitution, we have seen that courts deem them to be judi-cially unenforceable (though judges sometimes recognize and help to define them). By contrast, the issue posed by the values or principles that underlie written constitutional provisions is precisely whether they are as judicially enforceable as their explicit legal examples.

In other words, while it is undeniable that explicit constitutional pro-visions reflect underlying values or principles, the question is whether, or to what extent, these principles are themselves judicially enforceable constitutional law. There exists an expansive view of constitutionalism according to which explicit provisions are mere examples of broader zones of constitutional protection based on underlying values (Walters 2008). This view, which sees a judicially applicable constitutional dimen-sion in most issues of public importance, obviously extends the reach of legal constitutionalism. Political constitutionalists take a more restric-tive view, insisting that only the explicit examples are judicially enforce-able. This restrictive view distinguishes between the legitimate use of underlying values to construe explicit provisions and their illegitimate use to create entirely new constitutional rules. According to political

constitutionalists, some publicly important issues lie beyond the reach
of the judicially applicable constitution. The issues in this debate are
not limited to Canada's jurisprudential quarrels about labour law; they
crop up regularly and in a variety of contexts and regimes positioned
along a continuum of approaches to constitutionalism. Below, I use five
cases – two from the United States (*Griswold v. Connecticut* and *Alden v.
Maine*), two from Canada (the *Provincial Judges Reference* and the *Secession
Reference*), and one from New Zealand (*Hosking v. Runting*) – to flesh out
what is at stake between those advocating expansive conceptions of constitutional reach and those attempting to constrain it.

Griswold v. Connecticut (1965)

At issue in *Griswold* was a Connecticut law prohibiting the sale of contraceptives. The law was no longer generally enforced in the 1960s, but
opponents eventually manufactured the standing necessary to challenge
it. A majority of the Supreme Court found that the law infringed the
right to privacy, especially marital privacy. But where in the US Constitution was this right to be found? The answer was in the "penumbras
formed by emanations from" a set of explicit constitutional rights that
protect particular aspects of privacy (484). The First Amendment's protection of freedom of religion and speech, for example, arguably has
privacy dimensions. So do the Third Amendment's constraint on sol-
diers being quartered in private homes and the Fourth Amendment's
protection against unreasonable search and seizure. Similarly, the Fifth
Amendment's guarantee against self-incrimination can be seen as a
kind of privacy right. Finally, the Ninth Amendment's acknowledgment
of rights "retained by the people" could include privacy rights. According to Justice Douglas's majority opinion in *Griswold*, the penumbras of
these explicit rights create a "zone" of constitutionally protected privacy.
Or, to restate the claim, underlying the various explicit privacy rights is
the more general principle or value of privacy. This unwritten underlying principle gives meaning and coherence to the explicit rights, which
should be seen as examples of a broader zone of constitutional protection. Other examples of the underlying principle can and should be
made explicit, and brought to the surface, over time. These include the
kinds of privacy needed to invalidate laws against contraception and
later (and even more controversially) against abortion.

Critics of this jurisprudential approach have always resisted its elastic
potential to constitutionalize (and hence judicialize) almost everything.
In these critics' view, *Griswold* goes far beyond using the underlying principle (or value) of privacy to give interpretive meaning and

stronger protection to explicit privacy protections, such as the prohibition of unreasonable search and seizure; instead, it justifies the creation of entirely new constitutional rights. As Justice Stewart wrote in dissent in *Griswold*, the facts of the case did not involve:

> any abridgment of "the freedom of speech, or of the press; or the right of the people peaceably to assemble, and to petition the Government for a redress of grievances." No soldier has been quartered in any house. There has been no search, and no seizure. Nobody has been compelled to be a witness against himself. (529)

Not that Justice Stewart favoured the anti-contraception law at stake in *Griswold.* He considered it an "uncommonly silly law," and asserted his own view that "contraceptives in the relationship of marriage should be left to personal and private choice, based upon each individual's moral, ethical, and religious beliefs" (528). Like Justice Douglas, in other words, Stewart clearly considered the law to be a regrettable infringement of privacy. But the Court had not been asked whether the law "is unwise, or even asinine"; it had been asked only whether it "violates the United States Constitution," and in Justice Stewart's view it did not. In other words, not all "silly," "unwise," or even "asinine" laws were unconstitutional. Privacy was a good thing, but the Constitution protected only some aspects of it, leaving the rest to legislatures, which were free to enact silly laws. The remedy provided by the Constitution for such laws was legislative and electoral, not judicial:

> If, as I should surely hope, the law before us does not reflect the standards of the people of Connecticut, the people of Connecticut can freely exercise their true Ninth and Tenth Amendment rights to persuade their elected representatives to repeal it. That is the constitutional way to take this law off the books. (531)

Alden v. Maine (1999)

Alden arose when employees of the state of Maine filed suit in their state court alleging that their employer had violated the federal Fair Standards Act. When the case reached the Supreme Court, the question was whether federal legislation could make non-consenting states liable for damages in their own courts. In a narrowly decided (5–4) judgment, the Court found that this unconstitutionally infringed states' "sovereign immunity." There are striking parallels between the judicial disagreement in this case and the earlier disagreement in *Griswold.*

The constitutional provision most obviously relevant to *Alden* was the Eleventh Amendment, which states that "the Judicial power of the United States shall not be construed to extend to any suit in law or equity, commenced or prosecuted against one of the United States by Citizens of another State, or by Citizens or Subjects of any Foreign State." This amendment certainly does protect a degree of sovereign immunity, but note that (leaving aside the "foreign state" clause) it explicitly prevents only "the judicial power of the United States" – i.e., federal courts – from being used by citizens of one state to sue another state. But in *Alden* citizens had sued their *own state* in its *own courts.* They did so on the basis of a federal law, which may raise questions of sovereign immunity, but not of the kind explicitly prohibited by the Eleventh Amendment.

Justice Kennedy's majority opinion conceded that the Eleventh Amendment did not reach the facts of the case before the Court, but it did find a violation of sovereign immunity anyway by "regard[ing] the Eleventh Amendment as evidencing and exemplifying" a "broader concept of immunity, implicit in the Constitution" (728). This approach is strongly reminiscent of the *Griswold* majority's extrapolation of a more general right to (marital) privacy from the provisions of the Bill of Rights protecting other, particular aspects of privacy. The majority in *Alden* saw sovereign immunity as "a constitutional principle" foundational to the understanding of the sovereign states that ratified the Constitution. For Kennedy, the Eleventh Amendment "confirms the promise inherit in the original document" (714) – or in "the structure of the original Constitution" (728) – and therefore "it follows that the scope of the States' immunity from suit is demarcated not by the text of the Amendment alone but by fundamental postulates implicit in the constitutional design" (728–9). For Kennedy and the majority, the Constitution's federal character would be undermined if they came to a different conclusion. To allow non-consenting states to be sued in their own courts based on federal statutes would be tantamount to saying, "the Congress may circumvent the federal design by regulating the States directly when it pleases to do so" (759). This would amount to Congress "treat[ing] these sovereign entities as mere prefectures" rather than with the "esteem due to them as joint participants in a federal system" (758).

In dissent, Justice Souter on behalf of his colleagues expressed deep skepticism towards the majority's argument in general, and in particular towards its claim "that the state-court action is barred by the scheme of American federalism" (761). The dissenters argued that if the majority were indeed correct in deducing a broader, and judicially enforceable, concept of immunity from the federal structure of the Constitution, this would mean "the Eleventh Amendment itself was unnecessary" (760). The amendment would be superfluous because other categories of suits it limits would also have been captured by broad underlying immunity retained by the states. For the dissenters, the majority's federalism argument is "demonstrably mistaken" (790). In their view, the Constitution only recognizes those aspects of sovereign immunity detailed in the Eleventh Amendment. Again, this is reminiscent of Justice Stewart's dissent in *Griswold*. Just as Stewart resisted treating explicit references to privacy within the Constitution as elaborations of a broader right to privacy, so the *Alden* dissenters resisted viewing the Eleventh Amendment as merely "exemplifying" a "broader concept of immunity implicit in the Constitution."

Provincial Judges Reference (1997)

In Canada, the essence of the *Griswold* and *Alden* debates is evident in the *Provincial Judges Reference*. This case arose because provincial lower-court judges, along with the public sector more generally, had been subject to across-the-board salary reductions as part of governmental deficit- and debt-reduction strategies. The case concerned whether provincial governments could cut judicial salaries in this way without violating "judicial independence." The Supreme Court of Canada decided that the Constitution required judicial salaries to be set on the recommendation of independent judicial compensation commissions. A government's decision to pay less than such a commission advised, moreover, would be subject to review and potential reversal by judges.

Where did this hitherto unknown constitutional requirement of judicial compensation commissions come from? Not from any explicit constitutional provision but from the principle of judicial independence underlying several constitutional provisions. Section 11(d) of the Charter guarantees the right "to be presumed innocent until proven guilty according to law in a fair and public hearing by an independent and impartial tribunal." Section 99 of the Constitution Act, 1867, states that "Judges of the Superior Courts shall hold office during good behaviour," and "shall be removable" only "by the Governor General on Address of the Senate and House of Commons" (though it was not these superior court judges whose salaries were being reduced). Section 100 of the 1867 Constitution Act specifies that the salaries of federally appointed judges "shall be fixed and provided by the Parliament of Canada." Finally, the statement in the 1867 constitutional preamble – that the Constitution was "similar in Principle to that of the United Kingdom" – has been understood to include the principle of judicial independence.

In Chief Justice Lamer's majority opinion in the *Provincial Judges Reference*, the "express" or "substantive" provisions of the Constitution "merely elaborate" (para. 95) "the underlying, unwritten, and organizing principles found in the preamble to the *Constitution Act, 1867*" (para. 107). As "the very source of the substantive provisions" of the Constitution, the underlying, unwritten principles are "not only … key to construing the express provisions," but may also be used to "fill out gaps in the express terms of the constitutional scheme" (para. 95). As does Douglas in *Griswold* and Kennedy in *Alden*, Lamer holds that provisions expressly protecting parts of a basic principle are "merely" components of a broader constitutional zone of protection for that principle, all of which is open to judicial enforcement. Accordingly, judges may bring new components to the surface from time to time, such as the right to marital privacy in *Griswold*, the state sovereign immunity at issue in *Alden*, and the right to judicial compensation commissions in the *Provincial Judges Reference*.

As in *Griswold* and *Alden*, this elastic view of the Constitution attracted opposition in the *Provincial Judges Reference*. Justice La Forest's dissent in the latter case closely resembles Justice Stewart's in *Griswold* and Justice Souter's in *Alden*. For La Forest, "the express provisions of the Constitution are not, as the Chief Justice contends, 'elaborations of the underlying, unwritten, and organizing principles found in the preamble to the *Constitution Act, 1867*.' On the contrary, they *are* the Constitution" (para. 319, emphasis in original). Like Stewart, La Forest resists the idea of a constitution that extends to everything that might in principle be desirable. Underlying principles can, to use Lamer's formulation, be helpful in "construing the express provisions," but for La Forest using them to "fill out gaps … in the constitutional scheme" amounts to rewriting that scheme rather than interpreting it. "Construing" express provisions is a democratically justifiable judicial function, in this view, but to add entirely new, previously unthought-of rights is "to subvert the democratic foundation of judicial review" (para. 319).[11]

---

11 History repeated itself in *Trial Lawyers Association of British Columbia v. British Columbia (Attorney General)* (2014). The majority invalidated court hearing fees as unconstitutional due to their adverse effects on access to justice. The majority relied on section 96 of the Constitution Act, 1867 (the federal government's power to make appointments to superior courts in the provinces), and the underlying constitutional principle of the "rule of law." Justice Rothstein, dissenting forcibly, channelled the political-constitutionalist perspective against the majority's elastic approach to constitutional reach: "In a constitutional democracy such as ours, courts must be wary of subverting democracy and its accountability mechanisms beneath an overly *expansive* vision of constitutionalism" (para. 83, emphasis added). It is worth quoting his critique of the majority reasoning at length: "the majority uses the rule of law to

Peter Russell, among others (Leclair 2002; Patenaude 2001), agreed with Justice La Forest. Not only did Russell find the "reading of our constitution" on which the Court based the new requirement for judicial compensation commissions "very far-fetched," but he noted that "the six Supreme Court justices who went along with this decision seemed not a bit disturbed by the conflict of interest inherent in their ruling" – namely, that it gives "judges the final word in deciding how much they should be paid" (2007, 68). Russell *was* disturbed – so disturbed, in fact, that he considered the *Judges Reference* his "top candidate" for reversal through the Charter's section 33 notwithstanding clause (67). Leclair, while not suggesting use of the notwithstanding clause, raised similar criticisms – mainly, that the ruling undermines rather than strengthens judicial independence:

> The creditability of the judiciary requires that judges not initiate recourse to the law, particularly in situations where they are personally or financially interested. This precaution should apply with even greater stringency in cases where a statute is challenged on the basis of a judicially created principle. (2002, 432–3)

Secession Reference (1998)

In Canada, the use of underlying unwritten principles to "fill gaps" in the constitutional scheme was taken to its "zenith" in the *Secession Reference* (Carter 2007, 357). In this case, the constitutional "gap" to be filled was arguably what Michael Foley has called a constitutional "abeyance,"[12] – i.e., a purposeful constitutional silence that places the object of that silence beyond the reach of the Constitution (1989, xi; LeRoy 2004).

---

support reading a general constitutional right to access the superior courts into s. 96. This provision of the *Constitution Act, 1867*, requires that the existence and core jurisdiction of superior courts be preserved, but this does not, for the reasons herein, necessarily imply the general right of access to superior courts described by the majority. So long as the courts maintain their character as judicial bodies and exercise the core functions of courts, the demands of the Constitution are satisfied. In using an unwritten principle to support expanding the ambit of s. 96 to such an extent, the majority subverts the structure of the Constitution and jeopardizes the primacy of the written text" (para. 93).

12　Foley (1989, xii) describes the seventeenth-century British Constitution as an "unsustainable mixture of royal absolutism, Parliamentary power and common law rights." This combination of principles was held together by a system of abeyances "by which the logically irreconcilable issue of final sovereignty was habitually and effectively evaded."

In Canada, the question of how a province might secede from Confederation is plausibly understood as such an abeyance. The potential secession of the province of Quebec was a key factor in launching the constitutional reform process that led to the Constitution Act, 1982, with its Charter of Rights and Freedoms and its newly domesticated (i.e., "patriated") amending formulae (Romanow, Whyte, and Leeson 1984, xix; Russell 2004, 99). Given the prominence of secession during this constitution-making process, the absolute silence of the new constitutional documents on how to secede speaks loudly in support of the claim that this was indeed a purposeful silence, an "abeyance." It strongly suggests that the architects of the 1982 amendments, knowing the secession issue would need to be addressed, preferred to deal with it through political rather than legal means.[13] On this basis, one might consider the issue of secession to be a gap in the constitutional order that should not be filled by judges.

However, the Supreme Court refused in the *Secession Reference* to declare the Constitution irrelevant to the question of secession. Determining that an issue as important as secession could not lie beyond the reach of the Constitution – i.e., that we enjoyed a "gapless constitution" with respect to secession – the Court declared a constitutional duty to negotiate in good faith upon an affirmative answer by a clear majority to a clear referendum question on secession (Howse and Malkin 1997). Significantly, the Court based this duty not on any explicitly relevant constitutional provisions, but on underlying and unwritten constitutional "values" or "principles" (the two terms are used extensively and interchangeably throughout the judgment) (paras. 50, 66–7, 78–80). The four main values or principles were federalism, democracy, the rule of law, and minority rights. Some of these are particular to the Constitution Act, 1867 (federalism); others infuse the entire Constitution (democracy, rule of law, and minority rights) (para. 34).

As with *Griswold, Alden,* and the *Provincial Judges Reference,* the unwritten principles and values highlighted in the *Secession Reference* were all embodied in "express" or "substantive" provisions of the written Constitution and could helpfully illuminate the interpretation of those provisions. Yet the express provisions of the Constitution played little role in the judgment.[14] Indeed, according to José Woehrling (1999), "the

---

13 When the federal government referred questions pertaining to secession to the
   Supreme Court, the Quebec government refused to participate as a litigant and an
   amicus curae was appointed by the Court in its stead. Quebec's refusal to participate
   reflected its view that this was ultimately a political question.
14 For a detailed examination for this aspect of the *Secession Reference,* see LeRoy (2004).

most remarkable part of the decision was how the court answered all the questions without ever referring to the actual specific provisions of the constitution" (see also Morton 2002, 37). The reason was that the Court clearly needed to go beyond normal constitutional interpretation and fill a "gap" with a new constitutional rule or right. If *Griswold* arguably created a new right to marital privacy, and the *Provincial Judges Reference* created a new constitutional requirement for judicial compensation commissions, then the *Secession Reference* "essentially amended the amending formula of the constitution by clarifying the legal procedures that would be required for a province to leave the federation" (Bakvis, Baier, and Brown 2009, 89).

Unlike *Griswold*, *Alden*, and the *Provincial Judges Reference*, the *Secession Reference* generated no dissent. The judgment came in the form of a unanimous, unsigned opinion of "The Court." This is not surprising given the highly controversial public issues at stake. Faced with issues of such sensitivity, the Court strives for the increased institutional legitimacy conferred by *per curiam* unanimity (McCormick and Zanoni 2019).

Hosking v. Runting (2004)

A New Zealand case, *Hosking v. Runting* (2004), also illustrates the use of underlying values to extend constitutional reach. This case concerned whether a prominent family could file an injunction to prevent a magazine from publishing photos of its infant children. Among the many matters addressed by the case was the issue that dominated *Griswold* – namely, whether the NZBORA implied a general right to privacy not explicit in the document.

The Hoskings were subject to considerable media attention and a magazine took photos of their infant children without their knowledge while shopping in public. When the couple became aware of the photos, they filed an injunction against the photographer arguing the photos invaded their children's right to privacy. The photographer, of course, claimed freedom of expression. This was, in other words, a classic example of clashing rights, one of which (freedom of expression) was explicitly codified in the NZBORA, while the other (privacy) was not. The Hoskings wanted the court to develop a new common-law tort of privacy, based in part on uncodified NZBORA values (2004, paras. 263, 265).

According to Justice Tipping, the absence of an explicitly codified right to privacy in the NZBORA was not necessarily fatal to the Hoskings' case. The "lack of any express recognition of a right to privacy in the Bill of Rights," wrote Tipping, "should not ... inhibit common law developments found to be appropriate" (para. 226). Such developments should be informed by the values of privacy implied by explicit NZBORA provisions. For example, section 21 of the NZBORA protects against unreasonable search and seizure, and this is "not very far from an entitlement to be free from unreasonable intrusions into personal privacy" (para. 224). Furthermore, "the values that underpin s.21" are for Tipping reinforced by New Zealand's *international* obligations (para. 226), especially as they relate to the International Covenant on Civil and Political Rights (ICCPR). The NZBORA's preamble states that rights and freedoms guaranteed in the act "affirms New Zealand's commitment" to the ICCPR, and that document contains an explicit privacy guarantee (article 17).

But should the NZBORA's explicitly codified guarantee of freedom of expression not prevail over uncodified privacy principles? Justice Tipping did not think so. He treated NZBORA's freedom-of-expression provision as itself no more than the exemplification of underlying principles. For Tipping, freedom of expression is "recognized" by the text of the NZBORA "only because it advances certain important underlying human values, the most relevant of which in this context is individual autonomy" (Geddis 2004, 700; *Hosking* 2004, para. 224). For Tipping – as for Justice Douglas in *Griswold*, Justice Kennedy in *Alden*, and Justice Lamer in *Provincial Judges Reference* – it is the underlying principles, not their currently codified exemplifications, that are truly important, and judges are free to bring as-yet uncodified exemplifications to the surface. Treating the judiciary's role in this case as one of "reconciling competing values," Tipping in effect collapses the distinction between codified and uncodified values.

Justice Tipping did not persuade all of his colleagues. Justice Keith was critical of the efforts to recognize an underlying right to privacy because a "provision on privacy was deliberately excluded from the Bill of Rights" (para. 181). Citing the government's preparations for the ICCPR ratification and the 1985 White Paper outlining the contents and scope of the NZBORA, Keith noted that a general right to privacy was deliberatively excluded in part because aspects of privacy had been protected in certain circumstances by other legislation. As Gavin Phillipson similarly notes, there was no "obligation" under the NZBORA for Tipping's "bold move," because it does not "incorporate Article 17, the privacy guarantee of the ICCPR" (2011, 147–8).[15] Justice Keith warned of the controversy

---

15 John Smillie believes that the New Zealand courts use "international agreements" and other external sources to "provide evidence of contemporary values that can be relied upon by way of 'analogy' to develop the common law along 'parallel' lines" but

associated with the American approach to this issue by pointing to cases like *Griswold* where "broader concepts of privacy (not expressed in the Constitution) were invoked amidst controversy to strike down prohibitions on the sale of contraceptives to married couples (*Griswold v Connecticut*) ... and to ... state abortion laws (*Roe v Wade*)" (para. 182). In contrast, Keith preferred a more politically constitutionalist approach that was admittedly "also heavily contested" but wherein "those aspects of privacy were dealt with by legislation" (para. 183). For Keith, privacy guarantees have been left to the parliamentary political process and should remain there.

Justice Keith, in other words, represents the view taken by Justice Stewart in *Griswold*, Justice Souter in *Alden*, and Justice La Forest in the *Provincial Judges Reference*. These judges all worry about the elastic and perhaps limitless judicial extension of constitutional reach based on underlying principles. They prefer to stick more closely to the explicitly codified examples of those principles, leaving the rest for the political process. To borrow Justice Souter's language in *Alden*, they think that if underlying principles are considered more important than their codified examples, the codification "itself was unnecessary."

Debating Unwritten Constitutional Principles

The five cases just considered – *Griswold*, *Alden*, the *Provincial Judges Reference*, the *Secession Reference*, and *Hosking* – all display the long-standing and persistent debate about the appropriate jurisprudential use of underlying, unwritten principles or values. That such principles and values exist, that they can be appropriately understood as the "source" of "substantive" or "express" constitutional provisions (to invoke Justice Lamer's formulation), seems beyond question. How else can one understand a constitutional rule against "unreasonable search and seizure" than as a protection of "privacy"? Or a guarantee of state sovereign immunity than as recognizing the federal character of the regime? Or the protection of judicial tenure during good behaviour than as promoting "judicial independence"? Or the constitutional provision of elected legislatures than as implementing representative "democracy"? The controversy concerns how much of an underlying principle is given constitutional protection. Does the Constitution protect (in a judicially enforceable way) only those features of a principle that it expressly articulates, or are the

---

"where the direction indicated by such materials is inconvenient, it is simply ignored" (1996, 261).

express provisions "merely" examples of a broader "zone" of constitutional protection justified by the principle?

Justice Rothstein's insistence in *Fraser* that the objective of constitutional interpretation "is not to simply promote, as much as possible, values that some subjectively think underpin the *Charter* in a general sense" (para. 252) clearly takes the more restrictive view of the Constitution's reach – i.e., that it does not substantively protect everything that might plausibly be entailed in or implied by its underlying principles or values. On this he stands with Justice La Forest's view in the *Provincial Judges Reference* that "the express provisions of the Constitution are not … 'elaborations of the underlying, unwritten, and organizing principles found in the preamble to the *Constitution Act, 1867*.' On the contrary, they *are* the Constitution" (para. 319). And Justices La Forest and Rothstein both echo the view of Justice Stewart in *Griswold* that a new, previously undiscovered privacy right could not legitimately be added to the explicitly protected privacy rights. The same goes for the dissenters in *Alden* and *Hosking*, who are concerned that their colleagues in the majority risk making explicit legal features – like the bill of rights itself – logically redundant. This fits with Justice McIntyre's 1987 caution that "the *Charter* should not be regarded as an empty vessel to be filled with whatever meaning we might wish from time to time" (*Reference Re Public Service* 1987, para. 151). So, too, does the perspective of commentators who, however much they might admire the "bold statecraft" of the *Secession Reference*, think there is something questionable about jurisprudence that uses unwritten principles to amend the Constitution's explicit amending provisions in order to overcome a constitutional abeyance (Monahan 2000; Russell 1983a).

Despite the formal similarities between the debate as it occurs in *Fraser* and in the other cases, it is important to acknowledge a relevant difference. In all of the cases discussed above, the opponents of expansive constitutionalism resist what Justice Rothstein in *Fraser* calls "stand-alone" rights added to the Constitution by judges. Rothstein thinks *Health Services* created such a stand-alone right to collective bargaining and wants to undo it, a conclusion echoed by Peter Hogg. At the same time, a right to collective bargaining might be considered less dramatically stand-alone in relation to freedom of *association* than marital privacy is to the right against self-incrimination, or the duty to negotiate in good faith after a successful secession referendum is to any of Canada's explicit amending formulae. By the same token, collective bargaining (insofar as it is plausibly part of freedom of *association*) is more difficult to describe as an addition to the Constitution than, say, the requirement of judicial compensation commissions. In other words, *Health Services* perhaps comes closer than the other cases to the line between construing constitutional provisions and adding to them, and observers will be more apt to disagree about which side of that line it inhabits. For present purposes, the fact that the right to collective bargaining was seen by some Supreme Court judges and some leading authorities to be a stand-alone addition testifies to the ongoing vitality of the debate. The growing international prevalence of this expansive view of constitutional reach may also explain the short shrift given by Justices McLachlin and LeBel to the reservations about it expressed by Justice Rothstein in *Fraser*. In 2005, Justice McLachlin went to great lengths, in a well-known speech in New Zealand,[16] to defend the kind of elastic constitutional approach described by Robertson. By the time of *Fraser*, she thought it unnecessary to say more than "that a value-oriented approach to broadly worded guarantees of the *Charter* has been repeatedly endorsed by the *Charter* jurisprudence over the last quarter century" (2011, para. 96). This exhibits the confidence of victors in a debate, who can simply assert their victory without feeling the need to substantively rebut the few remaining losers.

Conclusion

Has the debate really been settled? Certainly, McLachlin's side is dominant these days, not only in Canada but, as Robertson shows, around the world. Nevertheless, the controversy continues to a significant degree, and one may doubt that it will subside entirely.

Driving the expansive view of constitutional reach is the legal-constitutionalist idea that the judicially supervised Constitution must have something to say about every question or issue that is deemed to be of significance or importance (Gardbaum 2013, 37). Under the influence of this view, even constitutional conventions, which were traditionally considered to be wholly political instruments that lay beyond judicial reach, are now authoritatively defined by judges. Similarly, sensitive matters of foreign policy and international relations are no longer considered to be "political questions" beyond judicial competence. And if existing constitutional provisions fail to address a matter of importance, judges often recruit underlying values or principles to generate new constitutional authority.

And yet, even judges who participate in the expansion of judicially applicable constitutional reach are often hesitant to go too far. Recall the unwillingness of courts to explicitly "enforce" constitutional conventions,

---

16 The text of the speech was later published; see McLachlin (2006).

even as they assume a supervisory responsibility for defining them, or their reluctance to aggressively constrain executive discretion over highly sensitive "political questions," even as they reject the idea that such questions lie beyond judicial reach.

A similar hesitancy sometimes occurs when judges use underlying principles to generate new constitutional rules. For example, although the *Secession Reference* judgment based the hitherto unrecognized constitutional duty to negotiate on underlying principles, the Court was obviously reluctant to intrude too heavily into the politically contentious issue of secession. If its judgment filled an apparent "gap" in the judicially enforceable Constitution, it did so more by supplying a guideline than anything approximating a "rule." The duty to negotiate in good faith when a clear majority answers "Yes" to a clear secession referendum question obviously leaves – and was intended by the Court to leave – a great deal to political determination. What is a clear question? What constitutes a clear majority? What needs to be negotiated in good faith? How is "good faith" determined? While the Court could not envisage a "gapless constitution" or a "court free" zone on a matter as important as secession, it was reluctant to over-specify the answers to such highly contentious political questions. Again, we see a dramatic advance of legal constitutionalism accompanied by some hesitancy and ambiguity.

In other cases, judges use underlying principles to develop much clearer constitutional rules, which they apply with less hesitancy. But such rulings often attract dissenting opinions expressing the political-constitutionalist desire for limitations on constitutional reach. The idea that important matters can never be left wholly to the non-judicial branches of government regularly attracts at least some skepticism and opposition. Peter Hogg's claim that, "without any clear [constitutional] prescription," some important questions should be left "to elected legislative bodies (and the sanction of the ballot box)" – essentially the political-constitutionalist view expressed by Justice Stewart's dissent in *Griswold* – is unlikely to die away entirely. Neither is Justice La Forest's view that going as far beyond "express provisions" as the Court's majority did in the *Provincial Judges Reference* "subvert[ed] the democratic foundation of judicial review."

Justice McIntyre, as we have seen, expressed this political-constitutionalist view of constitutional reach when he insisted in the *Reference Re Public Service* (1987) that "the *Charter* should not be regarded as an empty vessel to be filled with whatever meaning we might wish from time to time." A year later, in *R. v. Morgentaler* (1988, 141), McIntyre elaborated this perspective by quoting the late US Supreme Court justice John Marshall Harlan. "The Constitution," wrote Harlan in *Reynolds v. Sims* (1964), "is not a panacea for every blot upon the public welfare," and the Supreme Court "ordained as a judicial body [should not] be thought of as a general haven for reform movements." Harlan continued that "when, in the name of constitutional interpretation, the Court *adds* something to the Constitution that was deliberately excluded from it, the Court in reality substitutes its view of what should be so for the amending process." This political-constitutionalist perspective may be in the minority today, but it is by no means moribund. The Rothsteins of this world may more often be on the losing or dissenting side of jurisprudential debates, but they refuse to let the issue die.

Early in the Charter's history, W.R. Lederman warned about the need for "severe" limits on what is to be considered "constitutional," and to ensure we did not "constitutionalize the whole legal system." With respect to the Charter, he insisted that we should not "turn every legal issue into a specially entrenched Charter issue" (1991, 119). Clearly, Lederman's desire for "severe limits" on constitutional reach has been thwarted. While the ongoing resistance of political constitutionalists means that we have not gone all the way to "constitutionalizing everything," we have certainly travelled far in the direction of at least "state action" constitutional totalism. What about the even more comprehensive, "post liberal" version of constitutional totalism, which seeks to extend constitutional reach into the private sector? That is the subject of the next chapter.

Chapter Four

Constitutional Reach: The Private Sphere and the Clash between Liberal and Post-Liberal Constitutionalisms

Political and legal constitutionalists disagree not only about how far the judicially applicable constitution reaches across the public sector (or "state action"), but also about how far it reaches into the private sphere. How one answers the question of whether, and to what extent, the private sphere is a constitution-free zone depends in part on what side one takes in the second "clash of constitutionalisms" of interest in this study – namely, the clash between liberal and post-liberal constitutionalism (Bateman 2000, 1998; Peacock 2002; Rush 2002; Smithey 2002). Liberal constitutionalism emphasizes individual liberty, embraces governmental restraint, and takes a narrow approach to constitutional application, seeing the private sector as a constitution-free zone; this is one manifestation of contemporary political constitutionalism. Post-liberal constitutionalism, by contrast, emphasizes substantive equality, sees positive government action as a necessity for (rather than a threat to) the protection of individual freedom, and would expansively apply the judicially applicable constitution to the private sphere (Bateman 2000, 1–2; Rush 2002, 69); this perspective obviously fosters legal constitutionalism.[1]

---

1 Because of the emphasis on substantive equality and the necessity of government action, post-liberal constitutionalists share many beliefs with those who support a "positive" approach to rights, whereby a bill of rights necessitates government action. However, those in favour of positive rights do not necessarily need to approve of the application of the constitution to private activities. A related question concerns whether the text of the constitution recognizes "wide" or "narrow" range of rights. While she does not distinguish between negative and positive rights, Dixon (2015) refers to narrow versions as "partial bills of rights." This chapter does not directly address questions of positive rights or of what constitutes a "partial" bill of rights. For a fuller discussion of positive rights, including social and economic rights, see Tushnet 2008a, chs. 6 and 7. For the Canadian context, particularly sections 7 and 15, see Macfarlane 2017, 2018.

With respect to the issue of constitutional reach, political constitutionalists tend to be more sympathetic to liberal constitutionalism, whereas legal constitutionalists lean more to post-liberal constitutionalism.

Liberal and post-liberal versions of *constitutionalism*, according to Thomas Bateman, are not identical to the broader political theories of classical liberalism and post-liberalism. While "many liberal constitutionalists are [indeed] classical liberals critical of the post–New Deal state ... there is no necessary connection" between the two positions. Bateman continues,

> It is possible to make a political or moral argument for an interventionist, redistributive state while still adhering to the liberal constitutionalist principle ... Likewise, many egalitarian liberals may incline toward postliberal constitutionalism – and there are good reasons why this relationship does exist – but, again there is no necessary connection between the two positions. (2000, 30)

Indeed, this lack of ideological and institutional connection is demonstrated by Richard Bellamy (2007), one of the leading theorists of political constitutionalism, who is well known for his social democratic politics (Hirschl 2016, 6). Legal and political constitutionalism are amenable to any political program and can be a vehicle for "liberal" or "conservative" policy ends. For example, one could consider the *Lochner* era of the American Supreme Court as an example of a kind of conservative legal constitutionalism (Teles 2012). We shall encounter examples of these nuanced differences below. It is best to begin, however, with the very strong associations between each constitutional position and the broader political orientations to which they owe their names.

Liberal Constitutionalism

Certainly, liberal constitutionalism is historically grounded in, and derives its name from, classical liberalism (Schochet 1979, 4).[2] For classical liberals, a key goal is to prevent government power from trespassing on the negative rights of individuals, and constitutionalism exists primarily to achieve this goal; its central purpose is to protect the private sphere of liberty from state intrusion (Peacock 2002, 20). Accordingly, classical liberals understand a constitution primarily as "a legal limitation

---

2 The philosophical works of John Locke ([1690] 1999), Montesquieu ([1748] 2002), and the *Federalist Papers* (Hamilton et al. [1788] 2003) spring to mind.

on government" (McIlwain 2005, 24) or "state action." This is the key contribution of classical liberalism to liberal *constitutionalism* – namely, the "principle that constitutions bind government" in the name of liberty (Bateman 2000, 30).

For liberal constitutionalism, the constitution properly establishes and constrains the branches of government in their interactions with each other, and the orders or levels of government in federal systems (Manfredi 2001, xii–xiii). The "checks and balances" instituted by such state-oriented constitutionalism are, from the classical liberal perspective, intended to promote private liberty (Montesquieu [1748] 2002, 150). Constitutionalism can also promote private liberty through bills or charters of rights – a constitutional (sometimes quasi-constitutional) mechanism that has, over time, swept the world (Epp 1998; Erdos 2010; Hirschl 2004). For liberal constitutionalists, such rights documents exist to protect private liberty from state intrusion, not to protect private actors from or against each other (Manfredi 2001, 49). This means that the offices of the state are held to the higher standard of constitutional norms while private actions are not.[3] Bateman explains the distinction with this example: "If you want to exclude women from your fraternal organization's membership, the liberal constitutionalist may resent your sexism but would defend your right to discriminate in this fashion in your private dealings" (2018, 25). The state, by contrast, cannot similarly discriminate without running afoul of constitutional standards.

From the perspective of this liberal constitutionalism, rights documents govern only the relations between individuals and the state, not the relations between and among citizens in the "private sphere." In this sense, rights have only "vertical" application (Gardbaum 2003, 388; Tushnet 2008b, 196) – i.e., they govern only the "vertical" relations between government and individuals, not the "horizontal" relations of individuals with each other. Those "horizontal" relations may, of course, be governed by legislation and common law – indeed, to some extent they must be so governed (as classical liberals concede) lest the "private sphere" become the proverbial war of each against all. But the constitution, in this view, does not compel particular government regulation of the private sphere – it does not, for example, compel (though it may allow) anti-discrimination legislation to address the kind of private discrimination referred to by Bateman. Moreover, sub-constitutional legislation is itself subject to constitutional oversight on behalf of individual

---

3 Several scholars have noted that the Supreme Court of Canada has had difficulty in drawing lines between what is "government" and what is "private" or "commercial" (Bateman 2000; Hughes 2003; Hutchinson and Petter 1988).

liberty, while the constitution does not directly apply to the individuals it protects. Among other things, this means that while citizens can invoke constitutional provisions in challenging state action, they cannot use those provisions to sue each other as private individuals.

The extent to which the framers of the bills of rights in Canada, New Zealand, and the United Kingdom advocated liberal or post-liberal constitutionalism varies. Many observers have noted that the framers of the Charter did not intend for the new bill of rights to apply to private common law (Bateman 1998, 9; Dodek 2018, 354; McLachlin 2002, 198; Reichman 2002, 364). In contrast, the White Paper outlining the scope and purpose of the NZBORA "was explicit" that the common law, including the private common law, would be applied and updated with reference to the NZBORA (Rishworth 2003, 99; see also Geddis 2004, 686). The text of the United Kingdom's HRA is silent on its relationship to the common law. Both the House of Commons and House of Lords legislative debates concerning the passage of the HRA reveal that the common law was not thought to be affected by the HRA. For example, the home secretary responsible for the bill stated, "We decided that Convention rights should be available in proceedings involving what might be very broadly described as 'the state,' but that they would not be directly justiciable actions between private individuals" (quoted in Phillipson 1999, 827).

Scholars in all three countries can point to some support for the liberal-constitutional view. In the Canadian context, liberal constitutionalists find support for their view of constitutional application in section 32 of the Charter, which states that the Charter "applies to the Parliament and government of Canada in respect of all matters within the authority of Parliament" and "to the legislature and government of each province in respect of all matters within the authority of each province." For the liberal constitutionalist, this clearly indicates that the Charter binds only "state action" (be it federal or provincial in its source). In New Zealand, liberal constitutionalists point to section 3 of the NZBORA, which states that it applies only to "acts done" by the three traditional branches of government and by persons or bodies performing public functions. During the parliamentary debate to adopt the NZBORA, Prime Minister Geoffrey Palmer stressed that "citizens will not be able to invoke its provisions in order to sue one another" (quoted in Stemplewitz 2006, 198). Similarly, liberal constitutionalists in the United Kingdom can point to the HRA's section 6(1), which states that "It is unlawful for a *public authority* to act in a way which is incompatible with a Convention right" (emphasis added).

This liberal constitutionalism has received support in the jurisprudence of all three countries. In Canada, Justice McIntyre found in

Dolphin Delivery (1986) that section 32 was "conclusive" (para. 33) in limiting the Charter's scope to regulating "the relationship between the individual and the Government" (para. 26). The Charter, he insisted, "was intended to restrain government action and to protect the individual. It was not intended in the absence of some governmental action to be applied in private litigation" (para. 26). In *McKinney v. University of Guelph*,[4] Justice La Forest similarly read section 32 as giving "a strong message that the Charter is confined to government action" (1990, 261). "The exclusion of private activity from the *Charter*," he continued, "was not a result of happenstance. It was a deliberate choice which must be respected" (262). Among the reasons for this choice was that

> only government requires to be constitutionally shackled to preserve the rights of the individual. Others, it is true, may offend against the rights of individuals. This is especially true in a world in which economic life is largely left to the private sector where powerful private institutions are not directly affected by democratic forces. But government can either regulate these or create distinct bodies for the protection of human rights and the advancement of human dignity. (262)

In New Zealand, the liberal constitutionalist's restriction of constitutional reach to state action appears in *R. v. H* (1994), an early ruling where the Court of Appeal stated that the NZBORA was "directed to the exercise of the powers of the state and the conduct of governmental agencies." As such, "wholly private conduct is left to be controlled by the general law [i.e., common law] of the land" (147).

The liberal-constitutionalist conception has garnered support in UK jurisprudence as well. Lord Rodger of Earlsferry, in a prominent House of Lords decision, notes the "obvious examples" for defining "public authorities" under section 6 of the HRA are "organs of central and local government" – though he did qualify this by noting, somewhat cryptically, that the section that identifies "the class of persons who are to read and give effect to the legislation in accordance with it" are "not confined to them" (*Ghaidan v. Godin-Mendoza* 2004, para. 106). The UK Supreme Court recently reiterated that "section 6(1) of the 1998 Act only applied

---

4 *McKinney v. University of Guelph* concerned whether a university's mandatory retirement policy infringed employees' section 15 Charter rights (equality rights). The Supreme Court needed to address whether or not a university was considered a "government" actor for the purposes of section 32 of the Charter. Ultimately, the Court ruled that universities were private rather than public institutions.

to 'a public authority', which is unsurprising, given that the Convention is intended to protect individual rights against infringement by the *state* or its emanations" (*McDonald v. McDonald* 2016, para. 37, emphasis added).

It is important to note that while classical liberals seek to protect the "private sphere" from unwarranted state intrusion, this does not mean that they see the "private sphere" as a lawless realm. There are no doubt some purely private relationships and actions that are not subject to law at all – e.g., decisions on who to date or marry – but a good many interactions between individuals need some degree of legal regulation. Some of this comes through statutes like criminal law or human rights legislation, which liberal constitutionalists certainly see as subject to constitutional constraints. But many interactions that are conventionally considered "private" – and that are certainly so considered by the classical liberals among liberal constitutionalists – are, as we have seen, governed by judge-made "common law." The common law governing contractual relations is a good example; the aforementioned Supreme Court case *Dolphin Delivery* provides another. In that case, the Retail, Wholesale and Department Store Union, which was on strike against Purolator courier, also picketed a second company, Dolphin Delivery, which it alleged was allied with Purolator and was receiving subcontracted work because of the labour dispute. Dolphin filed for an injunction against the union under a common-law rule preventing such "secondary picketing." The Court agreed, siding with Dolphin upholding the common-law rule against the picketing of a third party. Such common-law rules are certainly "law," but liberal constitutionalists resist subjecting them directly to constitutional control. From their perspective, these are "background" rules for "private" action and should thus lie beyond the normal bounds of constitutional reach. In the United Kingdom, liberal constitutionalists find support for this perspective in the fact that the HRA makes no reference to Convention rights applying to private litigation or to the common law; indeed, it does not mention the common law at all. In particular, the duty placed on courts by section 3(1) to employ Convention rights as an interpretive guide applies only to legislation and not to common law (Gardbaum 2003, 408). In New Zealand, by contrast, the White Paper outlining the scope and purpose of the New Zealand Bill of Rights "was explicit" that the common law, including the private common law, would be apply and be updated with reference to the NZBORA (Geddis 2004, 686; see also Rishworth 2003, 99). As we shall see, however, this has not settled the debate between New Zealand's liberal and post-liberal constitutionalists about just how far the NZBORA reaches the background common-law rules for private action.

In Canada, these background common-law rules have clearly been considered to lie beyond constitutional reach. They involve the kind of "private litigation" to which Justice McIntyre's *Dolphin Delivery* judgment said the Charter did not apply (1986, para. 26). Thus, while Justice McIntyre agreed that the rule preventing secondary picketing infringed freedom of expression, he found that the Charter's guarantee of that freedom did not apply in the context of this "private litigation." Yet we should recall McIntyre's qualification of this exclusion of "private litigation" from Charter control. To repeat the statement quoted above, he wrote that the Charter "was not intended *in the absence of some governmental action* to be applied in private litigation" (para. 26, emphasis added). For McIntyre, the emphasized clause addressed the fact that common-law rules can sometimes be the basis of executive action, in which case they are brought under constitutional control by section 32 of the Charter. However, there was no such action by the executive branch of government in the labour dispute at issue in *Dolphin Delivery*.

The situation is further complicated by the fact that common-law rules can be replaced by statutes, which clearly *are* subject to constitutional constraints for liberal constitutionalists. Thus, the government could have replaced the common-law rule regarding secondary picketing with legislation. Had it legislated the same rule, the Charter would apply (though for McIntyre, the result in *Dolphin Delivery* would have been the same because, as he explained in *obiter*, the infringement of freedom of expression would be justified as a "reasonable limit" under section 1 of the Charter – see *Dolphin Delivery* 1986, para. 21). Among other things, the ability to replace common law with legislation means that constitutional reach expands with legislative replacement of common law, though for classical liberals the purpose of expanded constitutional reach would be to prevent unwarranted intrusions of constitutional liberty.

Post-Liberal Constitutionalism

For many post-liberal constitutionalists, such increasingly fine and nuanced distinctions are meaningless because what they seek to preserve – the distinction between "public" and "private" realms – is ultimately untenable. One reason for this conclusion is the breadth of the administrative or "embedded state" (Cairns 1995). Even among those who think the constitution applies primarily to "state action," there is wide disagreement over where the state starts and ends in an era characterized by the embedded state. As Mark Tushnet notes, "the thick statutory regulation of private life ... means that private life is already not *that* private" (2008b, 208, emphasis in original). Or, in the words of Seidman and Tushnet, "the

New Deal revolution has left us unable to believe in the naturalness of the public-private distinction" (1996, 70).

Some post-liberal theorists reject the liberal distinction between public and private for a deeper reason: they see state *inaction* as a form of unconstitutional state *action*. Yves de Montigny, for example, argues that "if the law is silent on a particular subject matter, the resulting situation constitutes a delegation of authority from the state to the individual, as much as if the state had expressly permitted the action" (1985, 594). This approach would radically expand the scope of rights documents by applying their rights and freedoms to what the executive and legislative branches of government have failed to do, in addition to their positive actions.

Even if post-liberals do not go as far as Montigny in defining government inaction as government action, they generally favour broad application of rights documents because they see them as protecting "equality and freedom from domination, whether that domination is rooted in the state or in society" (Bateman 2000, 203).[5] For example, Geddis notes that for most citizens "it makes little difference" if their "rights are potentially infringed by some 'public' authority" via a mandatory breathalyzer test at a police checkpoint, or by "another 'private' actor" requiring employees to be subject to a mandatory drug test (2004, 684). In this view, even if one accepts the "private" character of certain actions, rights documents would not actually protect rights and freedoms very effectively unless they reached "private" threats to the protected rights and freedoms. If they are understood in the narrow fashion of liberal constitutionalism, in other words, the impact of protected rights "on our daily lives would be considerably reduced" (MacIvor 2006, 20). Or as Robertson observes, the point is to spread "the values set out in the constitution throughout [both] state and society," an "idea of what a constitution is [that] does not always fit well with the orthodox idea of a liberal constitution" (2010, 1). The logical outcome of such thinking, according to Bateman, is a kind of constitutional totalism, whereby "the personal becomes the constitutional" (1998, 13).

The broad, post-liberal approach to the application of rights documents has several possible variants. First, and most radically, these documents could be interpreted as applying directly to the "horizontal" relations between individuals (Leigh 1999, 62; Gardbaum 2003, 393; Robertson 2010, 27). This is what Tushnet calls "direct horizontal effect."

---

5 Bateman makes this statement with respect to the Canadian Charter of Rights and Freedoms, but it describes a line of post-liberal thinking with respect to rights documents more generally.

To illustrate, Tushnet uses the example of sex discrimination (as Bateman did to explain vertical, liberal constitutionalism):

> Consider an employee who alleges that her employer fired her because she would not accede to her supervisor's sexual demands. Assume that the nation's constitution bans discrimination on the basis of sex, that the employee's claim describes an example of such discrimination, and that there is no applicable antidiscrimination statute. Under a constitution with direct horizontal effect, the employee would have a claim against her employer based directly on the constitution. (2008b, 197)

From this perspective, it might be better if legislatures enacted appropriate anti-discrimination legislation. If they do not, however, then under a doctrine of "direct horizontal effect," courts should step in and remedy discriminatory situations on the basis of constitutional standards (Gardbaum 2003, 397–8).[6]

All three regimes under consideration have steered clear of such "direct horizontal effect." In the Canadian context, Justice McIntyre rejected the view that "an individual may found a cause of action or defence against another individual on the basis of a breach of a Charter right" (*Dolphin Delivery* 1986, para. 26), or that "one private party owes a constitutional duty to another" (para. 39). He insisted that where "private party 'A' sues private party 'B' relying on the common law and where no act of government is relied upon to support the action, the *Charter* will not apply" (para. 39). Amnon Reichman agrees with McIntyre's *Dolphin Delivery* opinion. "Individuals," he writes, "should not possess a Charter-based cause of action against their fellow citizens, or, more accurately, citizens should not be under a direct Charter duty owed to their fellow citizens" (2002, 358). A key reason, as Justice McIntyre makes clear, is to avoid the kind of constitutional totalism in which "all private litigation would be subject to the *Charter*" (*Dolphin Delivery* 1986, para. 36).

New Zealand judges have also eschewed direct horizontalism (Rishworth 2003, 106–7). Recall *R. v. H* (1994), the case mentioned above as endorsing the liberal-constitutionalist view that the NZBORA was "directed" only to state action and to not "wholly private conduct." This case concerned the allegation that a company had engaged in bribery. When a whistle-blowing employee seized the company's transaction

---

6 In Canada's experience, the creation of anti-discrimination legislation and later human rights commissions were legislative responses in light of the *judiciary's* parsimonious approach to rights (Tarnopolsky and Pentney 2004, 2–3).

records, the company argued that this was an "unreasonable search and seizure" under the NZBORA. The Court responded that "the Bill of Rights does not extend to any search or seizure undertaken privately by a private individual" (147) – in other words, that the rights document did not have direct horizontal effect on the relations between private actors. In subsequent cases, the Court has reiterated this view. For instance, it has declined to apply the NZBORA when one citizen detains another (see *R. v. N. (No. 2)* 1999), or when a citizen searches the property of another (*R. v. Holford* 2001).

In the United Kingdom, too, the direct-application approach runs counter to the HRA's section 6(1) statement that the document applies to public rather than private authorities, and it has generally been the case that lower courts and the House of Lords have declined to take up a direct horizontal approach (Gardbaum 2003, 408). Nevertheless, there is some ambiguity. Lord Justice Mummery has written in an opinion that "the general question of horizontality has not yet been resolved by a court. Indeed, it may never be resolved judicially at the same high level of abstraction on which the debate has conducted in law books and legal periodicals" (quoted in Hoffman, Phillipson, and Young 2011, 6). Similarly, in *Campbell v. MGN Limited* (2003), a case concerning privacy rights, some of the judges participating in the decision made *obiter* statements that imply that British courts should not completely rule out the possibility that citizens owe each other positive duties based on the HRA.[7] Such statements would no doubt please such scholars as Murray Hunt, who see the HRA as leaning away from a "classical liberal model" of rights protection and towards a model with horizontal effect (1999, 89). In Hunt's view, HRA rights should be "all pervasive ... including in the proceedings between purely private parties" under the HRA (1999, 100). Hunt would be disappointed, however, that the matter has not been settled in favour of horizontal effect, and that the general trend has run in the opposite direction.

An alternative to direct horizontal effect as a way of achieving post-liberal ends through litigation would be for the courts to compel the

---

7 Baroness Hale's concurring judgment implies that there could be some support for a more direct approach: "The 1998 Act does not create any new cause of action between private persons. But if there is a relevant cause of action applicable, the court as a public authority must act compatibility with both parties' convention rights" (para. 132). See also Lord Nicholls statement that "it [is not] necessary to decide whether the duty imposed on courts by section 6 of the Human Rights Act 1998 extends to questions of substantive law as distinct from questions of practice and procedure" (para. 18).

state to remedy constitutional sins of omission by enacting missing legislation (e.g., anti-discrimination legislation), or reading missing parts
into existing legislation (*Vriend v. Alberta* 1998).[8] In a sense, this can
be understood as turning the problem of horizontal relations between
citizens back into an issue of appropriate relations between citizens
and their government – that is, back into an issue of vertical constitutional effect. It gets to the same "constitutional totalism" by a different
route.

A third approach to extending the reach of the constitution in a post-
liberal direction is what has become known as "indirect horizontal effect"
(Gardbaum 2003, 398; Mix-Ross 2009, 16; Tushnet 2008b, 197). Under
this doctrine, citizens do not owe each other constitutional duties, as
they would under a constitution with direct horizontal effect. In other
words, the courts will not enforce constitutional standards directly
against one individual at the behest of another. Nor does this approach
involve judges requiring governments to enact new remedial legislation
or themselves reading new standards into existing legislation. Instead,
under the doctrine of "indirect horizontal effect," courts undertake to
develop applicable "background" common-law rules to conform to constitutional standards.

In *Weak Courts, Strong Rights*, Tushnet illustrates indirect horizontal
effect with the now familiar example of private-sector sexual discrimination. Recall that under "direct horizontal effect," a female employee
suing her employer for sexual harassment could assert that her employer
violated the constitution's prohibition on sexual discrimination. Under
a constitution with *indirect* horizontal effect,

> the employee would have a claim founded on contract law against the
> employer. The courts charged with developing the contract law would be
> required to apply standard doctrines against wrongful discharge with an
> eye to the constitution's ban on sex discrimination. The nation's constitu-
> tional court would then examine the resulting law of wrongful discharge to
> determine whether it was appropriately sensitive to the nondiscrimination
> requirement (Tushnet 2008b, 197).

---

8 In *Vriend*, the Supreme Court "read in" sexual orientation into Alberta's Individual
Rights Protection Act. The Court's jurisprudence does not specify that governments
must enact such anti-discrimination legislation to comply with rights guarantees under
the Charter. This makes it unclear whether Parliament or a provincial legislature could
repeal their human rights acts entirely (the liberal-constitutionalist view) or whether
such repeal would violate the *Charter* (the post-liberal view).

The contract law at issue in this example is, of course, part of the judge-made common law. Indirect horizontal effect, in other words, involves judicial development of the common law "with an eye to" the relevant constitutional rights document. Given the fact that common law is what Reichman calls a *residual* regime – that it governs "all interactions not covered by statute" (2002, 348) – the doctrine of "indirect horizontal effect" has the potential of extending constitutional reach as far (or almost as far) into the "private sphere" as direct horizontal effect. From a liberal-constitutionalist perspective, however, it does have the virtue of having judges subject *laws* rather than individuals to constitutional standards.

If Canadian liberal constitutionalists can find some support for their doctrine of limited application in section 32 of the Charter, with its emphasis on the executive and legislative branches of government, post-liberal constitutionalists can point to section 52 of the Constitution Act, 1982, which states that "the Constitution of Canada is the supreme law of Canada, and *any law* that is inconsistent with the provisions of the Constitution is, to the extent of the inconsistency, of no force or effect" (emphasis added). The phrase "any law," say the advocates of indirect horizontal effect, must include judge-made common law governing allegedly "private sphere" interactions. Rhetorically, the point is not that individuals owe each other constitutional duties, but that their legal duties under the law, including common law, must be consistent with the Charter. This way of framing the issue is much more likely to be congenial to judges, even if the result is similar.

Post-liberal constitutionalists in New Zealand have pushed a similar "any law" rhetorical approach in hopes of expanding the scope of constitutional application. To the liberal-constitutionalist claim that the NZBORA's section 3 limits the document's application to only "acts done" by the three traditional branches of government, post-liberals reply that this includes "acts done" by the judiciary, which is thus "bound" to consider and apply the NZBORA in all of its "acts," including interpreting common-law rules regardless of whether they are public or private (Butler 2000). Taken to its extreme, this "judicially bound" view means a judge could be personally liable for behaving unconstitutionally, and that a dissatisfied litigant could claim the judge (a state actor) infringed the NZBORA in coming to the wrong conclusion about a private common-law rule (Rishworth 2007, 323). In support of this conclusion, post-liberal constitutionalists in New Zealand cite the above-mentioned foundational White Paper's "explicit" inclusion of common law, including the private common law, within the NZBORA's scope (Geddis 2004, 686; Rishworth 2003, 99). Unsurprisingly, liberal constitutionalists dispute this conclusion, arguing that there must be some conceptual separation between the rights document and the courts themselves, otherwise the judicial process would cease to function.[9] "It may possibly be that s. 3 requires the Courts to conduct themselves in accordance with the NZBORA," said the judgment in *TVNZ v. Newsmonitor Services Ltd.* (1994, 96), but only "in terms of their processes and procedures," and not in "the substance of their judgments and orders which flow out of those judgments."

Some UK scholars have similarly argued that the "public authorities" subject to the HRA by virtue of section 6 include the courts, who must act in accordance with the Convention rights, and develop the common law accordingly (Leigh 1999, 75; Phillipson 1999, 825). According to Hunt, the lord chancellor explained to the House of Lords during the parliamentary debate on the adoption of the HRA that the "degree of horizontal application the government [had] in mind" was based on the "principle that the courts ought to be under the duty to act compatibly with the Convention when developing the common law in deciding cases between individuals." Not only would this render the HRA "more in the nature of a social democratic than a classical liberal Bill of Rights," it also "require[d] a reconsideration of the public/private distinction in the prevailing culture" (1999, 100).

Balancing Liberals and Post-Liberals: The Indirect Effect

Not everyone who embraces the post-liberal rejection of the state/society or public/private distinctions is comfortable with the broad extensions of "constitutional reach" and the "constitutional totalism" implied by this rejection. Thus, although Seidman and Tushnet, as noted above, find it difficult "to believe in the naturalness of the public-private distinction," they find it just as difficult "to reconceive a system of individual rights without" it. Put another way, "we want to repudiate state action rhetoric because we know it blinds us to human suffering that the state might otherwise ameliorate. Yet we also want to embrace that it preserves a space for individual flourishing that the state might otherwise destroy" (Seidman and Tushnet 1996, 70). The result is the search for a middle-ground balance between the liberal and post-liberal perspectives. The jurisprudential expression of that balance tends to emphasize the "indirect horizontal effect" of constitutional documents.

---

9 This kind of expansive application of a rights document was dismissed in an early Supreme Court of Canada decision (see *Daganais v. Canadian Broadcasting Corp* 1994).

Consider the Supreme Court of Canada. On the one hand, we have already seen that the Court is reluctant to bring private common law within the reach of full Charter application. Indeed, even Supreme Court judges who reject the classical liberal, minimal-state perspective on "constitutionalism" have been reluctant to travel too far down the road of "post-liberal" constitutionalism. For example, in *McKinney v. University of Guelph,* Justice Wilson's dissenting opinion concluded "that a concept of minimal state intervention should not be relied on to justify a restrictive interpretation of 'government' or 'government action' for purposes of s.32 of the Charter" (1990, 357). "Governments," she wrote, "act today through many different instrumentalities depending upon their suitability for attaining the objectives governments seek to attain" (357). Thus, she was prepared to find that the Charter's prohibition on age-based discrimination applied to universities (understood as state actors for this purpose). At the same time, on the question whether the Charter is "the intermediary between the citizen and government only or [is also] the intermediary between citizen and citizen," Justice Wilson remained "of the view that it was aimed at government action" (340–1). Even in dissent, Justice Wilson was prepared to apply the Charter to university employment policies because she saw universities as state actors, not because she thought the Charter applied directly to relations between actors that remained legitimately "private."

On the other hand, the Supreme Court has been unwilling to exclude "private" common law entirely from the ambit of constitutional influence. Justice McIntyre made this clear in the same *Dolphin Delivery* opinion that was at such pains to protect the private sphere from constitutional control. It "would be wholly unrealistic and contrary to the clear language employed in s. 52(1) of the Act," he wrote, to "exclude from *Charter* application the whole body of the common law which in great part governs the rights and obligations of the individuals in society" (1986, para. 25).

This presents a conundrum. On the one hand, the Charter will not apply to litigation based on common law where "no act of government is relied upon to support the action" (*Dolphin Delivery* 1986, para. 39). On the other hand, the judiciary cannot "exclude from *Charter* application the whole body of the common law which in great part governs the rights and obligations of the individuals in society" (para. 25). Justice McIntyre reconciles the tension between these propositions in the following way: That the "Charter will not apply" in the absence of government action, he says, "is a distinct issue from the question whether the judiciary ought to apply and develop the principles of the common law in a manner consistent with the fundamental values enshrined in the Constitution ... The answer to [the latter] question," he asserts, "must be in the affirmative" (para. 39). This is developing the common law "with an eye" to the Charter – precisely what the literature defines as indirect horizontal effect.

McIntyre concludes that the Charter is therefore "far from irrelevant to private litigants whose disputes fall to be decided at common law" (para. 39). Moreover, it will presumably be relevant even if those disputes do not involve government action. This point was underlined in a subsequent case, *R. v. Salituro*, in which Justice Iacobucci, writing for a unanimous panel of five Supreme Court judges, affirmed that "the Charter will also be influential" in private common-law litigation "even in the absence of legislation or government action" (1991, 675).

It is worth unpacking what Justice McIntyre means by bringing judge-made common law into line with "the fundamental values enshrined in the Constitution." The part of the Constitution at issue in *Dolphin Delivery* was the Charter, so McIntyre has in mind "Charter values." The previous chapter noted how underlying principles and values, including Charter values, can be used to interpretively expand the meaning of explicit constitutional provisions. In addition to this "underlying values usage" of Charter values, the concept can also designate a jurisprudential approach to applying Charter provisions once they have been given their interpretive meaning. Under this approach, the Court chooses to bring a law into compliance with Charter *values* rather than invalidating it for unreasonably infringing Charter *rights and freedoms*. This strategy takes two forms. First, when reviewing sufficiently ambiguous legislation, the Court will resolve the ambiguity by choosing an interpretation consistent with Charter values. (I address this "statutory interpretation usage" of Charter values in chapter 7.) Second, the Court will invoke Charter values when it wants to renovate judge-made common-law rules. It is this "common-law usage" of Charter values that Justice McIntyre employs in *Dolphin Delivery*. It enabled him to negotiate a middle ground between making "all private litigation ... subject to the *Charter*" (1986, para. 36), which he was reluctant to do, and simultaneously ensuring that the common law is not beyond the Charter's reach. In purely "private litigation" – i.e., where no government action is involved – a common-law rule will not be found to be an unconstitutional violation of Charter "rights and freedoms"; rather, it will be interpreted or developed in accordance with Charter "values."

The New Zealand judiciary has developed a similar middle-ground approach. Referencing the Canadian approach of "holding that the common law is not literally subject to the Charter ... yet is to be informed by its 'values,'" New Zealand public law authority Paul Rishworth maintains that "New Zealand cases in fact exemplify a broadly similar approach, albeit without fully articulating it" (2003, 105). Often the language turns on the type of dispute: whether it is of a private or public nature. In many instances, under public common-law rules, the NZBORA's *rights* and *freedoms* apply directly, but if the dispute arises under private common-law rules, the *values* of the Bill of Rights are used to review the existing laws. And even in the private common-law cases, the courts find "a public element is similarly present ... where the substance of the common law appears to have been influenced, to some extent, by Bill of Rights *values*" (Rishworth 2003, 106, emphasis added). Leading cases like *Lange v. Atkinson* are synonymous with the doctrine that "the common law must be developed in light of Bill of Rights *values*" (Rishworth 2003, 100n176, emphasis added). In *Lange*, the Court even went so far as to favourably refer to the Supreme Court of Canada's approach of not applying the Charter directly to common-law rules, but instead bringing them into line with the "values of the Charter" (1998, 451). *Hosking v. Runting* endorses the same middle-ground position. "The Bill of Rights is designed to operate as between citizen and state," Justice Tipping said, but "nevertheless it will often be appropriate for the values which are recognised in that context to inform the development of the common law in its function of regulating relationships between citizen and citizen" (2004, para. 229).[10]

Similarly, Tom Hickman writes that the UK HRA influences the development of the common law "where it does not *require* common law change but it does *support* such change" (2010, 50). The HRA "signals to judges" to make "the values [of] the general law" (i.e., the common law) suitable for a "modern democracy" (50). The UK courts, according to this interpretation, have endeavoured to create a weaker, Canadian-style duty whereby, in adjudicating existing common-law causes of action, courts must simply take Convention values into account (Gardbaum 2003, 409).

The middle-ground, values-based approach has been seen as "confused" and unsatisfying by many commentators (Hutchinson and Petter 1988, 283), even through the mechanism of indirect constitutional effect. It has certainly come under attack from both liberal and post-liberal constitutionalists. In Canada, for example, Christopher Manfredi argues that bringing "Charter values" into the interpretation of private

---

10 In his discussion of *Hosking*, Geddis (2004, 701) observes how some of the cross-pollination between Canada and New Zealand courts on the indirect effect has been done without attribution. "Although Tipping J cites no authority for his approach, obviously it is influenced by the Supreme Court of Canada's methodology in cases such as *RWDSU v Dolphin Delivery* and *Hill v Church of Scientology*."

common law "push[es] the objectives of the Charter beyond the central purposes of liberal constitutionalism" (2001, 45–6). Canadian post-liberals, by contrast, criticize the Court's reluctance to bring the full weight of Charter application to bear on common-law rules in private litigation (Howse 1988; Hughes 2003; Slattery 1987).

Not all post-liberals favour extensive judicial power, however. For example, left-leaning Canadian Charter critics Hutchinson and Petter (1988) believe the public/private distinction to be nonsensical, but they are not led by this belief to support Charter-based judicial power; indeed, they would prefer no Charter-based judicial power at all (Hutchinson 1995; Petter 2010). These scholars are examples (as alluded to hypothetically above) of post-liberals supportive of political constitutionalism.

More interesting for our purposes is Reichman (2002), who was cited above on the issue of the "residual," hence very extensive, reach of the common law. Reichman, too, denies the existence of a "stateless" private realm, noting, in a manner akin to Montigny, that the alleged private activity is typically legally endorsed and/or protected, if only by judge-made common law (or by the failure of judges to make relevant common law) (345–6). For Reichman, we recall, the common law "governs *all* interactions not governed by statute" (348, emphasis added), meaning that the apparent absence of any rule governing an interaction is itself an official decision.

Like Tushnet, Reichman would challenge Bateman's formulation of the sexist exclusion of women from a fraternal organization as reflecting only "private dealings." Reichman argues that both the state and the law are ubiquitous to the extent that the "state governs all transactions and all legal entities, individuals and associations alike" (347). Unlike Aharon Barak, the former president of Israel's Supreme Court, however, Reichman does not take the fact that "the world is filled with law" to mean that "anything and everything is justiciable and '[n]othing falls beyond the purview of judicial review'" (quoted in Hirschl 2004, 169). To the contrary, despite the ubiquity of law, Reichman would not apply the Charter to common law, preferring instead to restrict its judicially enforced application to "state action" as traditionally conceived – i.e., to legislative and executive action. Despite his rejection of the classical liberal distinction between public and private, Reichman retains the orientation of liberal *constitutionalism* and remains an opponent of constitutional totalism. He does so not primarily out of reverence for private freedom but because he insists on the "democratic" side of the "liberal-democratic" coin. He maintains that if constitutional review were to fully extend to one's private actions,

The citizen would be told by the state which position on any given issue is right and in turn would be expected to reiterate her or his affirmation of the values which the state is promoting ... Under such conditions of total moral control, *the democratic regime loses a leg upon which its legitimacy stands – the meaningful consent of the governed.* (2002, 347, emphasis added)

Reichman is not a classical liberal who advocates using the Charter to dismantle welfare-state initiatives. However, neither does Reichman want the Constitution to *require* such positive state initiatives, not even in the manner of "indirect horizontal effect." For Reichman, the initiatives of the active (and activist) state in areas traditionally governed by "private" common law need the democratic legitimacy of legislation. "The justification for the product of the political process in a democracy," he insists,

is that it represents the will of people, namely the aggregation of the positive volition of the citizens, after all compromises have been made to secure a majority. The actual will of the people matters because through the expression of such will the people assume responsibility over their governance. (2002, 340–1)

Among other things, this democratic orientation leads Reichman to argue that sections 32 and 52 of Canada's Constitution Act, 1982, need to be interpreted in light of each other, and in a manner that maintains and protects the limited-application doctrine that is manifest on the face of section 32. Section 32 is part of the "supreme law" established by section 52. It follows that the section 32 application of the Charter – to only the actions of the executive and legislative branches – is entitled to section 52 "supremacy." This means "limiting the application of the Charter so as not to reach individuals or the common law" (2002, 360) in purely "private litigation" (i.e., where the common law at issue has not generated executive action). Given the extensive reach of the common law as the "default legal regime," which governs everything not governed by statute, subjecting all common law to the Charter is, for Reichman, indistinguishable from subjecting individuals directly to the Charter: "Because the common law is where we legally 'exist,' beyond any statutory definition, subjecting the common law to direct Charter-based review is tantamount to subjecting us, as individuals, to direct constitutional review" (2002, 359).

Likewise, Derek Mix-Ross worries that the proliferation of the indirect effect risks "creating a system of 'direct horizontally' in which private citizens are bound by the same constitutional duties, albeit cloaked in 'values' terminology, as the state" (2009, 47). His concern is for the Court's vague distinction between (for an example) "equality" as a right as codified in section 15 and "equality" as a value. If any Charter right can also be a Charter value, "doesn't the line between private law and public law disappear?" (47). Similarly, Timothy Macklem's article "*Vriend v. Alberta*: Making the Private Public" (1999) argues that the Supreme Court's Charter values jurisprudence has in effect extended Charter application to private action, effectively overturning the statement in *Dolphin Delivery* that "Charter rights don't exist in the absence of state action" (219–20). In this view, Justice McIntyre's denial in *Dolphin Delivery* that "one private party owes a constitutional duty to another" logically entails the corollary that the Charter does not apply to the common law in purely private litigation.

Conclusion

According to W.R. Lederman, one should not "constitutionalize the whole legal system" (1991, 119). For liberal constitutionalists, this means that the "private sphere" (or the common law that typically governs the private sphere) should not be covered by the relevant rights document. This perspective emphasizes those aspects of the rights documents in each of the three countries under consideration that arguably apply protected rights and freedoms only to governments and legislatures, not to individuals. For post-liberal constitutionalists, by contrast, it is futile to maintain an increasingly irrelevant distinction between public and private or to ignore the reality that private power can also diminish rights and freedoms. Taken to its logical conclusion, post-liberal constitutionalism would make the rights documents under consideration directly applicable to individuals in their "horizontal" relations with each other as well as to the "vertical" relations between individuals and the state.

Courts in all three countries have tried to stake out a middle ground between these two constitutional perspectives. On the one hand, they are reluctant to declare the private sphere (and, more particularly, the common law governing it) to be a zone altogether untouched by documentary rights. On the other, they have also been loath to apply their rights documents directly to relations between individuals (i.e., "direct horizontal" application). As far as "private common law" is concerned, it is not directly subject to the rights documents (unless it becomes the basis of executive action), but it may be indirectly influenced and developed by the courts on the basis of "rights values." Using rights values, judges in Canada, New Zealand, and the United Kingdom have paved an ambiguous middle road in the "clash of constitutionalisms." One of the ambiguities of this middle road concerns how well it secures an "appropriate balance between judicial and legislative action" (*Bell ExpressVu Ltd. v. Rex* 2002, para. 61) in the development of the common law. This question of inter-institutional balance – including balanced inter-institutional "dialogue" – is the topic of the next chapter.

Chapter Five

Balancing Institutional Relations:
The Common Law and Bills of Rights

"Despite the effort to keep the Charter out of the [private] common law," remarked Chief Justice Beverley McLachlin in 2002, "it has arguably come in through the back door" (2002, 199). The sign on that door reads "Charter values." Chapter 4 showed how the Canadian "Charter values" door was opened, in the case of "private common law," by the judicial unwillingness either to subject the private sphere to the full weight of Charter application (as post-liberal legal constitutionalists advise) or to declare the private sphere a Charter-free zone (as liberal political constitutionalists prefer). In effect, Canadian judges tried to chart an ambiguous middle ground between legal and political constitutionalism with respect to private common law.

Chapter 4 also observed that judges in the weaker-form UK and New Zealand systems have similarly refused to read the textual emphasis on state action (or "vertical application") as making their rights document irrelevant to the horizontal relations governed by private common law. Like their Canadian counterparts – and often with explicit reference to the Canadian example – they will invoke the "values" of their rights documents in developing and modifying private common law. Here, too, we see the ambiguous use of rights values as a middle-ground alternative to the direct application of protected rights.

A similar interpretive approach has also been used in all three systems to inform the judicial modification of "public" common law – that is, those areas of non-statutory law that govern vertical relations between the state and individuals. All three rights documents apply directly to state action in the form of public common law, so no indirect "back door" approach is strictly necessary. Nevertheless, using bills of rights to revise public common-law rules poses its own difficulties and conundrums. On the one hand, such revision seems consistent with the traditional role of courts in keeping the common law in tune with contemporary values, and why Wilfrid Waluchow (2007) argues precisely for a "common law conception" of constitutional judicial review.[1] On the other hand, framing the change as required by possessing constitutional weight risks upsetting the traditional balance of institutional relations between courts and legislatures. This issue of institutional balance, in fact, arises with respect to both public and private common law. How has this tension been managed in our three case countries? That is the question addressed in this chapter. As we shall see, the issues are more complicated and controversial in stronger-from Canada than in weaker-form New Zealand and the United Kingdom.

Bills of Rights and the Common Law

The central difference between Canada and its weaker-form cousins is, of course, the existence of a judicial invalidation mandate in Canada but not in the other two regimes. In the weak-form UK and New Zealand systems, both the indirect application of the rights document to private common law (via the expedient of rights "values") and its direct application to public common law are limited to interpretive adjustments of common-law rules. In Canada, by contrast, the direct application of the Charter to non-statutory rules of public law can take the strong-form option of invalidating (rather than interpretively reforming) them, leaving it to the legislature to respond (subject later, of course, to the possible judicial review of that response).

Despite possessing the invalidation option, however, Canadian judges tend not to use it when they find that a public common-law rule violates the Charter. In *R. v. Swain*,[2] where just such a violation was found, Chief Justice Lamer proclaimed that

> it is not strictly necessary to invoke s. 52(1) of the Constitution Act, 1982, in order to challenge a common law, judge-made rule on the basis of the

---

1 Because "we do *not* in fact know, in advance, what our rights and freedoms are in many cases," Waluchow argues for a "common law, case-by-case method" of resolving constitutional disputes that accords judges the same type of flexibility as in common law cases. One critique of Waluchow's common-law theory of judicial review is that it arguably conceives of courts primarily as oracular proclaimers of fundamental (democratic) morality in constitutional cases, yet another example of how legal constitutionalists often "prefer majoritarianism in the courtroom to majoritarianism in the electoral and legislative arena" (Knopff 2003, 210).

2 This case concerned the common law governing the Crown's power to raise an insanity defence, over objections by the accused. This rule violated section 7 ("the right to life, liberty and security of the person and the right not to be deprived thereof except in

rights and *values* guaranteed by the Charter – if a common law rule can be reformulated so as to attain its objectives while removing any inconsistency with basic principles, a judge is entitled to undertake such a reformulation and is not obliged to seek jurisdiction for this action under s. 52(1). (1991, 979, emphasis added)

In other words, even when the Charter applies directly to common law, it may be better to bring a delinquent rule into line with Charter "values" and "principles" than to invalidate it as an infringement of Charter rights. This bears more than incidental similarity to the Charter values approach to private common law set out by Justice McIntyre in *Dolphin Delivery* – namely, that where the Charter does "not apply" – i.e., to the participants in private litigation – "the judiciary ought [nevertheless] to apply and develop the principles of the common law in a manner consistent with the fundamental values enshrined in the Constitution" (1986, para. 39). In both cases, rather than bringing the full weight of the Charter to bear by invalidating an unconstitutional law, the Court prefers a less dramatic adjustment of the law, one that avoids a direct clash between the law and the Charter by interpretively making the law more Charter-compliant. As Kent Roach has observed, this practice makes the "Charter more like the interpretative bills of rights found in New Zealand and the United Kingdom" (2005, 735).

The Canadian treatment of public common law bears a particular resemblance to the New Zealand situation because, as noted previously (chapters 1 and 2), both rights documents contain virtually identical provisions permitting "reasonable limits" on protected rights and freedoms (section 1 of the Canadian Charter; section 5 of the NZBORA). In principle, a public common-law limitation of rights can be defended as a "reasonable limit" in both countries, but in practice this is not a significant prospect in either country.

In Canada, this is another feature of the *Swain* judgment discussed above. Not only did that judgment underline the judicial role in Charter-based common-law innovation, but it also maintained that when judges change the common law to make it more Charter-compliant, they "need not ascertain whether [the old] common law rule is reasonable under section 1," the "reasonable limits" section of the Canadian Charter (Hiebert 2002, 98). A challenged statute can always be defended under

---

accordance with the principles of fundamental justice") and was therefore modified to comply with the Charter. Section 52(1) states that "the Constitution of Canada is the supreme law of Canada, and any law that is inconsistent with the provisions of the Constitution is, to the extent of the inconsistency, of no force or effect."

section 1, but in the case of common law, Chief Justice Lamer saw "no conceptual problem with the Court's simply enunciating a [more Charter-compliant] rule to take the place of the old rule, without considering whether the old rule could nonetheless be upheld under s. 1 of the *Charter*" (*R. v. Swain* 1991, 978). The different treatment of legislation and common law is justified by the fact "that the common-law rule was fashioned by judges and not by Parliament or a legislature" (978). For this reason, "judicial deference to elected bodies is not an issue" (978). June Ross elaborates this line of thought:

> When a court is considering common law, none of the concerns as to relative institutional competence arise. The appropriate balance of competing claims will still frequently be disputable, but it must be recalled that the court is reconsidering an earlier court ruling. There is no fear of upsetting the democratic process where the legislature has not acted or has merely acquiesced in a common law rule. (1996, 130)

In *Swain*, Justice Lamer concludes that "if it is possible to reformulate a common-law rule so that it will not conflict with the principles of fundamental justice, such a reformulation should be undertaken" without considering whether the rule being reformulated could be justified as a "reasonable limit" on the relevant Charter rights (1990, 978).

The situation is similar in New Zealand. As noted in chapter 2, "reasonable limits" analysis is much less systematic there than in Canada and rarely determines the outcome of cases. As Rishworth puts it, "there is precious little indigenous jurisprudence that expounds upon or even applies the test of reasonable limits in s. 5." Among other things, this means that the NZBORA's reasonable limits clause "has no 'bite' in cases about common law" (2007, 346).[3] The same is true of the equally undeveloped "proportionality" analysis in the United Kingdom.

In sum, because courts in all three jurisdictions are unwilling either to apply their rights documents directly to those parts of the common law that regulate horizontal relations between private entities or to treat their documents as entirely irrelevant to the private sphere, they have chosen what McLachlin called the "back door" approach of using

---

3 The courts have been inconsistent in applying section 5 to the common law, and even when it is applied the analysis is superficial. For example, in *Gisborne Herald Co Ltd. v. Solicitor General*, the Court stated that "s. 5 recognizes explicitly that there are limits on those rights and freedoms," but the substance of the reasonable limits analysis was thin: "The result of balancing process will necessarily reflect the Court's assessment of society's values" (1995, 573).

the rights values inherent in the documents to adjust and develop the background rules of private common law. In the case of public common law, the documents all apply directly, but in the weak-form systems of the United Kingdom and New Zealand, this again entails making common law rights-compliant only through interpretive means. In stronger-form Canada, courts have the option of simply invalidating a public common-law rule. Instead, however, Canadian judges often interpretively reshape common-law rules to make them Charter-compliant, much in the manner of their weak-form cousins. When doing so, few judges in these jurisdictions give much weight to the possibility that the challenged common-law rule might be a "reasonable" or "proportional" limit on protected rights. How do these interpretive approaches affect (and how are they affected by) concerns regarding the appropriate institutional division of labour with respect to common-law reform and innovation? In other words, how, and to what extent, has the relationship between legislatures and courts changed with respect to common-law development in the era of rights documents? To answer that question, we need to know more about the traditional institutional division of labour.

The Traditional Institutional Division of Labour

New Zealand and Canada (except for the Canadian province of Quebec) possess common law because of their colonial inheritance, and thus the common law's origins are in the United Kingdom. Common law originated when the British monarch replaced the previous patchwork of law that differed from village to village by permitting judges to base their rulings on the customs and practices "common" to the entire realm (Hausegger, Hennigar, and Riddell 2015, 11; Malcolmson et al. 2016, 147). The adoption of similar approaches to "like cases" led to the creation of legal precedents. However, if there was no similar case to look to, the judge was free to make a new rule "in the manner that seemed most consistent with the underlying principles of the case law that existed" (Malcolmson et al. 2016, 147).

Over time, as Parliament emerged as a significant institution, disputes arose about whether laws passed by Parliament would prevail over common law created by the king's judges. With the Glorious Revolution of 1688, Parliament emerged supreme, and thereafter statutes enacted by representative legislatures became "hierarchically superior to the common law" (Reichman 2002, 340). That is, statutes could displace judicially produced common-law rules. Despite legislative superiority, however, common law continues to exist. Why?

One reason, noted by Amnon Reichman, is that a legislatively displaced common-law rule "still exists beyond the actual legislative will," because if the statute is repealed and not replaced, the original common-law rule re-emerges as the legal status quo.[4] The common law, in short, is what Reichman calls the *residual* or *default* legal regime. Second, even if legislatures tried to enact statutes to cover everything, novel situations inevitably end up in court and require a legal response. Perhaps some piece of legislation can be interpreted to cover the situation, but it may also make sense to develop a common-law rule, as happened in *R. v. Dudley and Stephens* (1884), where a British judge needed to determine whether the necessity of an extreme survival situation was an adequate legal defence for cannibalism (Hutchinson 2010, ch. 2). The legislature can, of course, step in and codify or alter a common-law rule created for novel circumstances, but arguably the judge-made rule has in the meantime usefully filled a legal gap.

However, legislatures do not always rush to codify the common law. They often leave well-established common law in place. One explanation is that there is no need to waste scarce legislative time and resources replacing common-law rules of which the legislature approves. "If our elected representatives are satisfied with certain common law rules," writes Mark Carter, "then there is no reason for them to enshrine or alter them in statute" (1995, 262). Indeed, suggests Carter,

> If there is any currency left in Edward Coke's view that the common law represents "that which hath been refined and perfected by all the wisest men in former succession of ages," legislators may be acting prudently by leaving it as unaltered as possible. (1995, 262)

In a sense, this legislative-approval explanation for the persistence of well-established common law may count against judicial change of that law. True, judges originally created the common law, but if it remains in place because it is what the hierarchically superior legislature would have enacted, courts should perhaps refrain from changing it, leaving further changes to the superior legislature.

But "legislative approval" may not always be a compelling explanation for the persistence of common law. Scarcity of legislative time and resources can explain not only why a rational legislature might leave in

---

4 Reichman argues that the common law, as the residual regime, "cannot tolerate a legal void ... [u]nlike statutory law, the statement 'this activity (or omission) is not legally covered' is unavailable to the common law; it *must* provide a legal consequence" (2002, 369, emphasis in original).

place common-law rules it likes, but also why it does not get around to changing rules it dislikes (or would dislike if it had the time and resources to notice everything) – i.e., when desired reform does not make it onto an overcrowded legislative agenda.

Just as the legislative-approval explanation for common-law persistence counts against judicial innovation, so the explanation of an overcrowded legislative agenda may count in favour of such innovation. Under such circumstances, in other words, judges should continue the development of the common law in ways the legislature would likely approve but does not have time to undertake. This is a common justification for the Supreme Court of Canada's 1959 decision in *Fleming v. Atkinson* (or the "Cattle Trespass case"). In this tort-liability case, Atkinson accidentally drove his car into a herd of cows, owned by Fleming, that were grazing on the road. Both litigants sought damages. One would expect that this would be a standard negligence case, but Fleming found an arcane common-law rule dating back to medieval England that made the carriage operator (i.e., the motorist in this case) responsible for injuring any cattle grazing on public highways (Weiler 1974, 58). It would seem obvious that this precedent was unworkable in modern circumstances. However, this rule had been recently upheld and left in place not only in the United Kingdom (in the 1947 British House of Lords decision, *Searle v. Wallbank*) but also in Canada (in the 1952 *Noble v. Calder* decision by the Ontario Court of Appeal).[5] On appeal, the Supreme Court of Canada overturned the "irrational legal anomaly" and updated the rule for modern conditions (Weiler 1974, 59). Justice Judson's majority opinion emphasized "that one of the virtues of the common law system is its flexibility, that it is capable of changing with the times and adapting its principles to new conditions" (*Fleming v. Atkinson* 1959, 535). However, he noted a "conspicuous failure to do this in this branch of the law" (535), and clearly thought the Supreme Court was justified in remedying this failure.

Paul Weiler approved of the *Fleming* judgment, arguing that the Cattle Trespass case represents the benefits of common-law flexibility, which liberates judges from blindly following established legal rules that are incongruent with their setting and purpose (1974, 60). In other words, judges, having always made the common law, should be able to continue to develop it in appropriate ways even under conditions of legislative

---

5 The Ontario Court of Appeal acknowledged that while the law was not satisfactory, it was bound to adhere to the House of Lords decision until the civil liability law was revised by the legislature (Weiler 1974, 58).

supremacy. After all, if the legislature truly disagrees with the change, it remains free to overrule it and return to the previous rule (or adopt some other alternative). Assumptions of "legislative approval" can cut both ways, working as readily in favour of judicial common-law innovation as against it.

If that is the case, why not encourage habitual judicial innovation on the grounds that the legislature will intervene when necessary to repair any damage? The answer lies in the fact that legislative change of a legal status quo is never easy (Flanagan 1997; Morton 2001), and that the possibility of judicial "mistakes" counsels judicial caution. Not all judicial reform of the common law will seem as self-evidently obvious as the decision in *Fleming v. Atkinson* (indeed, there were dissents even in that case). Recognizing this, the judiciary generally seeks a balance between stability and change in the common law – i.e., between overly adventurous reform of what may be legislatively approved common law and sensibly saving a busy legislature some law-reform effort. Lord Bingham, an influential House of Lords jurist, described this balance as "preclud[ing] excessive innovation and adventurism by the judges." "It is one thing" he continues, "to alter the law's direction of travel by a few degrees, quite another to set it off in a different direction" (quoted in Phillipson and Williams 2011, 888).

Has the advent of rights documents changed the balance aimed at by this traditional division of labour with respect to common-law development? Not according to the courts charged with applying the new documents. In the spirit of Lord Bingham, these courts often insist that they will not use rights values "to alter the law's direction of travel by [more than] a few degrees." Canada's Supreme Court, for example, has recognized the possibility of going too far in its Charter-based adjustment of the common law. Thus, in its post–*Dolphin Delivery* private common-law cases, the Court has regularly added an important qualification to the *Dolphin* doctrine that "courts should apply and develop the rules of the common law in accordance with the values and principles enshrined in the Charter" – namely, that such Charter values common-law development should occur only "*where it will not upset the appropriate balance between judicial and legislative action*" (*Bell ExpressVu Ltd. v. Rex* 2002, para. 61, emphasis added). A slight variation on this formulation appears in both *R. v. Salituro* (1991, 675) and in the following quote from *Hill v. Church of Scientology of Toronto* (1995):

> *If it is possible* to change the common law rule so as to make it consistent with Charter values, *without upsetting the proper balance of judicial and legislative action* ... then the rule ought to be changed. (para. 85, emphasis added)

In other words, a common-law rule ought *not* to be brought into line with "Charter values" by the courts whenever such reform would "upset the appropriate balance between judicial and legislative action." Similar issues arise with respect to public common law. The Court places particular emphasis on the difference between small or "incremental" common-law changes, which can legitimately be undertaken by the courts on the basis of Charter rights or values, and larger, more extensive reform, which should be left to the legislature (*Hill v. Church of Scientology* 1995, para. 92). In *Salituro*, the Court noted that "complex changes to the law with uncertain ramifications should be left to the legislature, [while] the courts can and should make incremental changes to the common law to bring legal rules into step with a changing society" (1991, 666).

New Zealand courts have struck the same note of caution regarding the use of rights values to change the common law, acknowledging on various occasions that they are "institutionally unsuited to be making more than incremental adjustments to the common law" (Rishworth 2003, 101). The previous chapter noted that New Zealand jurisprudence under the NZBORA has adopted the Canadian practice of developing the common law "in light of Bill of Rights values" (Rishworth 2003, 100). Recall that the leading case of *Lange v. Atkinson* explicitly relied on the Canadian example. Here it is important to add that *Lange* also emphasized the Canadian concern about preserving "the proper balance of judicial and legislative action." Citing *Hill v. Church of Scientology*, the *Lange* judgment emphasized that "courts have traditionally been cautious regarding the extent to which they will amend the common law," and that this tradition should be maintained under the NZBORA (1998, 451).[6] Indicating that judges "must not go further than is necessary" in using NZBORA values in common-law development, the Court emphasized that "far-reaching changes to the common law must be left to the legislature" (451).

While courts have obviously been at pains to present their use of rights values to interpretively adjust the common law as entirely consistent with the judiciary's traditional role in common-law development, not everyone is persuaded. Mix-Ross, for example, expresses a common worry that, while courts "have always been free to take into account new ideas and changing social circumstances in developing the common law,"

---

6 Huscroft – citing and recommending a comparison of *Lange* and *Hill* – says "there is little difference between the [New Zealand] Bill of Rights and the Charter" in this respect since, "like the Charter, the Bill of Rights can be invoked to help shape the development of the common law" (2002, 113–14).

things change when they begin "labeling these values 'constitutional'" (2009, 50). A problem occurs if courts "upset the proper balance" by setting the common law's "direction of travel" too far "off in a different direction." Traditionally, the legislature could step in and enact a statute reversing such a ruling. To what extent is this option still available when the values driving the court's ruling are labelled "constitutional"? Mix-Ross is right to say that the "constitutional" label changes things, but it does so in quite different ways in strong-form Canada than in weak-form New Zealand or the United Kingdom.

In New Zealand and the United Kingdom, an NZBORA- or HRA-based modification of a common-law rule arguably has greater moral force than the same modification would have had in the pre–bill of rights era. Nevertheless, a committed legislature can reverse both in the same way – i.e., by ordinary statute. Let us assume that the same constitutional considerations that led the court to modify the common-law rule also lead it to declare the reversing statute to be "unreasonably" or "disproportionately" inconsistent or incompatible with the rights document. That statute, as we have seen, enjoys the "burden of inertia," meaning that it prevails if the legislature chooses to ignore the judicial ruling against it. Applying the "constitutional" label in these circumstances no doubt changes things, but ultimately, the traditional division of labour is maintained – as, indeed, the designers of these weak-form rights documents intended. The idea of these "*parliamentary* bills of rights" was precisely "to conceive of judicial power in a manner that is consistent with the principle of parliamentary sovereignty" (Hiebert and Kelly 2015, 3, emphasis in original; see also 7). The Canadian situation is more complicated and controversial, as the rest of this chapter demonstrates.

Institutional Relations after the Charter: A *Salituro*-Based Thought Experiment

When Canadian courts update common-law rules based on Charter values, what happens to the traditional power of the legislature to override judicial innovation? A thought experiment, in two versions, based on the facts of *R. v. Salituro* (1991), a Charter values–based private common-law ruling, will serve to clarify the issue. *Salituro* dealt with whether "irreconcilably" separated spouses could testify against one another in court. The common-law "spousal competence rule" precluded such testimony in order to preserve and promote marital harmony. If the rule were maintained, Mr. Salituro would escape a conviction of fraud against his wife. Should the Court change the rule?

Salituro 1 (Counterfactual)

In the first version of our thought experiment, we imagine that *Salituro* arose not in the Charter era, but just prior to the adoption of the Charter. As it did in the actual Charter case, the Court in our counterfactual, pre-Charter version changes the rule. Emphasizing the legitimacy of the judiciary continuing to develop its own judge-made law, the Court concludes that in modern circumstances, it makes no sense to apply this rule to irreconcilably estranged and separated spouses. Since there was no marital harmony left to preserve between the Salituros, the judgment concludes, there was "no sound policy reason to apply the rule in this case" (*R. v. Salituro* 1991, 660).

Now suppose that the legislature – still in the pre-Charter period – disagrees and re-enacts the original rule. The legislature points out that it had recently revamped this area of law and had left the "spousal competence" rule intact. In the legislature's view, the Supreme Court should have listened to the dissenting justice in the Ontario Court of Appeal, for whom the legislative failure to reform this rule signified its approval of the rule.[7] Had the Court followed this advice, the legislature would not now have to waste its scarce resources in reversing the judicial error.

Soon after the old rule is re-established (now in statutory form), the Charter comes into force, and before long the statute is challenged as violating Charter guarantees of sexual equality. The Court, repeating much of the reasoning of its earlier common-law innovation, agrees that Charter rights are infringed, and then considers the government's argument that the law is nevertheless demonstrably justified as a reasonable limit on rights under section 1 of the Charter. At this point, the Court either upholds the legislation as a reasonable limit or invalidates it because it cannot be justified as a reasonable limit. If it chooses to invalidate, the ball is back in the legislature's court, so to speak. The legislature may accept the new legal status quo that results from the court's invalidation, or it may undertake a legislative sequel to the judicial ruling, taking advantage of whatever room for manoeuvre the Court provided in

---

7 A dissenting judge for the Ontario Court of Appeal argued that the Court ought to be deferential on the issue of spousal competence. Parliament had revisited the issue when it amended the Canada Evidence Act in 1985 – just six years prior to the Supreme Court's ruling in *Salituro*. Since the rule was not updated by Parliament, Justice Carthy assumed that Parliament preferred the status quo by not renovating the common-law rule (*Salituro* 1991, 663–4). Although this represents a deferential approach to the common law – Carthy called the rule "anachronistic and inappropriate" (663) – he still defended the rule on the grounds that parliamentary approval could be inferred from the legislative pattern of the relevant statutes.

the "minimal impairment" component of the *Oakes* test. Alternatively, if it fundamentally disagrees with the judicial invalidation, the legislature can choose to re-establish the invalidated statute by re-enacting it, this time including a clause that it shall operate "notwithstanding" relevant Charter rights and freedoms under section 33 of the Charter.

The above interaction between court and legislature is, of course, the inter-institutional dialogue discussed in chapter 2. Such dialogue involves the opportunity to (1) defend legislation on section 1 grounds, (2) redesign invalidated legislation in light of the "reasonable limit" standards established by the Court, and (3) re-establish invalidated legislation via a section 33 notwithstanding clause (Hogg, Thornton, and Wright 2007, 3). This entire set of dialogic opportunities is available whenever legislation is subject to a Charter challenge.

But what happens to this dialogic model when a common-law rule is changed on the basis of "Charter values"? We have seen that the courts may not consider whether the old rule can be defended as a "reasonable limit" (*Swain*). Does the legislature have the opportunity to re-enact the old rule in statutory form in order to test the section 1 issue in a subsequent challenge? If not, what happens to the section 1 component of inter-institutional "dialogue," and with what effect on the "proper balance between legislative and judicial action"? Our exploration of this question begins with the second version of our *Salituro* thought experiment – the actual, real-life version.

Salituro 2 (Factual)

All elements of the real *Salituro* occurred post-Charter (and in the wake of *Dolphin Delivery* and *Swain*). That is, the Court undertook its initial consideration of the common-law "spousal competence" rule with the Charter in place. Reichman might well argue that this should change nothing, that the Court should simply base its decision on traditional common-law reasoning without adding the weight of the Charter to its analysis. Reichman discourages the application of the Charter to the common law because he holds that it collapses any distinction between common and constitutional law (2002, 329–30). He would prefer the legal issue to be tested through the distinct layers of the legal hierarchy (common law, statutes, and constitutional law), with the Charter coming to bear only if and when the legislature enacted a conflicting statute and that statute was challenged – i.e., in exactly the circumstances of the first version of our thought experiment, circumstances in which the conflicting policy could at least be defended as a reasonable limit under section 1 of the Charter.

That is not how the Court proceeded in the actual *Salituro* case, however. In addition to seeing no good policy reason to apply the traditional "spousal competence" rule, the judges in the post-Charter circumstances found that "preserving the rule would be contrary to this Court's duty to see that the common law develops in accordance with the values of the Charter" (*R. v. Salituro* 1991, 671). In excluding estranged spouses from the rule's application for this reason, moreover, the Court, in the spirit of *Swain*, did not consider whether the old rule could be defended as a "reasonable limit" under section 1. It ignored the lower court judge who saw legislative approval of the old rule in its having survived a recent round of related law reform, preferring to see the rule's survival as a legislative oversight in a small matter, the judicial repair of which the legislature would no doubt approve. Major reform of the common law, the Court conceded, should be left to the legislature rather than being judicially implemented in the name of Charter values (670). The Court presented its modification of the spousal competence rule, however, as the kind of small or incremental "Charter values" change that could be judicially undertaken "without upsetting the proper balance of judicial and legislative action" (675). In 2015, the federal government through Bill C-32 (Canadian Victims Bill of Rights) amended the Canada Evidence Act, eliminating the spousal competence rule: "No person is incompetent, or uncompellable, to testify for the prosecution by reason only that they are married to the accused."

Analyzing the differences between the two different versions of our *Salituro* thought experiment raises doubt over whether the Court, in the second version, can sustain its ability to update the common law "without upsetting the proper balance" between the legislature and the Court. In the first version of *Salituro* (the one that hypothetically began pre-Charter) the legislature was able to enact a statue that disagreed with the Court's common-law interpretation, and it later had the opportunity to defend its statute as a reasonable limit on Charter rights and freedoms. In the actual *Salituro* case – the second version of our thought experiment – the Court's common-law interpretation (and innovation) was based on Charter values and the section 1 question of reasonable limits was not addressed. This returns us to Mix-Ross's concern about things changing when courts label values "constitutional" (2009, 50). Might the added weight of the Constitution mean that the legislature no longer has the opportunity to pass legislation that can be defended under section 1? Put another way, can the legislature in such cases express its disagreement only via a section 33 notwithstanding clause, in which case it is immune to litigation involving a section 1 defence? If so, what most commentators consider an important step in the legislative-judicial "dialogue" would be lost in the common-law context.

Rights Values and Section 1

Before pursuing this issue further, it is important to consider some nuances with respect to the role of section 1 when courts use the Charter to assess (and perhaps change) common-law rules. Although *Swain* held that the judiciary need not consider section 1 when reviewing the public common law, it did not preclude such considerations. Indeed, the *Swain* judgment itself conducted a reasonably full section 1 analysis, even though it did not consider it strictly necessary.[8] If this part of the *Swain* precedent were always followed, section 1 considerations would remain a significant part of the dialogic equation, at least at the stage of considering the constitutionality of the common-law rule itself, and part of the problem identified above would diminish. In fact, however, other prominent Charter-based common-law cases – such as *R. v. Daviault* (discussed below) – have followed the main part of the *Swain* precedent and devoted little or no attention to section 1.

When the Court *does* address section 1 in such public common-law cases as *Swain*, the government is at least a party to the litigation, and is thus present in court to mount a section 1 defence of the existing rule. But notice that in such cases the government is defending the reasonableness of a judge-made rule, not a statute that has passed through the legislative process. In other words, even when section 1 questions are fully addressed in public common-law cases, the basic question remains: If the Court changes the common-law rule on Charter values grounds, is it possible for the *legislature* to re-enact the rule and potentially have its *statute* defended as a reasonable limit in subsequent litigation? Or is it only constitutionally legitimate for the legislature to enact legislation if it contains section 33's notwithstanding clause? Does the legislature retain or lose the dialogic opportunity illustrated in version 1 of our thought experiment? This question is obviously more acute when the Court changes a public common-law rule on Charter grounds without fully addressing section 1 issues, but the question remains even if it elects to address those issues in response to the *executive's* defence of the old *judge-made* rule.

In purely private law cases, the government is not even present to defend the "reasonableness" of a challenged common-law rule. Does that task fall to the private litigant who stands to benefit from the existing

---

8 For instance, in *R. v. Clayton* the Supreme Court reaffirmed *Swain* that section 1 analysis is not strictly required for the common law, but just like *Swain*, the Court conducted section 1 analysis anyway (2007, para. 105).

rule? In *Hill v. Church of Scientology* (1995), the Supreme Court recognized that it would be unfair to expect the "defending" litigant to mount the kind of defence a government might in public law litigation. When two private parties are in conflict over a common-law rule, the Court said, the party relying "upon the existing law ... should not be placed in the position of having to defend it" (para. 98). The Court thus shifted the onus of demonstrating the "reasonableness" or "unreasonableness" of the rule. In all Charter litigation, the onus of demonstrating a conflict with the Charter falls on the party challenging the constitutional legitimacy of a law. If the challenger succeeds in establishing a conflict with the Charter in public law litigation, the onus of trying to save the law as a "reasonable limit" under section 1 falls on the government. By contrast, in litigation about the private common law, according to the *Hill* judgment, the onus is on "the party challenging the common law to bear the burden of proving *not only* that the common law is inconsistent with Charter values *but also* that its provisions cannot be justified" (1995, para. 98, emphasis added). This gives a *prima facie* advantage to the existing common-law rule, but that advantage is justified by the fact that the established existence of this rule has created settled expectations on which the defending litigant was entitled to rely. Established legal expectations among private actors should not be lightly or easily upset (*Hill v. Church of Scientology* 1995, para. 98; Ross 1996, 130).

However, the Court's assurance that Charter-based private common-law reform will not be lightly undertaken does not resolve the issue of what kind of legislative response is legitimate in the event that the Court *does* change the law and the legislature disagrees. As in the case of public common-law cases, the judicial nuances and qualifications that permit some degree of "reasonable limits" justification in private common-law cases leave intact the basic question posed by our *Salituro*-based thought experiment: Does the legislature retain the option of enacting a statute that could, in a subsequent dialogic step, be challenged, and defended *by the government* on section 1 grounds, or must it go directly to legislation including a section 33 notwithstanding clause?

If it is indeed the case that the legislature loses the option of non-section-33 legislation in response to Charter-based common-law reform, might this be defended as an inconsequential loss in light of the Court's assurance that it will only undertake such reforms if they are truly small or incremental? Perhaps, but that is not an obviously compelling defence. Who decides what is small or "incremental"? And what happens when successive "incremental" changes add up to major reform? If the legislature cannot enact conflicting legislation without the notwithstanding clause, then "the balance between judicial and legislative action" has certainly changed. Has "the proper balance" been "upset"? As the next section shows, this question remains controversial in Canada, both in case law and in the literature concerning the dialogical relationship between courts and legislatures.

Institutional Relations in Canada after the Charter: When Is a Notwithstanding Clause Required?

Throughout this study, we have seen political and legal constitutionalists disagree about matters of both constitutional reach and constitutional strength. Chapter 2 discussed how the two perspectives disagree about what kind of rights document best promotes inter-institutional dialogue: legal constitutionalists prefer a strong-form invalidation mandate, with its tendency towards judicial interpretive supremacy, while political constitutionalists' desire for coordinate interpretation (to generate more opportunities for inter-institutional dialogue) is associated with weak-form systems. The issue of when the notwithstanding clause is required captures an aspect of this perennial institutional debate. In each of the controversies described in this section, we see scholars arguing over different concepts of dialogue, either lauding a more enhanced parliamentary role or privileging the judicial perspective. On one side of the controversy are those who maintain that legislation overtly disagreeing with Charter-based judicial reform of the common law must include section 33's notwithstanding clause (Choudhry et al. 2005; Roach 2016). On the other side are those who would leave room for the intermediate dialogic step of non-section-33 legislation, which could then be defended under section 1 in a subsequent "second-look" court case (Baker 2010; Baker and Knopff 2002; Brudner 2005; Dixon 2019; Huscroft 2009; Knopff et al. 2017). In the language of dialogue theory, the issue concerns the legitimacy of certain kinds of legislative sequels.

The issue has come into focus most dramatically not with respect to cases like *Salituro* and *Hill*, which did not generate legislative sequels (or controversial sequel proposals), but with respect to *Daviault* (1994), *O'Connor* (1995), and the controversy about same-sex marriage following the *Same-Sex Marriage Reference* (2004). Each of these episodes generated considerable debate about how Parliament could permissibly disagree with Charter-based reform of the common law. Must legislative disagreement in such cases include a section 33 notwithstanding clause, or can the inter-institutional "dialogue" legitimately include the intermediate step of disagreement through ordinary (non-section-33) legislation? Such non-section-33 legislation, of course, could itself be subsequently challenged (and defended under section 1), as in our first version of the

Salituro thought experiment, and might well be struck down (at which point section 33 would be the only route to re-establishing the legislative preference). The question is whether an intermediate dialogic option is appropriate and legitimate.

Although the *Daviault, O'Connor,* and same-sex marriage episodes all raise this question, they do so in somewhat different circumstances. In *Daviault,* a legislative sequel re-established the policy represented by the previous common-law rule (and approved by the Supreme Court dissent), but the Court has not yet had an opportunity to revisit the issue in a "second-look" case. In *O'Connor,* the legislature disagreed with the Court's majority opinion by enacting legislation based on the common-law innovation preferred by the dissenting *O'Connor* minority (but considered unconstitutional by the majority); that legislation was itself subsequently challenged before the Supreme Court in the second-look case of *R. v. Mills* (1999). With respect to same-sex marriage, the debate focused on a proposed or hypothetical sequel to the *Reference Re Same-Sex Marriage.*

Daviault (1994) and Bill C-72

Daviault altered a common-law rule (confirmed in the pre-Charter case of *R. v. Leary* 1978) that excluded drunkenness as a legal defence against so-called general intent offences, such as sexual assault.[9] The *"Leary* rule" meant that Daviault, who had committed sexual assault while drunk, could not use his intoxication as a defence. But Daviault was not drunk in any ordinary way. He was so drunk as to be in a state of "automatism" that prevented him from forming the traditional legal intent (*mens rea*) required to commit a crime. He argued that in depriving him of a *mens rea*–based defence in such circumstances, the *Leary* rule violated the Charter's section 7 "right to life, liberty, and security of the person" and section 11(d) "right to be presumed innocent until proven guilty according to law in a fair and public hearing by an independent and impartial

---

9 The editors of *The Court and the Charter* explain that general intent offences arise when the offender possesses the intent to commit a crime, whereas in specific intent offences the offender possesses the general intent to commit a crime *and* a specific or ulterior purpose (Bateman et al. 2008, 252). The contrast between the two can be seen in assault (general intent) versus assault to inflict bodily harm (specific intent). Specific intent offenders will possess a higher mental awareness and therefore carry tougher punishments. Intoxication can inhibit this higher level of mental calculation and thus cast doubt on whether the accused could have possessed specific intent. The Supreme Court's *Leary* decision held that intoxication could not be used to diminish "general" criminal intent.

tribunal." The Court's majority agreed and overturned the *Leary* rule for cases of extreme intoxication, thereby making a *mens rea* defence available to the accused in circumstances like Daviault's.

Following *Swain*, moreover, the majority overturned the *Leary* rule with scant attention to whether it might be a section 1 "reasonable limit" on Charter rights. The majority judgment limited itself to asserting that the rule's violation of the Charter "is so drastic and so contrary to the principles of fundamental justice that it cannot be justified under s.1 of the Charter," and that "it cannot be said to be well tailored to address a particular objective and it would not meet either the proportionality or the minimum impairment requirements" (*R. v. Daviault* 1994, 92–3). This exceedingly brief reference to section 1 contrasts with the extensive role played by that section whenever legislation is found to violate a Charter provision (when, indeed, section 1 analysis sometimes dominates the judgment). To justify the extreme brevity of its comments on section 1, the *Daviault* majority immediately quotes *Swain* on the appropriateness of putting section 1 to the side in common-law cases (93).

The *Daviault* majority "invited" Parliament to confirm this ruling, and limit the *mens rea* defence to similar factual circumstances, by creating the new crime of "causing harm while extremely intoxicated" (Roach 2016, 309). Instead, Parliament, siding with the Court's dissenters and responding to public outrage (Hiebert 2002, 99–103), enacted Bill C-72, which effectively codified the previous *Leary* rule, thus returning to the pre-*Daviault* policy status quo. In siding with the dissenters, Parliament implied the *Daviault* "majority … was wrong to interpret the Charter as it did" (Roach 2016, 310). In effect, the legislature challenged the Court to reconsider and reverse its original judgment if and when the issue came before it again in a "second-look" case.

Of course, there is no guarantee that the Court would change its mind upon such a "second look." It could very well stick with its original judgment and strike down C-72, though in doing so it would have to consider at some length (and reject) a full section 1 "reasonable limits" defence. In that event, Parliament could continue its policy disagreement only via the section 33 notwithstanding clause. By not including a notwithstanding clause in C-72, Parliament was affirming the legitimacy of an intermediate dialogic step, at least in cases of Charter-based common-law reform by the Court. Such a step would be meaningless if the Court could never legitimately change its mind upon the "second-look" opportunity created by a non-section-33 legislative response. It follows that in enacting C-72, Parliament also affirmed the possibility and legitimacy of the judiciary being persuaded by its dialogic partner. As Janet Hiebert argues, Parliament was challenging "dominant legal assumptions that the judiciary has exclusive prerogative for interpreting the Charter" (2002, 117). In this view, Parliament is entitled to disagree with the Court about the best interpretation of the Charter, and there is no need to quickly concede a Charter violation that can only be maintained "notwithstanding" the Charter. The Court retains the interpretive upper hand in the sense that it can, if it chooses, force inter-institutional disagreement to the section 33 stage, but there is no need to jump to that stage after just a "first look" by the Court.

Although some commentators support the dialogic perspective embodied in C-72 (Baker 2010; Baker and Knopff 2002; Hiebert 2002), many others strongly reject it. To repeat Hiebert's formulation, C-72 challenges "*dominant* legal assumptions that the judiciary has *exclusive* prerogative for interpreting the Charter" (2002, 117, emphasis added). This "dominant" legal-constitutionalist view is well represented by Kent Roach, for whom legislation like C-72 represents an "in your face" legislative response to a judicial interpretation of the Charter (2016, 308, 317). It is "in your face" because it chooses to ignore and violate Charter rights (as the Court alone legitimately interprets them). For Roach, in other words, the inter-institutional disagreement represented by C-72 is not about how best to interpret the Charter, but about whether or not to abide by it. Such "in your face" disagreements are perfectly legitimate, Roach maintains, but only if they acknowledge the Charter violation by using the provision provided for that very purpose: the section 33 notwithstanding clause. Use of that clause, for Roach, alerts the public that Charter rights have been violated, so that they can debate and revisit Parliament's decision when the clause expires after five years (2016, 310).

For Roach, dialogic legislative sequels *without* a section 33 notwithstanding clause are appropriate only within the interpretive boundaries established by the courts, not as direct challenges to those interpretive boundaries. Roach has in mind especially judicial interpretations of section 1 "reasonable limits." If the Court strikes down a law as an "unreasonable limit" on the Charter, the legislature may enact a more "reasonable limit" without a notwithstanding clause. If the legislature wishes to enact what the Court (or its majority) have declared to be an unreasonable limit, the notwithstanding clause is essential.

Even if one accepts this distinction in general terms – and not everyone does (Baker and Knopff 2002; Huscroft 2009) – special difficulties seem present in cases when the judiciary undertakes Charter-based common-law reform with little meaningful section 1 analysis, as the Court did in *Daviault*. In such cases, Roach's dialogic model appears to accept the practical exclusion of section 1 analysis from the dialogic equation. Not only can the Court choose to sidestep the issue in the original common-law litigation, but, more importantly, the legislature has no opportunity to enact a statute that might then be fully defended as a "reasonable limit."

With respect to *Daviault*, the Supreme Court itself has not had an opportunity to comment on this controversy because, contrary to the expectation of many commentators, no second-look challenge to C-72 has reached that Court in the intervening two-plus decades (for a detailed analysis of this anomaly, see Baker and Knopff 2014). The Court did get that opportunity in *Mills*, which concerned the constitutionality of the sequel to *O'Connor*.

O'Connor (1995), Bill C-46, and *Mills* (1999)

In *R. v. O'Connor* (1995), the Supreme Court used Charter values to elaborate common-law rules regarding the access criminal defendants should have to the private medical records of the alleged victim in sexual assault cases.[10] The Court agreed that the private records were relevant to the accused's defence but were divided (5 to 4) over the process that determined their release. Both majority and dissenting opinions agreed that the trial judge should administer a balancing test for admitting the private records, but they disagreed over which considerations should be prioritized in the process. The dissenting opinion wanted to see a tougher test than the majority, and specifically one that emphasized equality rights and the need for sexual assaults to be reported (Baker 2010, 22). The dissenters wanted to make it more difficult than the majority for the accused to access the alleged victim's private records. From the majority's perspective, the dissenters' preferred policy was unconstitutionally restrictive.

After the *O'Connor* ruling, Parliament enacted a new legislative regime (Bill C-46) that essentially adopted the dissenters' view over that of the *O'Connor* majority. Like the *Daviault* sequel, Parliament's *O'Connor* sequel adopted a policy that was unconstitutional in the view of the Court's majority (what Roach calls an "in your face" legislative response), and it did so without using a section 33 notwithstanding clause. Unlike the

---

10 This case concerned a criminal trial of Bishop Hubert O'Connor, who was accused of sexually assaulting several students under his care at an Indian residential school. O'Connor's defence wanted medical and counselling records from his accusers. This meant there was a clash over the accused's right to a full answer and defence versus the victim's right to privacy. With an absence of legislation to address the circumstances, the case turned to common law.

Daviault sequel (C-72), the *O'Connor* sequel (C-46) provided the Court with a "second-look" opportunity in *R. v. Mills* (1999).

In *Mills*, the Court upheld C-46, essentially accepting the policy that its majority had rejected in *O'Connor*. "Tellingly," says Dennis Baker, "two justices from the *O'Connor* majority – Frank Iacobucci and John Major – joined the *Mills* majority, thus allowing parliamentarians to enact a policy they had voted against when it was originally put forward by the *O'Connor* dissenters" (2010, 23). Invoking the "dialogue" metaphor, the Court emphasized that we must "keep in mind that the decision in *O'Connor* is not necessarily the last word on the subject ... The law develops through dialogue between courts and legislatures" (*R. v. Mills* 1999, para. 20).

The Court was accepting as legitimate dialogue the kind of "in your face" response, without a section 33 notwithstanding clause, that the dialogue theorists represented by Roach consider illegitimate. Not surprisingly, those theorists launched a vigorous attack on the *Mills* judgment, arguing that the Court should reject such challenges to its interpretive finality over the Constitution (Cameron 2001, 1051; Roach 2016, 314–16). Roach argues that if the Court wanted to make room for dialogue, "the s.33 override also would have accomplished this task by preserving the Court's decision in *O'Connor* and ensuring that further public discussion of the difficult and evolving subject in five years time when the override would expire" (Roach 2001, 528–9). Baker summarizes Roach's disagreement with the outcome in *Mills* in the following terms:

> If judicial supremacy means that that Court gets the final word on policy, Roach rejects it. But he clearly thinks that judges must be supreme in matters of constitutional *interpretation*. Section 33 allows "in your face" derogations from rights; it does not allow legislatures to disagree with judges about the correct meaning of rights. *Mills* is deficient, for Roach, precisely to the extent that it departs from the *interpretative* judicial supremacy. (2010, 24, emphasis in original)

The above discussion of *Daviault* noted that with respect to Charter-based common-law reform, Roach's version of dialogue, by urging an immediate jump to the section 33 stage, threatens to exclude the step of *legislative* disagreement that might be fully defended as a reasonable disagreement under section 1. This would obviously be true of *O'Connor*, which also changed the common law on constitutional grounds. If Roach's model were applied, *Mills* would have found C-46 to be unconstitutional, thereby forcing inter-institutional disagreement to the section 33 stage. While Roach seems to ignore this problem in common-law cases, the Supreme Court in *Mills* did not. Very early in its opinion, the

Mills majority emphasized that the case was about "the relationship between the courts and Parliament when Parliament alters a judicially created common law procedure" (*R. v. Mills* 1999, para. 17). The Court emphasized the extent to which both sides on the issues in *O'Connor* and *Mills* could rely on "Charter standards" (para. 17), and that the balance struck by the *O'Connor* majority should not be the last interpretive word. At least with respect to Charter-based common-law litigation – and especially when competing Charter values are being balanced – the Court in *Mills* supports the kind of intermediate legislative step in the dialogic model that Roach rejects.

Same-Sex Marriage (2004)

Prior to 2005, Canadian law had never codified the definition of marriage in legislation, allowing the common-law rule defining marriage to persist. The common law defined marriage as "the voluntary union for life of one man and one woman to the exclusion of all others" (*Hyde v. Hyde and Woodmansee* 1866). In the early 2000s, several provincial courts (both trial courts and provincial courts of appeal) had established that this definition of marriage violated the Charter's equality rights on the grounds that it excluded same-sex couples, and had revised the common law to permit same-sex marriage.[11] Prior to introducing legislation to confirm these rulings, the federal Liberal government filed a reference to the Supreme Court (*Reference Re Same-Sex Marriage* 2004). In that reference, the Court ruled that the Constitution permitted changing the definition of marriage to include same-sex couples, but it refused to say whether such change was constitutionally required (i.e., whether the existing opposite-sex common-law requirement was unconstitutional).

The official Opposition, led by Stephen Harper, disagreed with the Liberal government's proposed same-sex marriage legislation and suggested a very different legislative response to the lower court rulings. Harper's Conservative Party proposed codifying the traditional opposite-sex common-law definition of marriage in statutory form, and at the same time creating statutory civil unions for same-sex couples. Unlike Bills C-75 (the sequel to *Daviault*) and C-46 (the sequel to *O'Connor*) – actual

---

11 The courts of appeal in Ontario (*Halpern v. Canada* 2003), British Columbia (*Barbeau v. BC* 2003), Quebec (*Hendricks and Leboeuf v. Quebec* 2004), and Yukon (*Dunbar and Edge v. Yukon* 2004) all ruled that the traditional definition of marriage was inconsistent with the Charter. After the *Halpern* ruling, the federal attorney general decided not to appeal these decisions, and "copycat" cases soon spread to the remaining provincial and territorial jurisdictions (Hennigar 2009, 226).

statutes that expressed legislative disagreement with Supreme Court decisions – Harper's proposed marriage law was a hypothetical sequel to overturn Charter-based lower court decisions in the absence of a Supreme Court ruling on the question at issue. Otherwise, the controversy generated by the proposal posed the same question as the controversies about the *Daviault* and *O'Connor* sequels: Could Parliament reject and overturn Charter-based revision of the common law? Harper insisted that Parliament need not include section 33 in an initial statutory opposition to the lower courts.

One hundred and thirty-four "constitutional experts" disagreed. In an open letter to Stephen Harper (Choudhry et al. 2005), this group of law professors argued that Harper's proposed legislation was unconstitutional and could thus be enacted only with a notwithstanding clause. In their view the accumulation of lower court rulings was enough to establish the unconstitutionality of the Harper proposal and to require a section 33 response from any government that wished to revert to the traditional heterosexual definition of marriage.

As Knopff and Banfield have noted, not all legal experts agreed (2009, 48–52). Most prominently, the University of Toronto's Alan Brudner (2005) – himself critical of Harper's proposed marriage policy – wrote an op-ed in the *Globe and Mail* in which he levelled two main criticisms at the open letter. First, Brudner argued there was no way to predict how the Supreme Court would treat the traditional definition of marriage in legislative form. This was problematic since the open letter "claimed to be stating the law, not predicting judicial behaviour" (A1). In Brudner's view the odds might be against Harper's hypothetical legislation, but "law professors and deans do not get to decide whether the laws of this country meet the requirements of the Charter. Courts do" (A1).

Brudner's second criticism of the open letter addresses precisely the issue we have been considering – namely, whether the legislation can disagree with Charter-based common-law change without including a section 33 notwithstanding clause (Knopff and Banfield 2009, 50). Brudner agreed with Harper "that the judicially-declared unconstitutionality of the traditional common-law definition of marriage does not entail the unconstitutionality of parliamentary legislation affirming the same definition" (2005, A1). The reason springs from the Supreme Court's decision in *Swain*. Brudner notes that "in *R. v. Swain*, the Supreme Court of Canada said that, where a common-law rule is challenged, the court will not show the same deference to the policy of the rule as it will when legislation is at issue, since no question of respect for the democratic will arises" (A1). It follows, for Brudner, that the Court *might* show more deference to legislation on the same issue, which means that it needs to have the opportunity to consider that option through legislation that does not include a Charter-immunizing notwithstanding clause. Brudner emphasizes the importance of section 1 analysis to a consideration of such legislation. "For all we know," he says, "courts may uphold heterosexual-only marriage as a reasonable limit on the right against discrimination when the restriction comes from a democratic body" (A1). Brudner agrees with the authors of the open letter that "the betting odds lie heavily against such an eventuality," but this is no reason for cutting the intermediate step of defending legislation on section 1 grounds out of the inter-institutional dialogue by jumping prematurely to section 33 legislation (A1).

Indeed, Brudner believes that section 33 should be invoked not preemptively to "protect laws suspected of being unconstitutional against judicial scrutiny," but only after the full process of judicial scrutiny has been completed, which means "only after the *Supreme Court* has ruled on the constitutionality of a law" (2005, A1, emphasis added). As Brudner notes, "neither [the Supreme Court], nor any provincial court outside Quebec has yet ruled on whether democratic *legislation* restricting marriage to heterosexual couples is valid" (A1, emphasis added).

The disagreement between Brudner and his colleagues features similar fault lines as the debates about *Daviault* and *O'Connor/Mills*. Here again we see one side, represented in this instance by the 134 signatories to the open letter, that denies the legitimacy of an intermediate dialogic response to Charter-based common-law change through normal (non-section-33) legislation, and another side, represented by Brudner (see also Knopff and Banfield 2009, 49–50; Petter 2009, 44–5), that believes that Parliament should be given the opportunity to justify the traditional definition of marriage as a reasonable limit under section 1 of the Charter.

In the end, this debate about inter-institutional dialogue on same-sex marriage remained largely hypothetical. Paul Martin's Liberal government responded to the Supreme Court's reference by passing the Civil Marriage Act (Bill C-38) in 2005, defining marriage to include both same- and opposite-sex couples and making Canada the fourth country in the world to extend marriage to same-sex couples. When the Harper-led Conservatives came to power in 2006, they held a free vote on whether to repeal this legislation and enact the traditional heterosexual definition of marriage (along with civil unions for same-sex couples). Supporters of the latter option lost the vote, and the issue has not been revisited by Parliament.

Conclusion

How much has the relationship between legislatures and courts changed with respect to common-law development in the bill of rights era? The question is more complicated in Canada than in New Zealand or the United Kingdom. The weak-form rights documents of the latter two countries explicitly retain legislative supremacy, allowing determined legislatures to pass ordinary statutes that overturn a common-law innovation they disagree with, even if the courts base that innovation on the values of their rights documents. No doubt, placing the weight of constitutional rights on the side of judicial common-law innovation makes statutory reversal more difficult than it would otherwise have been. At least formally, however, the traditional division of labour between courts and legislatures, which subjected judicial common-law development to ultimate legislative authority, is retained. Simply put, legislatures in the weak-form systems can re-establish in statutory form a common-law rule changed by the courts in light of rights values. If the courts then also find or declare the reversing statute to be unconstitutional, the legislature can maintain its preferred policy by ignoring that ruling.

Can Canadian legislatures similarly reverse judicial rulings that bring the common law into line with Charter values? The answer is clearly yes if a section 33 notwithstanding clause is included in the reversing statute. But a statute containing a notwithstanding clause is not the kind of "ordinary legislation" that the New Zealand and UK legislatures can use to reverse common-law innovation. Section 33 is so politically fraught in Canada that requiring it to reverse Charter-based common-law innovation – as legal constitutionalists insist – alters the traditional institutional balance much more than do the New Zealand or UK rights documents. While basing common-law innovation on rights values might make statutory reversal somewhat more difficult in New Zealand or the United Kingdom, it makes it almost impossible in Canada if the reversing statute must contain a section 33 notwithstanding clause. It follows that if Canadian legislatures must always use the notwithstanding clause in statutes that disagree with judicial reform of the common law – as legal-constitutionalist orthodoxy insists – then the traditional "balance between judicial and legislative action" has been significantly altered. Moreover, "the proper balance" in the Charter era has arguably been "upset."

Sensitive to this concern, the Supreme Court of Canada insists that judges should be cautious in using Charter values to transform the common law. The "appropriate balance" is maintained when judges leave "complex changes ... with uncertain ramifications ... to the legislature" and stick to making only smaller "incremental changes to the common law" (*Salituro* 1991, 666). In Lord Bingham's terms, courts may "alter the law's direction of travel by a few degrees," but they may not "set it off in a different direction." In making appropriately incremental changes, moreover, Canadian judges need not consider whether the rule they think runs counter to Charter values can be justified as a "reasonable limit," though they may sometimes choose to do so.

Such assurances tend not to satisfy political constitutionalists, partly because a series of incremental changes can add up over time to "complex" or "far-reaching" transformation, but more importantly because the line between incremental changes and complex and far-reaching ones is anything but clear. When legislatures strongly dislike a rights-based judicial reform of the common law, they obviously do not consider that reform to be small and insignificant. For example, Canada's Supreme Court presumably considered the changes it made in *Daviault* to be sufficiently small, but Parliament – to say nothing of the Canadian public – dramatically disagreed.

In such cases, can Canadian legislatures pass statutes reversing the judicial reform without including a section 33 notwithstanding clause? Can they, in other words, use the kind of "ordinary statutes" with which New Zealand and UK legislatures can reverse rights-based common-law innovation? If they cannot, and if the Canadian Court's reform side-stepped "reasonable limits" analysis (as *Swain* says it can), the opportunity to defend a legislatively preferred policy on section 1 grounds is lost. Even if the Court has undertaken a serious section 1 analysis of the common-law rule it is abandoning (as *Swain* permits), the *legislature* loses the opportunity for "reasonable limits" dialogue if it must use section 33 to register its disagreement. If Charter values–based reform of the common law eclipses the most important component of Charter dialogue, has the "appropriate balance" between courts and legislatures been "upset"? Is the balance better maintained by allowing legislatures to disagree without a section 33 notwithstanding clause – as Parliament did in its legislative sequels to *Daviault* and *O'Connor* – thus opening the door to serious section 1 analysis of a statute in subsequent "second-look" litigation? This is a matter of ongoing controversy between political and legal constitutionalists in Canada.

Rights-based common-law innovation is not the only part of the judicial "interpretive mandate" that engages the "appropriate balance between judicial and legislative action," however. The next two chapters address concerns about institutional balance raised by statutory interpretation in the bill of rights era. On these issues, too, political and legal constitutionalists are at loggerheads.

Strained Statutory Interpretation
in New Zealand and the United Kingdom

Having explored the controversies that judge-made common law raises under rights documents, we come to the issue of how those documents affect statutory interpretation. On this issue, which will occupy our attention for two chapters, political and legal constitutionalists disagree fundamentally about how to structure the legislative "burden of inertia" with respect to impugned statutes (Huscroft 2002, 125; Roach 2016, 70). Legal constitutionalists prefer to give judges the strong-form mandate to invalidate rights-infringing legislation, in which case the burden of legislative inertia – i.e., the legislature doing nothing in response to the judicial decision – favours the rights claimant who has succeeded in court. Political constitutionalists, by contrast, unwilling to concede judicial supremacy in determining whether rights have really been violated, prefer the weak-form judicial power to interpret legislation in a rights-compliant manner *if possible*. If such an interpretation is not possible, judges in weak-form systems can find or declare the law's incompatibility with the rights document, but such rulings leave the legislation in force and fully applicable, meaning that the burden of legislative inertia favours the impugned law, not the rights claimant.

But what happens if judges, reluctant either to strike down legislation in strong-form Canada or to find or declare it incompatible in weak-form New Zealand or the United Kingdom, engage in what the literature calls "strained interpretation" to "save" legislation that seems on its face, or by clear legislative intention, to infringe protected rights? In the weak-form systems, political constitutionalists worry that strained interpretation inappropriately escalates the system in the direction of legal constitutionalism. In stronger-form Canada, legal constitutionalists worry that strained interpretation distorts and undermines valuable features of dialogue under strong-form review. This chapter examines the New Zealand/UK version of the debate, while the next chapter focuses on the Canadian version. In this chapter, I find that the use of strained interpretations has been more prominent (and controversial) in the United Kingdom than in New Zealand. This is due to a combination of judicial interpretation, formal structural differences between the two rights documents, and differences in constitutional culture.

The Accepted Line between Legitimate and Strained Interpretation

In New Zealand and the United Kingdom, judges are generally *supposed* to interpretively "save" legislation from inconsistency with the relevant rights document. Section 6 of the NZBORA tells New Zealand judges to prefer a legislative "meaning that is consistent with" the document's protected rights and freedoms, and section 3 of the HRA tells UK judges to read and apply legislation "in a way which is compatible with the Convention rights." Recognizing that legislation will often be legitimately open to different interpretations, these provisions direct judges to choose the rights-compliant interpretation. In effect, this interpretive mandate reflects a "presumption of constitutionality." That is, the legislature is presumed to have acted in compliance with constitutional norms, and judges should resolve any ambiguities in legislative language accordingly.

However, the same provisions that set out this interpretive mandate, with its presumption of constitutionality, also place limits on it. A rights-compliant meaning may be chosen by New Zealand judges only when "an enactment *can* be given" that meaning, and by UK judges only "so far as it is *possible* to do so" (emphases added). The presumption of constitutionality extends only to legislation open to a rights-compliant interpretation. When an enactment *cannot* be given a NZBORA-consistent meaning, or when it is *impossible* to read legislation as rights-compatible under the HRA, the limits of presuming constitutionality have been reached and judges must forthrightly find or declare inconsistency. Any attempt interpretively to save such legislation is to engage in "strained interpretation," which is no longer really interpretation but judicial law-making. In both the New Zealand and UK rights documents, as noted in chapter 2, there is an explicitly "enacted line between [legitimate] judicial interpretation or construction and [illegitimate] judicial law-making" (Gardbaum 2013, 136).

The explicitly "enacted" line between legitimate and strained interpretation in the NZBORA and the HRA, moreover, finds support from judges in both countries. "We can interpret, but we cannot rewrite or legislate," wrote New Zealand's Justice Tipping (*Quilter v. Attorney-General* 1998, 572). In the United Kingdom, Lord Hope of Craighead similarly insisted that while interpreting statutes "belongs, as it has always done, to the judges ... it is not for them to legislate." The interpretative mandate enshrined in section 3 of the HRA, he adds, "does not give power to the judges to overrule decisions which the language of the statute shows have been taken on the very point at issue by the legislator" (*R v. Lambert* 2002, para. 79).

Where to Draw the Line between Legitimate and Strained Interpretation

Clearly, the distinction between appropriate rights-based interpretation of legislation and strained interpretation is well established and generally accepted. What is a well-accepted line in principle, however, is "a fine one in practice" (Gardbaum 2013, 136). Judges and commentators who agree that the line exists often disagree about where to draw it, which obviously affects judgments about when or whether it has been crossed.

Central to this line-drawing controversy in New Zealand and the United Kingdom is disagreement about the role of textual ambiguity in justifying a rights-compliant interpretation of legislation. While virtually everyone agrees that "the inherent ambiguity of language means that rules are necessarily uncertain at their margins, so that judges are frequently called upon to perform a creative interpretive role" (Smillie 1996, 255), not everyone agrees that judicial creativity under rights documents should be limited to resolving ambiguity or uncertainty at the "margins" of statutory language. Put another way, not everyone agrees that judges can choose a rights-compliant interpretation of a statute only when the statutory wording is sufficiently ambiguous to make that interpretation reasonably plausible. The contrary view holds that judges should adopt a rights-compliant interpretation of legislation even if it is *im*plausible as a matter of text or legislative intention, so long as it is a remotely "possible" reading of the statute. In the famous UK case *R. v. A.*, for example, Lord Steyn wrote that "the interpretive obligation under section 3 of [the HRA] is a strong one" that "applies even if there is no ambiguity in the language in the sense of the language being capable of two different meanings" (2002, para. 44). Aileen Kavanagh notes that Steyn's comments represent a "departure from the previous rule of statutory interpretation that judicial reliance on Convention rights was only allowed to resolve ambiguity" (2009, 24).

Whether statutory ambiguity is required for the legitimate exercise of the interpretive mandate is also debated in New Zealand. On the one hand, Justice Hardie in *Knight v. Commissioner of Inland Revenue* did not think interpretive creativity under section 6 of the NZBORA should occur "other than in cases of ambiguity or uncertainty" (quoted in Butler 2014, 11). Similarly, Justice Blanchard wrote in *R. v. Hansen* that judges can choose a rights-compliant interpretation of a statute "only" when that interpretation "is genuinely open in light of both [the statute's] text and its purpose" (2007, para. 62). On the other hand, Justice Elias, also writing in *Hansen*, insisted that "s.6 of the New Zealand Bill of Rights Act now makes it clear that *textual ambiguity is not required*" (2007, para. 13, emphasis added).[1]

Those in New Zealand and the United Kingdom who take Lord Steyn's "strong" view of the interpretive mandate think readings contrary to unambiguous text and legislative purpose are "*possible*" (HRA section 3) or "*can* be given" (NZBORA section 6) so long as the law does not, with absolute clarity, explicitly exclude them. This is why Justice Elias thinks section 6 of the NZBORA "makes it clear that textual ambiguity is not required" (*Hansen* 2007, para. 13). But as Lord Nicholls observes about the same issue in the UK context, "the word 'possible'" in section 3 of the HRA is itself "not free from ambiguity" and thus bears "more than one interpretation" (*Ghaidan v. Godin-Mendoza* 2004, para. 27). The other interpretation is to treat as possible only those interpretations that are at least reasonably plausible given a statute's ambiguity.

We can begin to flesh out what is at stake in this debate by considering the New Zealand case *Hopkinson v. Police* (2004). In 2003, Hopkinson participated in an anti-war demonstration outside of Parliament. He burnt a New Zealand flag and was fined $600 under the Flags, Emblems and Names Protection Act, which makes anyone who "uses, displays, destroys, or damages the New Zealand Flag in any manner with the intention of dishonouring it" guilty of an offence (section 11 (b)). Hopkinson was fined for destroying the flag "with the intention of dishonouring it." He challenged the fine as being inconsistent with the NZBORA's right to freedom of expression (section 14). At the High Court, Justice France agreed with Hopkinson and dropped the conviction. She achieved this result by reading the prohibition on "dishonouring" the flag as allowing for the destruction of the flag "so long as it is not done in a way that 'defiles' it" (Allan 2006, 8). Put differently, destroying the flag was not enough; the defendant had to disparage the flag in some other way to reach the standard of "defilement." Hopkinson, according to Justice France, had not reached that standard.

---

1 Justice Elias buttressed this conclusion by noting that "the common law had ... already evolved beyond requiring ambiguity before interpreting legislation to conform wherever possible with human rights instruments and fundamental values of the common law" (*Hansen* 2007, para. 13)

Is this an interpretation of the Flags, Emblems and Names Protection Act that should be judicially preferred because it "*can* be given"? Is it a "possible" interpretation? Justice France thought so, even though she conceded that the most natural meaning of "dishonouring" the flag was the one adopted by the lower court, which, in the words of Graeme Orr (2010: 514), held that " 'dishonour' would ordinarily embrace the indignity of being immolated in kerosene." Giving the statute this natural reading, however, would, in Justice France's view, bring it into direct conflict with the NZBORA's guarantee of freedom of expression. To avoid this conflict, she used the section 6 interpretive mandate to give "dishonour" the narrower meaning of "defile," which required more than mere burning. In her view, section 6 of the NZBORA "demands that" this unnatural, but possible, interpretation of the statutory language "must" be adopted (*Hopkinson* 2004, para. 60).

Eric Fish (2016, 138–9) suggests that the "creative interpretation" of the statute in *Hopkinson* is an "example" of "effectively rewriting" statutes to make them rights-compliant. For Orr, Justice France's transformation of "dishonour" into "vilification" "reads a heavily subjective element into what is otherwise a purely material offence of destroying an object in public" (2010, 515). This perceived "rewriting" opened the decision to "wide criticism" (Erdos 2009, 103) for crossing the line from legitimate construction to illegitimately strained interpretation. For example, Stephen Franks, "then justice spokesperson for the ACT party, ... attacked [*Hopkinson*] as a dangerous 'example of human rights induced judicial activism' " (quoted in Erdos 2009, 103).

For Steven Franks (2004), "not a single member of Parliament that passed the measure would have shared [Justice France's] view. Even members who opposed it ... would have thought that they were prohibiting precisely the kind of action Hopkinson indulged in." Erdos (2009, 114n36) agrees that this "is likely." For Huscroft and Rishworth (2009, 129–30), Justice France had "interpreted the prohibition on destroying a New Zealand flag 'with the intention of dishonouring it' so narrowly as to render it all but unenforceable." But wasn't one of the purposes of the NZBORA to allow a clearly inconsistent law to remain enforceable? Rewriting such a law to make it "all but unenforceable" was surely to subvert the balance between political and legal constitutionalism established by the act, tilting (or "escalating") the document in the direction of legal constitutionalism.

The above-mentioned UK case of *R. v. A.* (2002) poses the issues even more starkly. *R. v. A.* concerned a "rape-shield" provision under the Youth Justice and Criminal Evidence Act (1999). The law was designed to significantly protect complainants in sexual assault cases against being cross-examined about their sexual history, thus preventing the accused from raising unnecessary evidence concerning the victim's past sexual behaviour. Despite Parliament's hard work to protect the privacy concerns of victims, however, the judges in *R. v. A.* reinterpreted "seemingly categorical terms" in favour of the accused and the right to a fair trial (Roach 2005, 751). The Court held that the rape-shield provision needed to be understood alongside an "implied provision" permitting cross-examination of previous intimate encounters so as to ensure the right to a fair trial (para. 45). Lord Steyn admitted that this interpretation "may appear strained" (para. 44), but obviously considered it justified by his "strong" reading of the HRA's interpretive mandate.

Not everyone was persuaded that Steyn's ruling in *R. v. A.* merely "*appear[ed]* strained." For Janet Hiebert and James Kelly, "the Law Lords altered parliament's clear intention about how the rules of evidence are interpreted in the context of sexual assault trials" (2015, 267–8). Danny Nicol argues that the Court "strayed far from both the wording of the provision and Parliament's clear intention in introducing it" (2004, 276). Others characterize the challenged provision in question of being "effective[ly] rewritten" by the Court (Allan 2011, 108; Jackson 2007, 105). For many, this "high point of interpretative power" by the UK courts (Gardbaum 2010, 195) went altogether too far.

Two years after *R. v. A.* – in *Ghaidan v. Godin- Mendoza* (2004) – Lord Steyn elaborated on his "strong" approach to interpretation, making it clear that no statutory ambiguity is necessary to use section 3 to reach a possible legislative meaning (para. 44), and, indeed, that the interpretation need not even be a "reasonable one" (para. 44). As Lord Rodger said in support of Steyn, the Court can adopt any interpretation just short of "judicial vandalism" to the legislation (para. 111). Or as Lord Millett put it, the court can use section 3 to "do considerable violence to the language and stretch it almost (but not quite) to breaking point" (para. 67).

Note that such formulations still preserve a line between legitimate judicial interpretation and unwarranted judicial law-making. Courts may violently stretch statutory language *almost* to the breaking point, but not past that point. They may come close to, but must stop *just short* of, judicial vandalism. Interestingly, Lord Millett, who authored the "almost to the breaking point" formulation, did so in a case where he thought the Court's majority *had* gone past the breaking point. Writing that judges can "stretch" up to the "breaking point" by "read[ing] in and read[ing] down" or by "supply[ing] missing words," but only "so long as they [remain] consistent with the fundamental features of the legislative scheme" (para. 67), he argued (in dissent) that the traditional opposite-sex definition of "spouse" was a fundamental feature of the leg-islative scheme at issue, reading it to include same-sex couples stretched the law past the "breaking point." Lord Nicholls, by contrast, did not think reading "spouse" to include opposite-sex couples contradicted the "underlying thrust" of the legislation (para. 33). Clearly, even a view of the interpretive mandate "strong" enough to legitimize some degree of judicial "violence" or "vandalism" to statutory language leaves room for disagreement about when the line has been crossed.

Whatever disagreements might arise about when the "strong" form of the boundary between interpretation and law-making has been trans-gressed, this way of drawing the line clearly minimizes the number of statutes that will be found or declared inconsistent with the rights docu-ment. Statutory rules that would have been found inconsistent under the textual-ambiguity version of the line will be interpretively "fixed" under the just-short-of-judicial-vandalism version. The literature identifies stra-tegic reasons that might tempt judges to thus strengthen the interpre-tive mandate at the expense of finding or declaring incompatibility. One might think that judges would prefer to take the more dramatic or aggressive incompatibility route, but "extreme forms of judicial rewrit-ing" of statutes (McLean 2001, 435; see also Gardbaum 2013, 136) may actually be the more effective way of implementing their policy prefer-ences in the weak-form New Zealand and UK contexts. As we have seen, a finding or declaration of incompatibility can be ignored by legislatures, which means that the legislative burden of inertia favours the policy that judges consider incompatible with the rights document. By contrast, if judges interpretively "fix" legislation, legislatures who prefer the original version must act proactively to reinstate it; the legislative burden of iner-tia now favours the judicial interpretive innovation. By adopting some version of Lord Steyn's "strong" view of the interpretive mandate, judges ensure that the legislative burden of inertia favours impugned legisla-tion less often and judicial innovation more often.

R. v. A. itself illustrates the dynamics at work. Nicol (2004, 277) believes the UK Court chose to not issue a declaration of incompatibil-ity in *R. v. A.* precisely because the judges knew Parliament would dis-agree, leaving the rape-shield law on the books simply by doing nothing. Parliament also did nothing in response to the judicial "fixing" of the law (Hiebert and Kelly 2015, 267), but that now meant the victory of the judicial policy preference. The result of the "strong" version of "the enacted line between interpretation or construction and the judicial law-making" is arguably Tushnet's "escalation" of weak-form systems of judicial review into strong-form ones. "Through radical use of the inter-pretative power to rewrite legislation," in other words, "statutory bills of rights can ... come to resemble fully constitutional ones in practice, leading to de facto judicial supremacy" (Gardbaum 2013, 136). It should come as no surprise that legal constitutionalists will celebrate this development while political constitutionalists will deplore it.

Political constitutionalists in this debate argue that the "escalation" towards judicial supremacy undermines the most fundamental design of the weak-form rights documents – namely, placing the burden of legislative inertia on the side of legislation that judges consider inconsistent or incompatible with the rights document (Allan 2006; Huscroft 2002). The more judges "fix" legislation through creative (or "strained") interpretation, the less room there is for incompatible legislation that can benefit from the burden of legislative inertia. In effect, such judicial "fixing" reverses the intended burden of inertia.

Differences between New Zealand and the United Kingdom

For Lord Steyn, the political-constitutionalist concern about strained interpretation was less valid in the United Kingdom than it was in New Zealand. In his view, the interpretive mandate in section 6 of the NZBORA represented a "weaker model" than is found in section 3 of the HRA. Having the weaker New Zealand model before them, the drafters of the HRA "preferred stronger language," and "specifically rejected the legislative model of requiring a reasonable interpretation" (*R. v. A.* 2002, para. 44). Obviously, Lord Steyn considered the interpretations that "can be given" under the NZBORA to be more limited in scope than those that were "possible" under the HRA. While he thought the HRA allowed interpretations that "linguistically may appear strained," the "weaker" NZBORA might not.

New Zealand's Justice Elias disagreed with Lord Steyn on this point. As noted above, Elias thought judicial interpretations under NZBORA's section 6 required no more textual ambiguity than did interpretations under the HRA's section 3. In her view, "the direction to give an enactment a meaning that accords with the rights and freedoms contained in the New Zealand Bill of Rights Act where such an interpretation 'can' be given may as equally entail an interpretation which 'linguistically may appear strained,' as where such interpretation is 'possible'" (*Hansen* 2007, para. 13). Nor did she consider such interpretations to be "heretical" (para. 13.). Elias was thus "unable to accept that there is any material difference between the New Zealand and United Kingdom models" (para. 13). Both models established the "strong" interpretive mandate favoured by Lord Steyn.

Justice Elias knew, of course, that her view was controversial. Indeed, it was not accepted by her judicial colleagues in *Hansen* itself. Recall that Justice Blanchard's opinion in that case rejected strained interpretations, insisting that section 6 allowed only interpretations "genuinely open in light of both [the statute's] text and its purpose." He clearly saw section 6 as establishing a "weaker model" than Lord Steyn's version of the HRA's section 3.

In fact, there are other provisions of the NZBORA that can be called upon to support the "weaker model" perspective. As Rishworth notes, the framers of the NZBORA "pulled out all the stops to preclude every judicial technique that might elevate the Bill of Rights over other enactments" (2004, 258–9) – often stops that were not pulled out by the framers of the United Kingdom's HRA. One such stop is the Canadian-style "reasonable limits" clause (section 5 of the NZBORA), which allows subjects rights "to such reasonable limits prescribed by law as can be demonstrably justified in a free and democratic society." For Justice Blanchard in *Hansen*, if the natural interpretation of a statute appears to infringe a protected right but is justified as a "reasonable limit," it is "not inconsistent with the Bill of Rights in the sense envisaged by s.6" (para. 60), and there is no need for remedial interpretation, and certainly not for the kind of strained interpretation that Justice Elias considered legitimate.

Not surprisingly, Justice Elias disagreed. Rejecting Blanchard's view "that s.5 of the New Zealand Bill of Rights Act forms part of the s.6 inquiry," she did "not accept that s.6 gives preference to a meaning consistent with limitations justified under s.5, if a meaning consistent with the unlimited right is tenable" (para. 15). And for Elias, we should recall, "tenable" interpretations included "strained" ones. Without attempting to resolve this debate, it seems clear that the very existence of the "reasonable limits" clause enabled Blanchard's view that it should be part of coming to a "reasonable interpretation" of the statute in question, thereby supporting the "model requiring a reasonable interpretation" that Lord Steyn rejected for the United Kingdom. No doubt, the absence of a reasonable limits clause in the HRA made it easier for Lord Steyn than for Justice Elias to arrive at this conclusion.

Another of the stops "pulled out" by the NZBORA's framers "to preclude every judicial technique that might elevate the Bill of Rights over other enactments" is found in section 4 of the document. Section 4, as noted in chapter 2, is a kind of "anti-primacy clause," instructing courts what not to do (Rishworth 2004, 259). Section 4 says that "no court shall ... decline to apply any provision of [an] enactment by reason only that the provision is inconsistent with any provision of this Bill of Rights."

As in the case of the section 5 "reasonable limits" clause, no such anti-primacy provision is found in the United Kingdom's HRA.

Does the section 4 anti-primacy provision not mean that if "courts apply the interpretative duty in section 6 robustly, in a way that modifies or distorts statutory language and/or parliamentary intent," they are "violat[ing] section 4's prohibition on courts declining to apply the legislature's inconsistent statutes" (Gardbaum 2013, 136)? Giving an affirmative answer to this question, political constitutionalists in New Zealand would not think interpretations that distort statutory language and/or parliamentary intent "can" reasonably "be given" under section 6. They insist, as we have seen, on legislative "ambiguity or uncertainty" as a precondition for interpretive choices under section 6, and thus leave more room for inconsistent legislation to enjoy its intended legislative burden of inertia. For their part, legal constitutionalists – as we have also seen – believe "textual ambiguity is not required," thereby leaving less room for inconsistent legislation favoured by the burden of legislative inertia.

That political constitutionalists in the United Kingdom cannot rely on explicit "reasonable limits" or anti-primacy provisions has made it easier for legal constitutionalists to invoke founding intention on *their* side of the argument. Thus, Lord Steyn's judgment in *R. v. A.* drew on the parliamentary debates around adopting the HRA to conclude that the interpretive mandate in section 3 "was the prime remedial measure" in the HRA, and that the section providing for a declaration of incompatibility (section 4) was "a measure of last resort" (2002, para. 46). Steyn was accordingly persuaded by the *Hansard* comments of the Lord Chancellor when the HRA was being debated: "in 99% of the cases that will arise, there will be no need for judicial declarations of incompatibility." Steyn further emphasized the home secretary's expectation "that, in almost all cases, the courts will be able to interpret the legislation compatibly with the Convention'" (quoted in *Ghaidan* 2004, para. 46). The legislative burden of inertia would rarely weigh on the side of legislation "declared" incompatible, because robust judicial creativity was intended to prevent that result. The burden of legislative inertia would almost always favour judicial interpretations under section 3 instead, even if those interpretations "appear strained." In New Zealand, by contrast, the anti-primacy section's insistence that courts must continue to apply inconsistent statutes seems to envision considerably greater scope for such inconsistent laws than Lord Steyn is willing to grant in the United Kingdom. And that, in turn, suggests a stronger animus in New Zealand against fixing laws through strained interpretation.

Considering these institutional differences, it is perhaps not surprising that "strained interpretations" are, in fact, less common in New Zealand than in the United Kingdom. They certainly occur in New Zealand, as *Hopkinson* shows, but there is a scholarly consensus that UK courts have been more prone to adopt strained interpretations than their New Zealand counterparts (Allan 2014, 68–70; Gardbaum 2013, 136; Geddis and Fenton 2008). The New Zealand judiciary's approach to statutory interpretation is "textualist," say Andrew Geddis and Bridget Fenton, and thus hews "closely to the wording Parliament has included in its enactment, even when this results in an outcome it considers inconsistent with individual rights" (2008, 736). New Zealand's textualists, in other words, shy away from "fixing" statutes through strained interpretation. In contrast, the UK judiciary's more "teleological" mode of reasoning (Geddis and Fenton 2008, 736) makes it "adventurous" or "aggressive" in using the "HRA to substantially rework the statutory language selected by Parliament in order to generate an outcome it regards as compatible with rights." The difference between textualism and teleological reasoning, in this view, helps explain why we do not see the same level of "judicial vandalism" or stretching of statutory language to the "breaking point" in New Zealand as in the United Kingdom.

The continuing strength of New Zealand's textualism, according to Hiebert and Kelly, is evident in that country's Interpretation Act, enacted in 1999, almost a decade after the NZBORA. According to section 5 of the Interpretation Act, the "meaning of an enactment must be ascertained from its text and in light of its purpose." This law, say Hiebert and Kelly, "clearly signals to the judiciary, when interpreting the NZBORA, that the courts must defer to parliament's stated purpose and not the effect of legislative enactments on rights and freedoms" (2015, 68).

The issue of "reverse onus" for drug trafficking nicely illustrates the difference between the jurisprudential approaches of New Zealand and UK judges. (Indeed, this issue also highlights the difference between these two weak-form regimes and stronger-form Canada.) Like Canada, both countries criminalize the simple possession of certain drugs as well as possession for the purposes of trafficking. The latter is more serious, and thus subject to significantly higher penalties, than is simple possession. In criminal law, the state bears the onus or burden of proving guilt "beyond a reasonable doubt," and in all three laws under consideration, this standard applied to establishing illegal "possession." Someone found guilty of possessing illegal drugs above a specified quantity, however, was deemed by these laws also to be guilty of trafficking, unless they could prove otherwise. This "reverses" the traditional onus of proof with respect to the trafficking charge.

In all three countries, the courts found this "reverse onus" to infringe the "presumption of innocence" guaranteed by the relevant rights document.

In *Oakes* – the Canadian case that established the famous *Oakes* test for implementing the section 1 "reasonable limits" clause of the Charter – Canada's Supreme Court struck down the reverse onus as unreasonably infringing the presumption of innocence. Canadian-style invalidation not being an option for the New Zealand and UK courts, judges in those countries considered whether they could interpretively soften implementation of the reverse onus. The issue concerned the standard of proof that the accused had to meet to be found not guilty on the trafficking charge. There was no question of the accused having to prove innocence "beyond a reasonable doubt"; none of the laws in question reversed onus to that extent. The issue, rather, was whether the accused had to disprove trafficking "on the balance of probabilities" (often called the "legal" or "persuasive" onus of proof) or whether it was enough to point to evidence raising a doubt about the purpose of the possessed drugs (often referred to as an "evidential" onus of proof). The evidential onus is less stringent, or softer, because if raising a doubt about the purpose of possession is enough to escape a conviction for trafficking, then the legal onus ultimately remains "on the Crown [to establish] beyond a reasonable doubt that [the accused] had such purpose" (*R. v. Hansen* 2007, para. 3). This is more consistent with the traditional presumption of innocence than the accused having to prove innocence "on a balance of probabilities."

Could judges use their interpretive mandate to implement this less stringent or softer interpretation of the reverse onus? The New Zealand and UK courts gave opposite answers to this question. In *R. v. Phillips* (1991), the New Zealand Court of Appeal concluded that the reverse onus clearly required the balance-of-probabilities approach and that the more relaxed evidentiary approach was "a *strained* and *unnatural* interpretation" of the law "which ... the Court would not be justified in adopting" (176, emphasis added). A little over a decade later, in *R. v. Lambert* (2002, para. 157), the UK House of Lords came to the opposite conclusion, finding that it "requires no straining of the language of [the reverse onus provision] to construe the references to proof as intending" the more relaxed evidentiary standard.

The issue was revisited in New Zealand in *Hansen* (2007), the case discussed above with respect to whether or not textual ambiguity was required to exercise the section 6 interpretive mandate. The New Zealand Supreme Court was asked in *Hansen* to reconsider the Court of Appeal's *Phillips* ruling in light of the UK's *Lambert* judgment. Although the judges in *Hansen* were divided, as we have seen, in their general approach to textual ambiguity – with Justice Elias arguing that "strained interpretation" is not always "heretical" – all of the judges agreed to uphold *Phillips* on the reverse-onus question rather than adopting the *Lambert* approach. For Chief Justice Elias, the New Zealand reverse onus imposes the balance-of-probabilities onus on the accused. She sees "no other tenable meaning" that can be reached, not even by using section 6 of the interpretative mandate (*Hansen* 2007, para. 5). Justice Tipping comes to a similar conclusion about not being able to use section 6 of the NZBORA to change law in the manner the complaint desires: "The language I have used earlier in these reasons, which inquires whether a suggested meaning is reasonably possible, seems to me to come as close as possible to capturing the way in which the statutory 'can' in s 6 must be applied" (para. 158).

Justice Tipping was revealingly critical of how his British counterparts used their interpretive mandate to handle the same issue in *Lambert*. Tipping thought the House of Lords judges arrived at an "unreasonably possible" view of the law that clearly "defeats Parliament's purpose" (*Hansen* 2007, para. 158). Tipping pulled no punches in describing how UK judges treated their interpretative mandate "as a concealed legislative tool" and ultimately "a judicial override of Parliament." Whether this is "appropriate in England is not for me to say," Tipping dryly concluded, "but I am satisfied it is not appropriate in New Zealand" (para. 158).

Tipping's critique is a striking feature of the *Hansen* decision. Of course, judges disagree among themselves frequently. But the *Lambert/Hansen* sequence is interesting because it features judges from different countries using similar weak-form rights documents to reach different conclusions about the same legal issue. The formal features of rights documents matter, but so does the constitutional culture of each regime.

In fact, broad differences in constitutional culture are what many scholars use to explain legal and jurisprudential differences between New Zealand and the United Kingdom. Geddis and Fenton, for example, note that "New Zealand's constitutional culture remains more deeply wedded to the orthodox idea of absolute parliamentary sovereignty than does the United Kingdom; with the latter being more receptive to the idea that 'rule of law' values ought to limit ... Parliament's power to legislate" (2008, 770). Hiebert and Kelly agree. Following Geiringer, they describe New Zealand as having a "judicial culture that avoids confrontations with parliament and a populace that embraces the principles of parliamentary supremacy without reservation," thus preventing "a robust dialogue of the kind that is emerging in the United Kingdom between the judicial and political branches of government" (Hiebert and Kelly 2015, 68–9). In their view, the 1999 Interpretation Act reinforces "the principle of parliamentary supremacy [and] severely curtails judicial participation in rights protections when courts review statutes passed by parliament."

Geddis and Fenton sum all this up in terms of the central conceptual framework of this study. "There is reason," they write, "to think that the tenets of legal constitutionalism have gained greater sway within the constitutional culture of the United Kingdom than in New Zealand" (2008, 775). This divergence surely helps to explain differences in both institutional design (e.g., reasonable limits and anti-primacy provisions in New Zealand but not in the United Kingdom) and subsequent application (e.g., more strained interpretations in the United Kingdom than in New Zealand).

Conclusion

Statutory interpretation in the bill of rights era provides yet another battleground in the clash between legal and political constitutionalism. In New Zealand and the United Kingdom, both rights documents explicitly instruct judges to interpret statutes in a rights-compliant manner whenever possible, but disagreement arises over what counts as legitimately "possible." Political constitutionalists insist that only interpretations made reasonably plausible by textual ambiguity are possible. Legal constitutionalists reply that even interpretations running counter to the natural and intended meaning of a statute's text are possible so long as the legal text does not clearly and explicitly exclude them; in other words, that "textual ambiguity is not required."

To achieve rights compliance, say the more dramatic legal constitutionalists, judges may "do considerable violence" to statutory language, coming close to "judicial vandalism" by "stretch[ing]" legal text "almost ... to the breaking point" (*Ghaidan v. Godin-Mendoza* 2004, paras. 67, 100). From this perspective, "strained interpretation" is acceptable – or not "heretical" (as New Zealand's Justice Elias put it in *Hansen* 2007, para. 13). Yet it *is* heretical to political constitutionalists, who see this expansive view of the interpretive mandate as establishing precisely the "judicial override of Parliament" that weak-form bills of rights were designed to avoid. Having been explicitly denied a strong-form invalidation mandate, judges should not smuggle something very like it in through the back door, thereby undermining the intention to leave clearly unconstitutional legislation in place unless and until the legislature chooses to change it. If virtually all legislation can be interpretively "fixed," say political constitutionalists, then finding or declaring incompatibility will become a negligible phenomenon. The result would be the illegitimate "escalation" of weak-form systems towards de facto judicial supremacy that observers like Tushnet and Gardbaum identified.

Declarations of incompatibility will indeed be negligible, reply such legal constitutionalists as Lord Steyn – and in the United Kingdom, at least, they *should* be negligible because the framers of the HRA intended declarations of incompatibility to be "a measure of last resort," and saw the interpretive mandate as "the prime remedial measure" in the HRA. Such arguments are more difficult to make in New Zealand, where the framers of the NZBORA "pulled out all the stops to preclude every judicial technique that might elevate the Bill of Rights over other enactments" (Rishworth 2004, 258–9). These "stops" include important provisions not found in the HRA, such as the NZBORA's reasonable limits clause and its explicit statement in section 4 (the so-called anti-primacy clause) that courts must continue to apply laws that are clearly inconsistent with the bill of rights. Despite these provisions, however, we have seen that strained interpretation is not heretical to all New Zealand judges and that cases such as *Hopkinson* have attracted charges of strained interpretation.

Although controversies about strained interpretation occur in both countries, the literature holds that UK judges are more inclined to an aggressive and adventurous approach to statutory interpretation than are their counterparts in New Zealand. No doubt, the formal institutional differences between the NZBORA and the HRA help explain this variation in the use of strained interpretation. But differences in constitutional culture also play a role. New Zealand, the literature agrees, is more oriented to the tradition of parliamentary supremacy and to a textualist jurisprudence that defers to Parliament. Ironically, the New Zealand constitutional culture is more traditionally British than the United Kingdom's is now. Put differently, in New Zealand political constitutionalism retains more traction in the clash of constitutionalisms than it does in the mother country. Let us now consider how the issue of statutory interpretation has played out under Canada's Charter of Rights and Freedoms.

Strained Statutory Interpretation in Canada

The Canadian Charter of Rights and Freedoms does not contain the explicitly "enacted line" between legitimate and strained interpretation found in section 6 of the NZBORA and section 3 of the HRA. Indeed, the Charter does not even mention the kind of interpretive mandate found in those sections; instead, section 52 of the Constitution Act, 1982, makes an invalidation mandate available to Canadian judges by declaring that "any law that is inconsistent with the provisions of the Constitution is, to the extent of the inconsistency, of no force or effect." Nevertheless, the Supreme Court of Canada has developed an implied interpretive mandate based on a "modern approach" to statutory interpretation that presumes legislation intends to be consistent with constitutional norms, including those guaranteed under the Charter (Sullivan 2007, 119). "If a legislative provision can be read both in a way that is constitutional and in a way that is not," the Court held in *R. v. Sharpe*, "the former reading should be adopted" (2001, para. 33).

Whether a provision *can* be read as constitutional turns out to be as difficult and controversial a question in Canada as in New Zealand and the United Kingdom, but for somewhat different reasons. This chapter explores the Canadian version of the controversy about "strained interpretation." It shows how the Supreme Court of Canada has used "Charter values" as an interpretative aid to resolve ambiguous statutory provisions. As with its common-law usage, the Court professes to limit its Charter values–based decisions to small and incremental changes. However, because Charter values–based legislative interpretation does not engage in section 1 reasonable limits analysis, this finding has important implications for inter-institutional dialogue. This development is particularly problematic for legal constitutionalists in Canada who would prefer not to see the invalidation mandate circumscribed.

Activism and Restraint: Distinguishing Canada from New Zealand and the United Kingdom

The interpretive choice between a constitutional and an unconstitutional reading of a statute can be cast as a choice between judicial deference and judicial activism. By activism, I mean the judiciary's readiness to veto or replace the policies of the elected branches of government, whereas restrained decisions express deference to other branches of government (Russell, Knopff, and Morton 1989, 18). In Canada, it certainly seems more activist to invalidate a statute than to give it a rights-compliant reading and uphold it. But what if that reading runs counter to the statute's unambiguous text and purpose? Is such "strained interpretation" any less activist than invalidating the statute? Might it be more problematically activist than invalidation?

We have seen that in New Zealand and the United Kingdom strained interpretation *is* often more activist than declaring incompatibility. Finding clear incompatibility with the rights document in those countries places the burden of legislative inertia on the side of impugned statute; the legislature can maintain what the judges consider unconstitutional simply by doing nothing. If judges engage in strained interpretation to "fix" the statute, the burden of legislative inertia favours that "fixing," which can be undone by the legislature only through a new statute. If the legislature does nothing, the judicially "fixed" law remains in place. In the weak-form context of New Zealand and the United Kingdom, strained interpretation is thus often the more activist option. This explains why legal constitutionalists, such as Lord Steyn, want to see the interpretive mandate as "the prime remedial measure" of their weak-form documents, and the declaration of incompatibility as a rare "measure of last resort."

The situation is quite different in Canada, where findings of clear statutory inconsistency with the Charter lead to the strong-form remedy of invalidation, thus placing the burden of legislative inertia on the side of the successful rights claimant. Legal constitutionalists in this context will be less attracted by the interpretive mandate than was Lord Steyn in the United Kingdom. One cannot imagine a legal constitutionalist in Canada adopting Steyn's argument that judges can (and should) avoid ruling statutes incompatible with the Charter "in 99% of cases that arise" because rights-compliant interpretations are possible "in almost all cases." Applied to Canada, this view would eviscerate the Charter's invalidation mandate.

It is certainly not in the interest of Canadian judges to eviscerate their invalidation mandate (nor, one suspects, would Lord Steyn have wanted to eviscerate the UK declaration of incompatibility, had it entailed the invalidation consequence). It should come as no surprise, therefore, that Canadian judges do not think their implied interpretive mandate should be "strong" enough to apply "even if there is no ambiguity in the language in the sense of the language being capable of two different meanings," as the United Kingdom's interpretive mandate does according to Lord Steyn. Judges in other weak-form regimes, such as New Zealand's Justice Elias, may be tempted to claim that "textual ambiguity is not required" to exercise their interpretive mandate, but Canadian judges have no such temptation. Their approach, as we shall see in detail below, is more like the dominant New Zealand view that judges can choose "only" interpretations that are "genuinely open in light of both [the statute's] text and its purpose" (*R. v. Hansen* 2007, para. 61). If a statute is clearly incompatible with the Charter, the appropriate form of judicial activism in Canada is invalidation, not strained interpretation.

The Statutory Usage of Charter Values

Summarizing the Court's approach to Charter-based statutory interpretation, Gaile McGregor writes that, unless "there is clear language to the contrary, [statutory] interpretations should be consistent with *Charter values*, and should include the assumption that Parliament did not intend an absurd or unfair result" (2002, 236, emphasis added). In using the language of Charter values, McGregor is following the Court itself. When the Court chooses to interpret the law in a Charter-compliant manner (thus avoiding the more "activist" route of invalidation), it often says it is interpreting legislation in accordance with "Charter values." Given the recurring importance of this terminology in this study, we need to consider its significance for the issue of statutory interpretation.

This is the third usage of "Charter values" that we have encountered. In chapter 3, we examined the "underlying values usage" of the terminology – namely, employing underlying values that do not appear directly in the Canadian Charter of Rights and Freedoms (e.g., "dignity," "autonomy," or "privacy") to develop new judicially enforceable constitutional rules. In chapters 4 and 5 we observed how Canada's Supreme Court, reluctant to apply Charter rights directly to judge-made common law, prefers to "develop ... the common law in a manner consistent with the [Charter's] fundamental values" (*Dolphin Delivery* 1986, para. 39); this is the "common-law usage" of Charter values. In this chapter, we come to the "statutory interpretation" usage of Charter values – i.e., bringing a statute into compliance with Charter *values* rather than invalidating it for unreasonably infringing Charter *rights and freedoms.*[1]

In chapter 5, we saw the Court insisting that the Charter values approach should be employed with respect to common-law development only "where it will not upset the appropriate balance between judicial and legislative action" (*Bell ExpressVu* 2002, para. 61; see also *R. v. Salituro* 1991, 675; *Hill v. Church of Scientology* 1995, para. 85). The Court is similarly worried that the statutory-interpretation usage of Charter values can "upset the appropriate [institutional] balance," particularly through its potential effect on the legislature's ability to mount a reasonable limits defence of a law under section 1 of the *Charter.* As Kent Roach puts it, the Charter values approach threatens to "eclipse ... the ability of governments to justify reasonable limits on *Charter* rights" (2005, 746). In doing so, he claims it undermines valuable aspects of dialogue between Canadian courts and legislatures. As with respect to Charter-based common-law innovation, the concern with institutional balance involves issues of inter-institutional "dialogue," especially section 1 "reasonable limits" dialogue.

The Supreme Court is acutely aware of the difficulties raised by using Charter values as a tool of statutory interpretation. In *Bell ExpressVu Ltd. v. Rex* (2002, para. 61), the Court's leading decision on this question, Justice Iacobucci cited *Dolphin Delivery* (1986) and *Salituro* (1991) on the need to preserve the "appropriate balance" between legislative and judicial functions. Reiterating Justice Lamer's distinction between the common law and legislation, Justice Iacobucci underlines the appropriateness of judicially developing the common law in accordance with Charter values. The common law, he insists, "is the province of the judiciary [with] the courts ... responsible for its application, and for ensuring that it continues to reflect the basic values of society" (*Bell ExpressVu* 2002, para. 61). The same is not true of legislation and "the courts do not ... occupy the same role vis-à-vis statute law" (para. 61). Statutes "embody the legislative will" and they "supplement, modify, or supersede

---

1 A fourth usage of Charter values involves their consideration in the area of administrative law. In 2018, the Supreme Court was heavily divided on the desirability of Charter values to inform provincial law societies' decision not to accredit Trinity Western University's proposed law school (*Law Society of British Columbia v. Trinity Western University* 2018). Many of the justices' arguments for and against the use of Charter values in the administrative context raise interesting implications for matters related to both constitutional strength and constitutional reach. However, since there is not an analogous jurisprudential development in New Zealand and the United Kingdom, I do not elaborate on those implications here.

the common law" (para. 62). Acknowledging that it may sometimes be "appropriate for courts to prefer [statutory] interpretations that tend to promote ... [Charter] principles and values over interpretations that do not," Iacobucci advises caution in using this interpretive strategy (para. 62). He is particularly concerned that "Charter values" not be used to *change* statutes in the way that they can be legitimately used to change the common law (the province of the judiciary). Not even the small or "incremental" changes to which judges ought to limit themselves in the common-law realm are appropriate with respect to legislation. In the statutory context, Charter values should be used not to change a law that clearly infringes those values (as the *Daviault* Court thought the *Leary* rule did, for example), but only to choose between interpretations of a law sufficiently ambiguous for both the Charter-compliant and the Charter-infringing readings to be equally plausible. The " '*Charter* values' interpretive principle," says Iacobucci, "can *only* receive application in circumstances of genuine ambiguity, i.e., where a statutory provision is subject to differing, but equally plausible, interpretations" (para. 62, emphasis in original). Iacobucci notes this has been the Court's policy at least since *Hills v. Canada* (1988) (*Bell ExpressVu* 2002, para. 63). In the absence of the required legislative ambiguity, he insists, the legislature's clear intent must be given effect (para. 62), even if it conflicts with the Charter. A similar conclusion in New Zealand and the United Kingdom would lead to a finding or declaration of incompatibility, which the legislature could ignore. In Canada, it likely leads to invalidating the statute.

For Canada's Supreme Court, the criterion of "genuine ambiguity" plays the same role with respect to a "Charter values" interpretation of legislation as the incremental-change criterion plays with respect to a common-law innovation based on Charter values. Both criteria purport to prevent Charter values from "upset[ting] the appropriate balance between judicial and legislative action."

To allow Charter values to change unambiguous legislation, says Justice Iacobucci, entails a "presumption of Charter consistency" strong enough not only "to frustrate true legislative intent" (*Bell ExpressVu* 2002, para. 64) but to make it impossible for the government ever "to justify infringements as reasonable limits under s.1 of the Charter, since the interpretative process would preclude one from finding infringements in the first place" (para. 64, quoting *Symes v. Canada* 1993). In other words, "if statutory meanings must be made congruent with the Charter even in the absence of ambiguity," the courts could only "consult the values of the Charter," they could never "apply" Charter rights directly, subject to section 1 justification (para. 64., quoting *Symes v. Canada* 1993). To repeat Kent Roach's formulation, an overly strong "presumption that statutes will respect the constitution [can] eclipse the whole machinery of Charter adjudication and, in particular, the ability of governments to justify reasonable limits on Charter rights" (2005, 746). Even more dramatically than in the common-law context, the Charter values approach to statutory interpretation threatens the section 1 component of inter-institutional dialogue.

Indeed, Justice Iacobucci's *Bell ExpressVu* opinion makes explicit use of dialogue theory to justify caution in the Charter values approach to statutory interpretation. A strong Charter values–based presumption of constitutionality would, in his view, diminish the process of the "dialogue and mutual respect" between the courts and legislatures and undermine the "certain measure of vitality" that full application of the Charter "brings to the democratic process, in that it fosters both dynamic interaction and accountability amongst the various branches" (2002, para. 65). Interpreting all legislation in a manner that made it congruent with the Charter "would wrongly upset the dialogic balance" and would "pre-empt judicial review on Charter grounds, where resort to the internal checks and balances of s.1 may be had" (para. 66). "In this fashion," Iacobucci continues, "the legislatures would be largely shorn of their constitutional power to enact reasonable limits on *Charter* rights and freedoms, which would in turn be inflated to near absolute status" (para. 66). Iacobucci speculates on how legislatures might "avoid this result," but finds their only option to be unworkable:

> Quite literally, in order to avoid this result a legislature would somehow have to set out its justification for qualifying the *Charter* right expressly in the statutory text, all without the benefit of judicial discussion regarding the limitations that are permissible in a free and democratic society. Before long, courts would be asked to interpret *this* sort of enactment in light of *Charter* principles. The patent unworkability of such a scheme highlights the importance of retaining a forum for dialogue among the branches of governance. (para. 66)

He concludes that, "where a statute is unambiguous, courts must give effect to the clearly expressed legislative intent and avoid using the *Charter* to achieve a different result" (para. 66).

Eclipsing the Whole Machinery of Charter Adjudication?

Despite Justice Iacobucci's worry in *Bell ExpressVu* that a strong Charter values–based presumption of constitutionality might entirely "eclipse" section 1 analysis, it should be noted that this need not always be the case. Such a presumption can sometimes work alongside a section 1 analysis in the sense of interpretively bringing legislation to the point where it can be justified as a "reasonable limit." The famous censorship case of *R. v. Butler* (1992) is a good example. Butler challenged the Criminal Code's censorship of obscenity as violating the Charter. There was little doubt that the law infringed the section 2(b) guarantee of freedom of expression,[2] and that the law would stand or fall on the section 1 "reasonable limits" question. *Butler*, in other words, was clearly not a case that, to repeat Justice Iacobucci's formulation, "pre-empt[ed] judicial review on Charter grounds, where resort to the internal checks and balances of s.1 may be had" (*Bell ExpressVu* 2002, para. 66). Before reaching the section 1 question in *Butler*, however, the Court, as noted in chapter 2, interpretively brought the law into line with modern Charter values, finding that rather than criminalizing "erotica" on moralistic grounds (its original purpose), it had now come to prohibit only pornographic harm to women and children (1992, 493). Only on this modern harm-based reading, based on Charter values, could the law be justified as a reasonable limit.

   Butler was decided ten years before *Bell ExpressVu*, and there is some risk in retroactively reading the former case in light of the latter. Nevertheless, using *Bell ExpressVu* categories, the censorship law challenged in *Butler* presumably exhibited the kind of "genuine ambiguity" that allowed for both the traditional and the new Charter values–based interpretations. Indeed, Justice Sopinka's majority opinion in *Butler* was at pains to emphasize that he was not radically changing the law to make it Charter-compatible. As opposed to "shifting" the law's purpose,[3] his opinion constituted no more than a "shift in emphasis" in how best to understand the law's perennial concern with preventing "harm" (para. 86).

   Sopinka's attempt to deny that he was significantly changing the law in *Butler* is debatable – some observers thought the judgment, which upheld the censorship law, had nevertheless engaged in a "world historical"

2 Section 2(b) of the Charter protects "freedom of thought, belief, opinion and expression, including freedom of the press and other media of communication."

3 In one of the Supreme Court's earliest Charter decisions, *R. v. Big M Drug Mart* (1985), it rejected the "shifting purposes" doctrine. That case concerned the constitutionality of the Lord's Day Act that outlawed Sunday shopping. In an attempt to preserve its legislation against the charge that it violated freedom of religion, the government argued that the religious intentions of the legislation's drafters were irrelevant since the law had evolved into a secular day of rest rather than endorsing any one religious observance. The Court rejected this argument by claiming that "such a finding cannot justify the conclusion that its purpose has similarly changed" (para. 93).

transformation of that law[4] – but for the moment the point is that his decision essentially agrees with Justice's Iacobucci's later concern in *Bell ExpressVu* that "Charter values" be used only to choose between plausible interpretations of a statute, not to fundamentally change that statute (and, indeed, Justice Iacobucci had earlier joined Sopinka's *Butler* opinion). As long as a plausible interpretation occurs, bringing a law into line with Charter values can save it. Sometimes, as in *Butler*, this interpretive stage occurs in the context of a normal Charter challenge, in which case "the whole machinery of Charter adjudication" remains in place, including "the ability of governments to justify reasonable limits on Charter rights" (Roach 2005, 746). In such cases, the effect of the prior interpretation is to ensure that the law will be upheld as a reasonable limit. At other times, as in *Bell ExpressVu*, the normal "machinery of Charter adjudication," including the section 1 stage, is eclipsed.

Why was "the whole machinery of Charter adjudication" not available in *Bell ExpressVu*? Because the case was not launched as a Charter challenge at the outset. At trial and through all appeals before reaching the Supreme Court, the case was argued simply as a matter of statutory interpretation. It was only at oral argument in the Supreme Court that one of the parties challenged the constitutionality of the legislation (2002, para. 60). The Court declined to address the Charter issues because its procedural rules prohibit addressing issues for which there is an insufficient "Charter record" – that is, where the relevant evidence and argument have not been tested in lower courts (para. 59). Conceding this, the party making the Charter claim argued that "Charter values" should inform the interpretation of the legislation (para. 60). As an alternative to striking the legislation down for violating the Charter, in other words, the Court was asked to choose an interpretation that respected "Charter values." It was being asked to do this, of course, in a context where none of the normal components of Charter analysis, especially section 1 analysis, would be present. It is this context that prompted the concerns of Justice Iacobucci and Kent Roach about what Roach calls "eclips[ing] the whole machinery of Charter adjudication and, in particular, the ability of governments to justify reasonable limits on Charter rights" (2005, 746).

As Roach makes clear, however, essentially the same concerns arise in cases like *Butler*, where the full "machinery of Charter adjudication" is

---

4 Bateman et al. (2008, 93) note that while the new definition of obscenity was lauded by many prominent feminist activists, it casts some doubt on whether this "world historic innovation [had] been in the minds of the legislators who enacted" the original definition of obscenity in 1959.

very much present (i.e., in no sense "eclipsed"), but where the stage of Charter values interpretation, embodying a "presumption of constitutionality," still undermines the appropriate dialogic interaction between courts and legislatures. As noted in chapter 2, Roach describes the kind of interpretive strategy employed in *Butler* as the judiciary's attempt "under the Charter to fix laws through creative and strained interpretations" (Roach 2005, 735; see also 748–50). In his view, this "spurious technique of statutory interpretation," which often involves the "fiction that the court is not departing from the words and intent of the legislature when it applies a presumption that the legislature intends to respect rights," fails "the test of judicial candour" (735, 752). In other words, Roach is highly skeptical of the claim that the Court is simply choosing between two equally plausible interpretations of a sufficiently ambiguous statute. Perhaps that sometimes happens, but it is more often a disguising "fiction," as Roach certainly thought it was in *Butler*. While Roach did not resort to the language of "world historic" change used by some to describe *Butler*, he clearly thought the Court had changed the law rather than choosing among equally plausible interpretations (2005, 749–50).

For reasons much like those expressed by Justice Iacobucci in *Bell ExpressVu*, Roach deplores the damage done to inter-institutional dialogue when courts fundamentally change a statute in the guise of merely interpreting it. The kind of "Charter values" interpretive remedy under consideration, says Roach, often fails "to provoke the full democratic debate and dialogue about the treatment of rights that can follow a more forthright judicial invalidation of laws that violate rights" (2005, 735). The interpretive remedy used by the Court in *Butler* (and similar cases) "avoided the controversy that would have accompanied striking down the impugned law but also avoided the democratic debate that would have occurred had such a result effectively required Parliament to revisit the matters in question" (750).

"It is true," says Roach, "that Parliament could still enact legislation" in response to *Butler* (2005, 750). We saw in chapter 5 that he would insist on a section 33 notwithstanding clause in legislation that disagrees with Charter-based common-law innovations. In the discussion of legislative interpretation under consideration here, Roach does not make the same claim. Instead, he emphasizes the sense in which "the idea that the Court has 'fixed' controversial legislation and made it Charter-proof may very well ensure that the issue is not placed on an already crowded legislative agenda" (750). The section 33 notwithstanding clause, of course, is the way of getting around judicial "Charter-proofing," so perhaps Roach is referring to the natural reluctance to place a notwithstanding clause on the crowded legislative agenda. However that may be, he emphasizes how the greater "candour" of invalidation might force issues onto the democratic agenda:

> In contrast [to interpretively "curing" legislation], the invalidation of legislation under the Charter may frequently operate so as to put questions of principle on the legislative agenda, literally forcing our representatives to vote on how they wish to treat rights. Interpretive remedies that fix unconstitutional legislation can let the legislature off easy. (750)

Clearly, the use of Charter values in legislative interpretation poses problems for the "appropriate balance" between courts and legislatures – whether or not the full "machinery of Charter adjudication" is present – if it is used to fundamentally transform laws, as opposed to choosing between equally plausible interpretations of the law. Both the Court (through judgments such as *Bell ExpressVu*) and legal commentators such as Roach agree on this. Just as clearly, the line between changing or "fixing" law and interpreting it is not a self-applying bright line. It can be a matter of considerable controversy whether a Charter values-based reading of a statute falls on one side of the line or another. Presumably Justice Iacobucci, who so clearly set out the criterion in *Bell ExpressVu*, did not think he had violated it by participating in the main *Butler* opinion. Roach, by contrast, saw the *Butler* opinion as changing the law under the "fiction" of interpretation. The remainder of this chapter situates this controversy within a more detailed analysis of three Supreme Court decisions: *Bell ExpressVu* (2002), *Hills v. Canada* (1988), and *Harvard College v. Canada* (2002). All three lacked a "Charter record" in the lower courts, and thus raised the issue of "Charter values" interpretation in the absence of the full "machinery of Charter adjudication."

Bell ExpressVu (2002)

Bell, a telecommunications company, was licensed to sell television signals to Canadians. The signals were encrypted and subscribers paid to have them decoded. As the appellant in this case, Bell objected to an American competitor, licensed in the United States but not in Canada, selling signals to Canadian viewers. At issue was section 9(1)(c) of the Radiocommunications Act, which specified that "No person shall ... decode an encrypted subscription programming signal or encrypted network feed otherwise than under and in accordance with an authorization from the lawful distributor of the signal or feed." Bell argued that this provision prohibited all decoding of signals not authorized by a lawful Canadian distributor (such as Bell), which meant that it was illegal for Canadians to buy signals from American distributors not licensed in Canada.

The respondents identified an alternative and more restrictive interpretation of section 9(1)(c). In their view, the provision should be read as prohibiting only the *theft* by viewers of a signal from a Canadian distributor, not the *purchase* of signals from non-Canadian competitors. The lower courts had applied both interpretations of the act, thus requiring the Supreme Court to harmonize the interpretations (paras. 22–4). At the Supreme Court, the respondents also raised the question whether section 9(1)(c) of the Radiocommunications Act infringed their Charter section 2(b) guarantee of freedom of expression. While the Court refused to address this question directly (because of the lack of a "Charter record"), it was invited to use the Charter value of free expression to give the legislation the interpretation preferred by the respondents. For Justice Iacobucci, as we have seen, this would be an option "*only* ... in circumstances of genuine ambiguity, i.e., where a statutory provision is subject to differing, but equally plausible, interpretations" (para. 62, emphasis in original). The presence or absence of such "genuine ambiguity" was thus the issue on which the fate of a "Charter values" interpretation would turn.

Justice Iacobucci, speaking for a unanimous panel of seven judges, denied that "genuine ambiguity" was established by the "mere fact that several courts – or, for that matter, several doctrinal writers – have come to differing conclusions on the interpretation of a given provision" (as the lower courts had on this provision):

Just as it would be improper for one to engage in a preliminary tallying of the number of decisions supporting competing interpretations and then apply that which receives the "higher score," it is not appropriate to take as one's starting point the premise that differing interpretations reveal an ambiguity. (para. 30)

Instead, a careful "contextual and purposive" interpretive exercise must be undertaken by the Court to determine if "the words are ambiguous enough to induce two people to spend good money in backing two opposing views as to their meaning." Iacobucci did not think that "money ... backing [the] two opposing views as to [the] meaning" of section 9.1(c) of the Radiocommunications Act was well spent. He considered the provision to unambiguously support the interpretation preferred by Bell, even though that interpretation was more restrictive of freedom of expression, and was prepared to give effect to the clearly expressed "legislative intent and avoid using the *Charter* to achieve a

different result" (para. 66). Iacobucci emphasized that this decision did
not dispose of the Charter issue. He conceded that the section 9.1(c)
might eventually be found unconstitutional, but insisted that such an
outcome should come only via what Roach called the "whole machinery
of Charter adjudication." "It may well be," said Iacobucci,

> that, when this matter returns to trial, the respondents' counsel will make
> an application to have s. 9(1)(c) of the *Radiocommunication Act* declared
> unconstitutional for violating the *Charter*. At that time, it will be necessary
> to consider evidence regarding whose expressive rights are engaged, whe-
> ther these rights are violated by s. 9(1)(c), and, if they are, whether they are
> justified under s. 1. (para. 67)

This process, Iacobucci insists, should not be short-circuited by the judicial renovation of the statute through "Charter values" interpretation.

Bell ExpressVu is thus an instance in which the Court refused to engage
in Charter values–based interpretation. Roach approved of the Court's
restraint in this instance, indicating that the judgment exhibited no
"spurious technique of statutory interpretation" involving the "fiction
that the court is not departing from the words and intent of the legislature when it applies a presumption that the legislature intends to respect
rights" (2005, 735; see also Roach 2007, 463). The judgment did not fail
"the test of judicial candour" because it was prepared to leave a possibly
unconstitutional provision in place, pending full Charter litigation, with
all of its dialogic checks and balances.

Hills v. Canada (1988)

A very different picture is presented in *Hills v. Canada* (1988). This case
came much earlier in the Charter's history, but, as noted above, it was
cited by Justice Iacobucci in *Bell ExpressVu* as one of the "occasions" on
which the Court has "striven to make ... clear" that the Charter values
interpretive principle "can *only* receive application in circumstances of
genuine ambiguity" (2002, para. 62.) Justice Iacobucci's citation on this
point was in reference to Justice L'Heureux-Dubé's majority opinion in
Hills that, unlike the later *Bell ExpressVu* judgment (in which she also participated), found enough statutory ambiguity to give the law a "Charter
values" reading. The Court was sharply divided, with Justice L'Heureux-
Dubé's four-judge opinion prevailing over Justice Lamer's three-judge
dissent. While Lamer did not follow L'Heureux-Dubé in explicitly
addressing the Charter values question, he found that the legislative

provision clearly and unambiguously had the meaning that L'Heureux-Dubé thought infringed Charter values.

Hills arose out of a claim for unemployment insurance benefits by Dennis Hills. Section 44(2)(a) of the Unemployment Insurance Act denied benefits to anyone whose work stoppage was "attributable to a labour dispute" unless the claimant can prove that "he is not participating or financing or directly interested in the labour dispute that caused the stoppage of work" (para. 1). Hills was laid off due to a strike at his place of employment that was initiated by a union separate from his own. He thus "was not participating ... or directly interested in" the dispute (para. 1). On those grounds he might be entitled to unemployment insurance. But was he "financing" the labour dispute? A portion of his union dues were being paid to the International Union, which placed the money into a strike fund that was being used in the current strike against his employer. If this meant that Hills was "financing" the labour dispute, he would be denied unemployment insurance benefits. The Supreme Court thus needed to determine whether payment of mandatory union dues, set aside for a strike fund, constitutes financing of a strike.

For Justice Lamer's dissenting group of judges, normal statutory interpretation meant that Hills should lose the case. Recognizing "that if a statute is not clear, interpretation becomes a necessity," Lamer denied that there was any such lack of clarity in this case (*Hills v. Canada* 1988, para. 101). The word "financing," he insisted, "is clear, unambiguous and in no sense confusing." He continued:

> Under section 44(2)(*a*), a person who finances a labour dispute is a person who provides money to assist in starting and sustaining a work stoppage. It does not matter whether this monetary contribution is made to finance a particular labour dispute or in anticipation of a possible strike. It is also irrelevant that the contributions are paid into a common strike fund. In all cases, the ordinary meaning of the verb "finance" must prevail. (para. 101)

For Justice L'Heureux-Dubé's majority, by contrast, a broad contextual reading of the law revealed enough ambiguity to allow for a narrower reading of "financing," one that would not apply to Hills's situation and would thus enable him to collect unemployment insurance benefits. She had no doubt that the law originally embodied the definition preferred by Lamer, but that "the evolution in Canadian labour relations, the labour movement, and the social and economic conditions of Canadian society" had made for a more ambiguous context in which a different interpretation became plausible (para. 55).

Lamer was not convinced. He noted that Canadian legislators "could not have been unaware of the constant changes in the labour relations panorama" to which Justice L'Heureux-Dubé referred (para. 54). Indeed, in response to these changes, the legislature had often amended the Unemployment Insurance Act. It had not, however, changed the "financing" provision at issue in this case. "Though aware of the changes that have occurred in labour relations," wrote Lamer, "Parliament has not felt it necessary to limit the application of a word of general import ["financing"]." Why? "Undoubtedly because [Parliament] intended to cover all situations to which the word might apply. We cannot assume that this is a mere oversight" (para. 108).

Despite such objections, L'Heureux-Dubé insisted that the law had acquired sufficient ambiguity to permit a non-traditional interpretation. In this context of ambiguity, moreover, the Charter had to be taken into account. Here, as in *Bell ExpressVu* many years later, there was no Charter record, and thus the full "machinery of Charter adjudication" was lacking. Nevertheless, Justice L'Heureux-Dubé insisted that, given legal ambiguity, "the values embodied in the Charter [in this case values of "freedom of association"] must be given preference over an interpretation which would run contrary to them" (*Hills v. Canada* 1988, para. 93).

Unlike the *Bell ExpressVu* judgment in which she later participated, Justice L'Heureux-Dubé's *Hills* judgment was not prepared to wait for an explicit Charter challenge to the legislation. Instead, she chose to bring the law into line with Charter values. The fact that her *Bell ExpressVu* colleague, Justice Iacobucci, later cited her *Hills* opinion in support of his view that the "'*Charter* values' interpretive principle can *only* receive application in circumstances of genuine ambiguity" may imply that he agreed that such ambiguity existed in *Hills* (*Bell ExpressVu* 2002, para. 62). But Lamer's strong dissent in *Hills* itself indicates that this is by no means an inevitable conclusion. From Lamer's perspective, *Hills* looks very much like Roach's "spurious statutory interpretation" based on the "fiction that the court is not departing from the words and intent of the legislature when it applies a presumption that the legislature intends to respect rights" (Roach 2005, 735). In this view, true "judicial candour" would have meant reading the law as Lamer did and awaiting a full Charter-based "dialogue" in subsequent litigation. Not only does the *Hills* judgment short-circuit a direct Charter challenge, but Roach might also worry about its effect on possible legislative sequels – namely, that "the idea that the Court has 'fixed' controversial legislation and made it Charter-proof may very well ensure that the issue is not placed on an already crowded legislative agenda" (750).

Harvard College (2002)

The Supreme Court's decision in *Harvard College v. Canada* (2002) demonstrates a curious application of the *Bell ExpressVu* approach, despite the fact that the precedent is hardly mentioned. The issue was whether Harvard University could secure a Canadian patent for the so-called oncomouse, a "transgenic animal" whose genetic make-up had been technologically altered to facilitate cancer research. Section 2 of Canada's Patent Act allowed patents for "inventions," defined as "any new and useful art, process, machine, manufacture or composition of matter." The central question in this case was whether the oncomouse came within the meaning of a new "manufacture or composition of matter." The Court split 5–4 on this issue, with the majority denying that the oncomouse was patentable under the legislation.

The debate between the two groups of judges turned in part on whether patenting a mouse was the beginning of a "slippery slope" that would eventually enable the patenting of transgenic human beings. All of the judges abhorred the idea of patenting human beings, but they disagreed about whether the door to that prospect would be opened by the patenting of a transgenic mouse. For the majority, mice and human beings both belong to the category of "higher life forms" (as compared to, say, yeast), and if one higher life form could be a patentable "manufacture or composition of matter," so could all others, including humans. In the majority's view, there is no way, as a matter of statutory interpretation, of drawing a legal line within the category of "higher life forms," a line that would allow patentable mice but not patentable humans. "Should this Court determine that higher life forms are within the scope of s. 2," said Justice Bastarache in his majority opinion, "this must necessarily include human beings ... There is no defensible basis within the definition of 'invention' itself to conclude that a chimpanzee is a 'composition of matter' while a human being is not" (*Harvard College v. Canada* 2002, para. 178). Thus, in order to prevent the patenting of human beings, one must deny that higher life forms, including the oncomouse, were the kind of "composition of matter" that was patentable under the Patent Act.

Justice Binnie's dissent summarizes the "slippery slope" claim: "Today the oncomouse; tomorrow Frankenstein's creature" (para. 102). Yet Binnie fundamentally disagrees that the slope is slippery. "There is a qualitative divide between rodents and human beings," he insists, one that most Western nations, who have patented the oncomouse under similar legislative wording, have had no trouble maintaining (para. 102). Binnie does "not believe that the issue of patentability of a human being even arises under the *Patent Act*" (para. 102). It does not arise because "ss. 7 and 15 of the *Canadian Charter of Rights and Freedoms* would clearly prohibit an individual from being reduced to a chattel of another individual" (para. 54).[5] In short, Binnie is using the Charter as an aid in statutory interpretation, one that allows him to narrow the meaning of "composition of matter" so as to exclude human beings.

Although Binnie did not use the term "Charter values" to characterize this Charter-based statutory interpretation, the Bastarache majority did use those terms, and denied that section 2 of the Patents Act exhibits the "genuine ambiguity" that could justify Binnie's interpretation. "As noted by this Court in *Bell ExpressVu*," writes Bastarache, "'*Charter* values' are to be used as an interpretative principle only in circumstances of genuine ambiguity, i.e. where a statutory provision is subject to differing but equally plausible interpretations" (para. 178). For Bastarache, there is no plausible interpretation of "composition of matter" that includes mice but excludes human beings. In Bastarache's view, Justice Binnie was using Charter values to rewrite a clear law. In Roach's terms, Bastarache was accusing Binnie of undertaking a "creative and strained interpretation" (2005, 735).

Bastarache also emphasized the way in which "strained" Charter values interpretations can undermine the section 1 component of inter-institutional dialogue. "To read legislation in conformity with the *Charter* in cases where there is no real ambiguity," he wrote (relying again on *Bell ExpressVu*), "is to deprive the government the opportunity to justify a provision that appears to conflict with the *Charter* under s. 1" (*Harvard College v. Canada* 2002, para. 178). Bastarache's invocation of the section 1 issue appears unusual. What is the apparent "conflict with the Charter" that can no longer be justified given Binnie's "Charter values" rewriting of the law? It can only be the patentability of human beings. But such patentability is not possible on Bastarache's own, even narrower interpretation of the law. So, how can Bastarache say that Binnie is precluding a section 1 justification of something neither side thinks the law includes? The answer may be that Bastarache thinks the unambiguous clarity of "a composition of matter" – the clarity that precludes Charter

---

5 Section 7 of the Charter states, "Everyone has the right to life, liberty and security of the person and the right not to be deprived thereof except in accordance with the principles of fundamental justice." Section 15(1) states, "Every individual is equal before and under the law and has the right to the equal protection and equal benefit of the law without discrimination and, in particular, without discrimination based on race, national or ethnic origin, colour, religion, sex, age or mental or physical disability."

values interpretation – is that the phrase "clearly" includes all higher life forms or none of them.

If this explanation of Bastarache's odd invocation of the section 1 issue is correct, it follows that if Binnie thought the oncomouse was patentable, he should have concluded that human beings were also patentable under the act and waited for a subsequent direct Charter challenge, as the Court was prepared to do in *Bell ExpressVu*. That would have allowed the government to defend the patentability of humans under section 1, or, more likely, to respond to a judicial invalidation with a legislative sequel that explicitly makes a distinction between human beings and, say, mice. What is illegitimate, in this view, is for the Court to use "Charter values" to enact intermediate distinctions in the face of what is (Bastarache seems to suggest) clearly "either/or" legislation. Such legislation certainly exhibits enough "genuine ambiguity" to allow for two interpretations, but only the two polar interpretations.

Bastarache, of course, chose an interpretation that is the polar opposite of the one he implies a more consistent Binnie – one who fully respected the Charter values criterion of *Bell ExpressVu* – should have chosen. It goes without saying that Bastarache's polar choice is entirely Charter-compliant and would not require section 1 justification. Yet it, too, leaves the field clear for the legislature to enact new intermediate legislation explicitly allowing mice but not humans to be patented. Perhaps the idiosyncrasies of Bastarache's opinion are explained by his desire to engage the legislature more fully in the inter-institutional dialogue. The role of Charter values in this form of dialogue is obviously complicated.

Conclusion

As with reforming the common law, using Charter values as a tool or strategy of legislative interpretation raises questions about the appropriate dialogic balance between Canadian courts and legislatures. Because common law is the "inherent province of the judiciary," the Supreme Court feels justified in changing judge-made rules on the basis of Charter values. Nevertheless, it acknowledges that major changes to the common law should be left to the legislature lest the "appropriate balance" between courts and legislatures be "upset." Accordingly, the Court professes to limit its Charter values–based reform of common law to small and incremental changes.

When it turns to legislative interpretation, the Court, now out of its inherent province, owes deference to the democratic will expressed in statutory form, and thus proclaims that it will interpret legislation along the lines of Charter values only when the statute is so "genuinely ambiguous" that the Charter values interpretation is as plausible as less Charter-friendly readings of the law. In circumstances of "genuine ambiguity," a Charter values interpretation preserves the "appropriate balance" between courts and legislatures. By contrast, using Charter values to change the clear (and possibly unconstitutional) meaning of a statute would "upset" the appropriate balance of inter-institutional dialogue. Where the meaning of a law is clear (and perhaps unconstitutional), appropriate dialogue is achieved only through the "whole machinery of Charter adjudication," including the opportunity for the government to defend the law as a "reasonable limit" under section 1 of the Charter, and for the Court (if the section 1 defence fails) to strike down the law. In terms of maintaining the "appropriate" dialogic balance between legislatures and courts, limiting the Charter values interpretive strategy to circumstances of "genuine" statutory "ambiguity" serves the same purpose in the legislative context as undertaking only small or incremental Charter values–based legal change does in the common-law context.

In theory, it seems sensible to use the presence or absence of genuine ambiguity to distinguish between legitimate and illegitimate uses of Charter values–based legislative interpretation. But in practice there appears to be a good deal of genuine ambiguity in the "genuine ambiguity" criterion itself. Judges who bring a statute into line with Charter values always claim that they are justified by genuine ambiguity, that they are in no sense using Charter values to actually alter the legislation. But those claims are, more often than not, seen as transparent "fictions" by others, both on and off the bench. From the latter perspective, Charter values interpretation tends to look like a "spurious technique of statutory interpretation," one that lacks "candour" because it casts what is significant legislative change as mere choice between equally plausible readings. What is really happening, from this perspective, is that an unconstitutional law has been judicially "fixed" without the government having adequate opportunity to defend that law as a section 1 "reasonable limit" on Charter rights and freedoms. The "eclipsing" of section 1 as a central, and critically important, step in Charter "dialogue" turns out to be as central to the debate about Charter values–based legislative interpretation as it is to the debate about Charter values–based common-law reform.

The use of strained interpretations in the Canadian context represents a novel episode in the clash of constitutionalisms insofar as legal and political constitutionalists consider strained interpretations to be problematic, albeit for different reasons. For political constitutionalists, judicial resort to strained interpretation is a negative development – one that makes Canada look more and more like a regime based on judicial supremacy. When the judiciary interpretively fixes a law, the political branches are not signalled, as they would be with judicial invalidation, that there is anything non-compliant about their laws. Full-throated judicial supremacy would have more candour than the subtle, back-door aspect of strained interpretations. Legal constitutionalists *also* lament the use of strained interpretations insofar as they would prefer to see robust inter-institutional dialogue, with the judiciary explicit about a statute's Charter inconsistency. From this perspective, strained interpretations make Canada more like weaker forms of judicial review such as New Zealand and the United Kingdom. As is the case in both of these countries, the Canadian judicial phenomenon of fixing laws through interpretation represents yet another feature of the ongoing clash of constitutionalisms.

Chapter Eight

Conclusion

E.E. Schattschneider (1960) observed that political institutions are not neutral. They are best conceived as forms of organized bias. We expect members of an institution to have an interest in shaping the direction of that bias. This means political institutions are not only arenas *for* politics but are themselves also the objects *of* politics. For example, in addition to occurring *within* Parliament, politics is often *about* Parliament – e.g., when and under what conditions prorogation or dissolution are appropriate and legitimate (Russell and Sossin 2009). Similarly, politicians compete not only *in* elections but *about* electoral systems – e.g., whether to replace a single-member plurality system with a more proportional alternative.

What is true of any particular institution is certainly true of a country's overarching institution: its constitution. Establishing the fundamental "rules of the game," constitutions provide the broadest arena for political life, shaping and constraining political actors' range of behaviour. Here, too, the participants compete not only within the rules of the game but also about whether and how to modify those rules. The "politics of constitutional modification," says Christopher Manfredi, "can be conceptualized as a competitive game of institutional design in which the objective is to alter the range of possible policy outcomes by modifying existing rules" (1997, 113).

How best to protect rights has been a central issue of such constitutional competition in recent decades. The contestants in this institutional politics are political and legal constitutionalism, and, relatedly, liberal and post-liberal constitutionalism. Political and legal constitutionalists fundamentally disagree about how much power to give judges in the political and policy process (Tomkins 2005). As far as rights protection is concerned, legal constitutionalists emphasize judicial power under a bill of rights, while political constitutionalists emphasize institutional checks and balances among the branches of government

(Bellamy 2007). Liberal constitutionalists want bills of rights to protect liberty in the private sphere against overly intrusive government or state action, while post-liberal constitutionalists want such bills to govern the private sphere in the name of equality (Bateman 1998; Smithey 2002; Rush 2002). This study has explored the clash of these intersecting constitutionalisms in (mainly) three countries: Canada, New Zealand, and the United Kingdom.

In addition to framing constitutional politics as part of a competitive game, Manfredi distinguishes between macro and micro constitutional change. "Macro" constitutional changes are formal enactments or amendments, typically involving contentious elite-level bargaining, complex procedural thresholds, and disagreements over whether popular consent has been reached. These factors cause "institutional rigidity," making this type of change rare. "Micro" constitutional change, in contrast, involves a politics of interpretation, often associated with litigation, which can be just as significant and drastic as macro-changes in many instances (Manfredi 1997, 114).

The clash of constitutionalisms examined in this study involves both macro and micro constitutional politics. Macro constitutional politics has led to the formal enactment of rights documents throughout the liberal-democratic world (Erdos 2010), including Canada's Charter of Rights and Freedoms (1982), New Zealand's Bill of Rights Act (1990), and the United Kingdom's Human Rights Act (1998). Although the original battle between political and legal constitutionalism – whether or not to have an explicit, judicially enforceable rights document – has been decisively won by legal constitutionalists, the clashing constitutional perspectives were manifest in the different designs of those documents. The "competitive game of institutional design," moreover, did not end with the original macro-level enactments. Rather, the new documents have generated an ongoing micro-level politics of interpretation about how best to understand and apply them. Bills of rights may now be ubiquitous, but the "clash of constitutionalisms" continues in the bill of rights era. At both the macro and micro levels, the central battles concern the strength and reach of those documents.

Constitutional Strength

Regarding strength, legal constitutionalists prefer strong-form rights documents, like the US Bill of Rights, under which legislatures can restore laws struck down by the courts only through such difficult processes as constitutional amendment or politicized judicial appointments (Tushnet 2002, 2016). Seeing altogether too much "judicial supremacy" in the US model, political constitutionalists prefer "weak-form" institutional designs that make it easier for legislatures to resist and reverse rights-based judicial decisions.

A prominent example of weak-form design is the section 33 notwithstanding provision in Canada's Charter of Rights and Freedoms, which eliminates the need to take the difficult course of either constitutional amendment or court packing in order to prevent or reverse certain judicial invalidations. The provisions of the Canadian and New Zealand rights documents that allow for "reasonable limits" on protected rights and freedoms also point in the weak-form direction. Weak-form design – and hence the influence of political constitutionalism – is most dramatically evident, however, in the explicit denial of a judicial invalidation mandate by the statutory rights documents in New Zealand and the United Kingdom. For the framers of these documents, the Canadian attempt to offset judicial invalidation with a notwithstanding provision had failed because the notwithstanding clause had become difficult to use. The NZBORA and the HRA thus reject the invalidation option and provide only the interpretive mandate to read statutes in a rights-compliant manner if possible. If judges cannot give the law a rights-compliant reading, if they find (or explicitly declare) it to be clearly incompatible with protected rights, the law remains in place and fully applicable, unless and until the legislature chooses to address the judicial concerns. At the level of formal, macro-level constitutional design, New Zealand and the United Kingdom clearly lean more strongly in the weak-form direction than does Canada.

But macro-level design is subject to modification through the micro-level politics of interpretation. In formally weak-form New Zealand and the United Kingdom, legal constitutionalists have worked to strengthen the interpretive mandate, so that a statute need not exhibit enough textual ambiguity to plausibly support a rights-compatible interpretation. Whereas political constitutionalists in New Zealand and the United Kingdom insist that judges can choose only interpretations that are "genuinely open in light of both [a statute's] text and purpose" (*R. v. Hansen* 2007, para. 61), their legal-constitutionalist opponents prefer the "possibility" of even interpretations that "do considerable violence" to statutory language or that stop just short of "judicial vandalism" (*Ghaidan v. Godin-Mendoza* 2004, paras. 67, 100). Following the United Kingdom's Lord Steyn, they see their "interpretive obligation … [as] a *strong* one" (*R. v. A.* 2002, para. 44, emphasis added). Among other things, this strong view of the interpretive mandate makes findings or declarations of incompatibility mostly unnecessary, and hence rare.

To political constitutionalists in New Zealand and the United Kingdom, Steyn's strong interpretive mandate justifies "strained" readings that turn "interpretation" into judicial legislation, and thus upset the balance between judicial and legislative power intended by a weak-form design. New Zealand's Justice Tipping – obviously writing from a political-constitutionalist standpoint on this issue – declares that when judges use the interpretive mandate "as a concealed legislative tool," they come close to establishing "a judicial override of Parliament" (*R. v. Hansen* 2007, para. 156); they approximate, in other words, the invalidation mandate that was so explicitly rejected by the New Zealand and UK rights documents. New Zealand and UK judges can only *approximate* invalidation, of course, because it remains true that the legislature can enact a new statute re-establishing in even clearer terms what the court considered unconstitutional. But this positive response to a strained interpretation is obviously more difficult than doing nothing in response to a judicial finding or declaration of incompatibility. And given the "staying power" of a newly created judicial status quo, it can be very difficult indeed (Flanagan 1997; Morton 2001; Manfredi 2007). In Tushnet's (2002, 2787) terms, such strengthening of the interpretive mandate is one way of "escalating" a weak-form formal design towards a strong-form reality. This speaks to the significance of the micro-level politics of interpretation.

In Canada, where a "judicial override of Parliament" is part of the macro-level strong-form design, there is no need to *approximate* invalidation by interpretively "fixing" statutes that could be struck down. Canadian judges thus reject the idea of giving a statute a rights-compatible reading even in the absence of textual ambiguity. They agree that they can bring a statute into line with Charter values "*only* … in circumstances of genuine ambiguity, i.e., where the statutory provision is subject to differing, but equally plausible interpretations" (*Bell ExpressVu* 2002, para. 62, emphasis in original).

Canadian judges, in short, agree on the criterion for legitimate rights-based statutory interpretation that appeals to political constitutionalists in New Zealand and the United Kingdom. This criterion obviously has a very different significance in Canada, however. Whereas it helps prevent the weak-form interpretive mandate from escalating towards strong-form invalidation in New Zealand and the United Kingdom, it protects the invalidation mandate in Canada. Limiting the interpretive mandate to circumstances of genuine ambiguity in New Zealand and the United Kingdom, in other words, leaves more room for findings or declarations of clear inconsistency with protected rights, in which case legislative inertia leaves the offending law in place. Limiting the interpretive mandate to circumstances of genuine ambiguity in Canada, by contrast, leaves more room for judicial invalidation. By the same token, the much stronger interpretive mandate favoured by legal constitutionalists in

New Zealand and the United Kingdom risks "eclipsing" the invalidation mandate in Canada (Roach 2005, 746). With respect to the "genuine ambiguity" criterion, the positions of legal and political constitutionalists are reversed in the two contexts.

It is important to note that the positions taken in the micro-level interpretive politics about the strength of the interpretive mandate can generate their own rounds of interpretive politics. Recall that in the very case in which he argued that judges can legitimately "stretch" a law up to "the breaking point," the United Kingdom's Lord Millett thought the Court's majority had gone beyond that point (*Ghaidan v. Godin-Mendoza* 2004, para. 67). Similarly, in the very case (*R v. Hansen* 2007, para. 13) in which New Zealand's Justice Elias adopted Lord Steyn's "strong" approach, declaring that "strained" interpretations were not "heretical," she refused to give her country's reverse onus for drug trafficking the more generous, accused-friendly reading given to a similar provision by the UK court in *Lambert* (2002). An interpretation that seemed entirely possible to her UK colleagues was simply not tenable to Justice Elias. In Canada, too, abstract agreement on the "genuine ambiguity" standard has not meant agreement about how to apply that standard in practice. We have seen that interpretations thought to be justified by genuine statutory ambiguity by some Canadian judges and observers appear to others as "spurious" attempts to "fix" laws that unambiguously infringe rights. However the micro-level constitutional politics of interpretation draws (or proposes to draw) the line between legitimate and illegitimate interpretation, the controversy about strained interpretation persists.

The Canadian version of this controversy raises some particularly intriguing issues about constitutional strength. Rather than engaging in "spurious" attempts to "fix" laws, say Canadian critics of strained interpretation, courts should strike down such laws unless governments can demonstrably justify them as "reasonable limits," an opportunity they lose when judicial legislation under the guise of interpretation precludes "finding infringements in the first place" (*Bell ExpressVu* 2002, para. 64). In this critique, strained interpretation risks "eclipsing" not only invalidation but also the opportunity for the political branches to justify "reasonable limits." It is the "whole machinery of Charter adjudication" (Roach 2005, 746), including both its strong-form invalidation component and its weak-form reasonable-limits dimension, that is threatened by overly adventurous statutory interpretation, and it is the whole package that must be defended against that threat. A blend of legal and political constitutionalism is on display here.

This blend is frequently expressed in terms of a balanced inter-institutional dialogue in which legislation can only be judicially struck down if it has not successfully been defended by government as a reasonable limit. If judges do strike the law down as an *un*reasonable limit, they generally leave room for the legislature to pursue its objective with a more carefully crafted statute, one that more minimally impairs the affected rights. In this "dialogue," it is argued, neither the judiciary nor the legislature are supreme. The possibility of strong-form invalidation, in other words, does not entail judicial supremacy, meaning that the perspectives of legal and political constitutionalism have been appropriately balanced.

Some political constitutionalists contest this denial of judicial supremacy (Huscroft 2002), pointing out that Canadian legislatures are generally expected to work within the interpretive parameters set by judges, including on such section 1 issues as minimal impairment, and that they can step outside those limits only by using the section 33 notwithstanding clause. To the extent that the notwithstanding clause has become politically rare, they argue, judges are practically supreme on the questions that really matter. It is for reasons such as this that political constitutionalists in New Zealand and the United Kingdom allowed legislatures to disagree with findings or declarations of unreasonable incompatibility by choosing not to correct the judicially discovered defects, rather than forcing them to respond proactively through something like Canada's notwithstanding clause.

Of course, this difference in constitutional strength between the Canadian document and its New Zealand/UK counterparts would have been smaller had the section 33 notwithstanding option retained greater vitality. In that case, Canada would have stayed closer to the weak-form end of Tushnet's continuum. Lord Steyn's "strong" interpretive mandate similarly diminishes the difference, but from the other direction, by establishing something closer to "a judicial override of Parliament" in the formally weak-form systems. Just as legal constitutionalists in Canada celebrate the Charter's strong-form invalidation mandate, so their counterparts in New Zealand and the United Kingdom favour a reading of their interpretive mandate strong enough to approximate invalidation. Just as political constitutionalists in Canada decry the rare usage of the section 33 notwithstanding clause, so their counterparts in New Zealand and the United Kingdom decry any decline in the ability of their legislatures to resist judicial rulings by doing nothing.

The differences between New Zealand and the United Kingdom also deserve mention. Although both the NZBORA and the HRA deny an explicit invalidation mandate, the New Zealand document went further in "pull[ing] out all the stops" to make its weak-form intentions as explicit as possible, including a so-called anti-primacy clause reminding courts that they must continue to apply laws that are inconsistent with the Bill of Rights (Rishworth 2004, 258–9). Such features of the NZBO-RA's macro-level design reflect a constitutional culture strongly oriented to the tradition of parliamentary supremacy, and that culture continues to affect the micro-level politics of interpretation in New Zealand (Geddis and Fenton 2008, 775). Strained interpretation certainly arises in New Zealand, but it does not feature as prominently there as in the United Kingdom (Gardbaum 2013, 136). Not only did the HRA's macro-level design pull out fewer stops to protect parliamentary supremacy, but its micro-level politics of interpretation has embraced a "stronger" interpretive mandate than has emerged in New Zealand. Ironically, the motherland of parliamentary supremacy has been somewhat less committed to it than its former colony in the antipodes.

The United Kingdom has, however, remained more committed to parliamentary supremacy than its former colony in the northern hemisphere. Canada clearly has the strongest-form rights document of the three under consideration, with its UK and New Zealand counterparts arrayed, in that order, in the weaker-form direction. Partly this reflects the continuing influence of the different macro-level institutional designs, with Canada's Charter embracing the invalidation mandate, New Zealand's NZBORA explicitly including an anti-primacy provision, and the United Kingdom's HRA positioned in between. The original macro-level designs matter. But so does the ongoing politics of interpretation, which has moved the United Kingdom's HRA in the strong-form direction by developing a "strong" reading of the interpretive mandate that justifies strained interpretations that approximate "judicial vandalism" (*Ghaidan v. Godin-Mendoza* 2004, paras. 67, 100). While this strong reading of the interpretative mandate is not as well established in New Zealand, it is certainly part of that country's politics of interpretation, with influential judges declaring that strained interpretations are not "heretical" (*R. v. Hansen* 2007, para. 13). In Canada, the Charter has moved in an even more strong-form direction with the delegitimation, over time, of its main nod towards parliamentary supremacy, the notwithstanding clause. Whatever the current institutional balance concerning constitutional strength, legal and political constitutionalists will continue the struggle to shift that balance in their preferred direction.

Constitutional Reach

Political and legal constitutionalists clash about constitutional reach as much as they do about constitutional strength. Even the most strong-form constitution, providing for difficult-to-reverse judicial invalidations, would not satisfy legal constitutionalists if, governing only a very limited set of matters, it did not reach very far. Ideally, "pure legal constitutionalism" wants the judicially supervised constitution to reach "virtually all rights-relevant issues and conflicts in a society" (Gardbaum 2013, 37), making it a "total constitution" (Kumm 2006) and giving rise to "constitutional totalism" (Bateman 1998, 13). "Pure political constitutionalism," by contrast, prefers all "rights-relevant issues and conflicts in a society" to be "resolved politically, through ordinary, non-constitutional laws made and executed by political actors who remain fully accountable for them to the electorate" (Gardbaum 2013, 37) – meaning no judicially supervised rights document at all, and hence no "constitutional reach." Even the most weak-form bill of rights will not satisfy the "pure" political constitutionalist.

As with constitutional strength, neither "pure" view of constitutional reach has prevailed in the three countries under consideration. Here again, the very existence of bills of rights signifies the defeat of pure political constitutionalism. At the same time, however, "constitutional totalism" has thus far been denied complete victory, although it has made significant advances. The battles about constitutional reach, like those about constitutional strength, are nowadays fought in the middle range between the two poles.

Sometimes these middle-range battles settle on middle-ground compromises. For example, even constitutional conventions, traditionally thought of as decidedly *political* parts of the constitution that exceed legal and judicial reach, have been brought under judicial guidance. As they define conventions in novel and controversial ways, however, judges continue to insist that they cannot "enforce" them. Conventions may be judicially supervised in new ways, but not enforced in the manner of the more clearly legal parts of the constitution. Perhaps one could say they have been increasingly *judicialized* without being fully *legalized*. While legal constitutionalism has won a partial victory, political constitutionalism retains some traction in this area. A compromise is also apparent regarding executive prerogative over foreign policy. Although political constitutionalists consider this an archetypical area of political discretion for the executive branch of government, judges in Canada, New Zealand, and the United Kingdom insist their rights documents reach this area of executive action in a judicially enforceable manner. At the same time, however, judges have been reticent to use their claimed power over executive discretion in an aggressive manner.

Judges of a legal-constitutionalist bent have been much less reticent in aggressively enforcing expansive constitutional interpretations applying underlying values, to the chagrin and pointed opposition of their political-constitutionalist opponents. The explicit textual provisions of rights documents often protect some part or aspect of a deeper underlying principle or value. For example, the guarantee against "unreasonable search and seizure" found in all rights documents can plausibly be understood to protect certain aspects of "privacy." Similarly, constitutional provisions guaranteeing judges tenure during good behaviour and giving the legislature authority to set their salaries are clearly designed as particularizations of the underlying value of "judicial independence." Does the constitution protect only those particularizations of the underlying value that its text explicitly codifies, or does it also protect uncodified particularizations whose importance becomes apparent over time? Legal and political constitutionalists give opposite answers to this question.

Legal constitutionalists give a strongly positive answer, insisting that the constitution's "express" provisions "merely elaborate" its "underlying, unwritten, and organizing principles," and that the principles themselves are fully constitutionalized and judicially enforceable (*Provincial Judges Reference* 1997, paras. 95, 107). Thus, judges can add to documented protections of judicial independence the hitherto unspecified requirement of judicial compensation commissions. Or they can add protections of sexual privacy to such explicit provisions as the guarantee against unreasonable search and seizure. Chapter 3 explored several other examples of this expansive use of underlying principles or values. As that chapter showed, legal constitutionalists have generally prevailed on the issue of expansive constitutional interpretation in recent decades.

The victories of legal constitutionalists have not, however, gone without regular and spirited opposition by political constitutionalists, who strongly object to the elastic view of constitutional reach. They deny that judges should "promote, as much as possible, values that some subjectively think underpin" explicit constitutional provisions (see Justice Rothstein in *Ontario (A.G.) v. Fraser* 2011, para. 252). The express provisions may indeed "elaborate" underlying principles, but they are not "mere" elaborations. To the contrary, those elaborations "*are* the constitution" (*Provincial Judges Reference* 1997, para. 319, emphasis in original), which does not reach any farther. Other elaborations or particularizations of underlying values lie beyond the judicially enforceable constitution. Judicial compensation commissions, protections of sexual privacy, and the like might very well be good ideas, but they must be left to the political process. This may have become a minority view among judges, but it is far from a moribund view.

Do constitutional provisions – however broadly or narrowly they are read – reach beyond the public sector into the private sphere? Political and legal constitutionalists also offer opposing answers to this question. And here we encounter the second clash of constitutionalisms of interest to this study: the clash between liberal and post-liberal constitutionalists. Liberal constitutionalists see constitutions chiefly as a way of protecting private liberty by constraining the state. In this view, bills of rights do not reach directly into the private sphere; they apply only to "state action." Post-liberal constitutionalism is skeptical of the public/private distinction on which liberal constitutionalism is grounded, arguing that rights documents should protect individuals "from domination, whether that domination is rooted in the state or in society" (Bateman 2000, 203). For some post-liberals, this means that state inaction can be as unconstitutional as state action because inaction amounts to "a delegation of authority" to private power, essentially enabling private domination by permitting it (Montigny 1985).

As noted in chapter 4, not everyone who denies the public/private distinction wants the judicially supervised constitution to reach into the private sphere. Some post-liberals are skeptical of judicial power and prefer to secure *politically* democratic legitimacy for their policy agendas (Reichman 2002). Some post-liberals, in other words, are political constitutionalists. More commonly, however, post-liberalism aligns with legal constitutionalism insofar as it wants to extend constitutional reach into the private sphere, just as liberal constitutionalism aligns with political constitutionalism insofar as it resists that extension of constitutional reach.

A central question in the debate about constitutional reach into the private sphere is whether – and if so, to what extent – rights documents reach those areas of judge-made common law that govern relations between private individuals, such as tort or contract law. Can private individuals use rights documents not only to sue the state but also to sue their private-sector employers in contract litigation when no state action is involved? To use Justice McIntyre's formulation in *Dolphin Delivery* (1986, para. 39), will the rights document apply where "private party 'A' sues private party 'B' relying on the common law and where no act of government is relied upon to support the action"?

On this question, the courts in all three countries have charted an ambiguous middle ground between the polar positions of liberal and post-liberal constitutionalists. On the one hand, they agree that private actors cannot use rights documents to sue each other for directly breaching constitutional duties in the absence of any state action. On the other hand, they also agree that private common law cannot be entirely untouched by the relevant rights document. The resolution lies in interpretively bringing the common law into line with "rights values." This approach, known as the "indirect horizontal effect" (Tushnet 2008b, 197), retains some of the vestiges of the public/private distinction while still allowing for some "private" wrongs to be addressed by the rights documents. This middle-ground convergence does not satisfy completely either liberal or post-liberal constitutionalists.

Does this middle ground make sense, or is it "confused," as Hutchinson and Petter allege (1988, 283)? Is Mix-Ross right in calling it a distinction without a difference "in which private citizens are bound by the same constitutional duties, albeit cloaked in 'value' terminology, as the state" (2009, 47)? Perhaps some of this skepticism is present in former chief justice Beverley McLachlin's comment that, "despite the effort to keep the Charter out of the common law, it has arguably come in through the back door" (2002, 199). After all, the door of entry does not change the character of what has entered, though it may make the fact of entry less noticeable. Whether or not that is the case, the "rights values" approach obviously reflects a judicial disinclination to simply take sides in the debate between liberal and post-liberal constitutionalism about the appropriateness of constitutional reach into the private sphere. While judges do not want to exempt private common law altogether from the reach of their rights documents, they want to be cautious rather than aggressive in how they extend that reach.

A significant aspect of this cautious approach is the view, expressed in New Zealand in the *Lange v. Atkinson* judgment that judges "must not go further than is necessary" in using rights values to develop the common law, leaving "far-reaching changes ... to the legislature" (1998, 451). In taking this view, the *Lange* judgment explicitly followed the Canadian Supreme Court, which insists that "complex changes to the law with uncertain ramifications should be left to the legislature," with the courts using Charter values to make only "incremental changes to the common law" (*Salituro* 1991, 666). Importantly, the distinction between smaller, "incremental" changes and "more complex" or "far-reaching" ones applies not only to private common law, but also to those parts of the judge-made common law that govern relations between the individual and the state, including important aspects of criminal law. Although the rights documents apply to such public common law much more clearly than they do to private common law, judges assert with respect to both realms that far-reaching changes would upset "the appropriate balance between judicial and legislative action." "Courts have traditionally been cautious regarding the extent to which they will amend the common law," said the *Lange* judgment (1998, 451), and preserving this traditional caution as much as possible under the new rights documents is evidently necessary to maintain "the appropriate balance between judicial and legislative action."

Of course, abstract judicial agreement on making only smaller, incremental changes to the common law is no more self-applying – or no less open to its own politics of interpretation – than are the criteria for appropriate rights-based statutory interpretation. Just as judges disagree about whether a statutory interpretation is justified by genuine ambiguity – or even by the stronger criterion of judicial violence up to the breaking point – so they disagree about whether a proposed judicial common-law innovation is sufficiently incremental or too far-reaching.

The question is what happens if the legislature thinks the courts have gone too far. In New Zealand and the United Kingdom, the answer is that the legislature can enact ordinary legislation to alter or reverse the ruling. Changing a policy status quo, including a judicially created status quo, is rarely easy, of course, and it arguably becomes more difficult if the judicial innovation invokes constitutional standards. Still, at least formally, this maintains the traditional inter-institutional balance in which the legislation supersedes judicial common law. It is true that the reversing legislation itself could subsequently be found by the courts to be incompatible with the rights document for the same reasons that led to their common-law innovation, but a legislature willing to enact such legislation would likely ignore an incompatibility ruling.

Can Canadian legislatures who oppose what they see as far-reaching Charter-based reform of the common law also pass reversing legislation that supersedes the judicial ruling? Absolutely, if that legislation includes an eligible section 33 notwithstanding clause. But should that be the legislature's first and only resort? Hypothetically, the judicial common-law innovation, following *Swain* (1991), might not have (or might only cursorily have) addressed whether the original common-law rule could be justified as a "reasonable limit" on affected rights and freedoms under section 1 of the Charter. If so, then resorting immediately to the notwithstanding clause in reversing legislation entails the loss of the "reasonable limits" stage of inter-institutional dialogue, just as "strained" statutory interpretation, by precluding the "finding [Charter] infringements in the first place," risks "eclipsing" the opportunity to justify those infringements under section 1.

For these reasons, political constitutionalists in Canada believe that legislatures should be free to reverse Charter-based innovations of the common law without including a notwithstanding clause in the reversing statute, as Canada's Parliament did in response to the controversial *Daviault* (1994) and *O'Connor* (1995) decisions. If and when such statutes are challenged in "second-look" cases, say political constitutionalists, the full "reasonable limits" stage of inter-institutional dialogue would be assured. Legal constitutionalists see it differently, considering reversing statutes without a notwithstanding clause to be based on the illegitimate assumption "that Parliament is entitled to act on its own interpretation of the constitution, even when it is at odds with that of the Court" (Roach 2016, 316). Such "in your face" reversing statutes, they insist, require a notwithstanding clause.

Political constitutionalists reply that the Court remains free to side with its original common-law innovation and invalidate the reversing statute, in which case a notwithstanding clause *would* become necessary. This ability of the Court to insist on section 33 means that it ultimately retains the upper hand, especially given the immense political difficulty of using section 33. In this context, political constitutionalists wonder what is wrong with first inviting the Court to reconsider and perhaps change its mind, as the Court's majority arguably did when it upheld Parliament's sequel to *O'Connor* in its 1999 *Mills* decision (Knopff et al. 2017, 640–1, 644). They argue that such intermediate dialogic invitations to reconsider – what Knopff et al. (2017) call "reconsideration dialogue" – can occur only if Parliament initially expresses its disagreement in statutory form without a notwithstanding clause.

The political-constitutionalist perspective on "reconsideration dialogue" is very much a minority view in Canada, however. Political constitutionalists can point to only two cases – *Mills* (1999) and *Hall* (2002) – in which the Court reconsidered and accepted legislative sequels that clearly reversed its Charter-based common-law innovation. The Court's approach in those cases came under such sustained criticism by legal constitutionalists that it has not been repeated (see Baker 2010, 6–8). Indeed, so cautious has the Court become on this issue, that for over two decades it has managed to avoid a much-anticipated second-look judgment at what legal constitutionalists consider the clearly unconstitutional legislative sequel to *Daviault* (Baker and Knopff 2014). Still, the *Mills* and *Hall* precedents exist, and political constitutionalists continue to defend them (Baker 2016, 8–11; Knopff et al. 2017, 636–44).

Final Thoughts

This study's main contribution is to integrate the theoretical distinction between political and legal constitutionalism into a systematic analysis of rights documents in Canada, New Zealand, and the United Kingdom. As a study of multiple cases, it contributes to the comparative literature on constitutional thought, demonstrating how political developments in these countries reflect two clashes of constitutionalisms – between liberal and post-liberal constitutionalism, on the one hand, and between political and legal constitutionalism, on the other. By applying Manfredi's (1997) distinction between "macro" and "micro" constitutional changes to questions of institutional design and development, it also contributes a better understanding of how these questions have developed (and continue to develop) at the micro level of judicial interpretation in each country. Moreover, by providing a theoretical distinction between constitutional strength and constitutional reach, it demonstrates how issues of interpretation, dialogue, legislative rights protection, and "rights values" play out differently in debates over public and private law. This study shows how some of these differences can be attributed to subtle variations in constitutional cultures within each national context. Future comparative scholarship can build on this study by applying these theoretical applications to countries ranging from those without a national bill of rights (such as Australia) to those with a much longer history of a judicially enforceable bill of rights (such as the United States).

In each of the three cases studied, on both the major dimensions of constitutional strength and constitutional reach, legal constitutionalism and its frequent ally, post-liberal constitutionalism, have made important advances, but political constitutionalism and its frequent ally, liberal constitutionalism, mount an ongoing and spirited opposition on virtually every front. And there are many fronts, ranging from common-law reform to strained interpretation of legislation to matters of constitutional convention and even executive prerogative.

On some issues, the relative balance between the two sides varies from country to country. For example, although all three countries have seen gains in constitutional strength – in Canada through the delegitimation of "reconsideration dialogue" and the related (though perhaps fading) delegitimation of the notwithstanding clause; in the United Kingdom and New Zealand through Lord Steyn's "strong" reading of the interpretive mandate, though the United Kingdom has not "escalated" as far in the strong-form direction as Canada, and New Zealand has not escalated as far as the United Kingdom. This owes much to the varying influence of political constitutionalism in the three countries (most influential in New Zealand, less influential in the United Kingdom, least influential in Canada). The different institutional designs produced by these constitutional cultures have a continuing effect. Legal constitutionalism can increase the strength of all three documents, but less in New Zealand than in the United Kingdom, and more in already strong-form Canada than in either of the countries that lack an explicit invalidation mandate.

On other issues, judges in all three countries strike very similar balances between the clashing competitors, sometimes tilting strongly towards the legal-constitutionalist camp (e.g., by using underlying values to extend constitutional reach), and sometimes attempting a middle-ground compromise. One such compromise involves extending constitutional reach to the common law governing private activity, but only via the ambiguous middle ground of the "indirect horizontal effect." Another involves approximating the traditional inter-institutional balance between courts and legislatures by making only small and "incremental" changes to the common law (both private and public), leaving more far-reaching changes to the legislature.

The striking of any particular balance or compromise is no more apt to end the micro-level politics of interpretation than were the original macro-level institutional designs. Judges and commentators who agree that far-reaching changes to the common law should be avoided will disagree about what counts as a far-reaching change. Even judges who think it legitimate to give "strained" interpretations to statutes up to the "breaking point" will disagree about when that breaking point has been reached. In these and a host of other ways explored in this study, the clash of constitutionalisms in the liberal-democratic world will continue.

The clash persists because liberal democracies are "compound regimes" (Ceaser 1990, 8) that attempt to blend competing institutional principles. There cannot be *liberal* democracy unless democratic legislatures are subject to constitutional constraints, but neither can there be liberal *democracy* unless some important matters lie beyond the reach of the judicially enforceable constitution and are left to legislative discretion. Where the correct balance lies will always be a controversial subject, guaranteeing a continuing battle between political and legal constitutionalism about how much of our political life we want to constitutionalize in the legal, judicially enforceable sense. Put differently, "everything" does not inevitably need to become constitutionalized and judicialized as long both perspectives in the clash of constitutionalisms persist.

This study has aimed to enhance our understanding of this important and ongoing clash. Its comparative analysis has clarified a complex and nuanced debate and shed light on such under-explored topics as the controversies about common law and strained statutory interpretation. The study's novel integration of the debate's many interrelated dimensions into a single, unified analysis has been especially illuminating.

Works Cited

Ajzenstat, Janet. 1997. "Reconciling Parliament and Rights: A.V. Dicey Reads
    the Canadian Charter of Rights and Freedoms." *Canadian Journal of Political*
    Science 30 (4): 645–62. https://doi.org/10.1017/S00084239000
    16462.
Allan, James. 2000. "Turning Clark Kent into Superman: The New Zealand
    Bill of Rights Act 1990." *Otago Law Review* 9 (4): 613–32.
– 2006. "Portia, Bassanio or Dick the Butcher? Constraining Judges in the
    Twenty-First Century." *King's College Law Journal* 17 (1): 1–26. https://
    doi.org/10.1080/09615768.2006.11427627.
– 2011. "Statutory Bills of Rights: You Read Words In, You Read Words Out,
    You Take Parliament's Clear Intention and You Shake it All About – Doin'
    the Sankey Hanky Panky." In *The Legal Protection of Human Rights: Sceptical*
    Essays, edited by Tom Campbell, K.D. Ewing, and Adam Tomkins. Oxford:
    Oxford University Press.
– 2014. Democracy in Decline: Steps in the Wrong Direction. Montreal:
    McGill-Queen's University Press.
Allan, T.R.S. 1993. *Law, Liberty, and Justice: The Legal Foundations of British*
    Constitutionalism. New York: Oxford University Press.
Baker, Dennis. 2010. *Not Quite Supreme: The Courts and Coordinate Constitutional*
    Interpretation. Montreal: McGill-Queen's University Press.
– 2016. "Checking the Court: Justifying Parliament's Role in Constitutional
    Interpretation." *Supreme Court Law Review* 73 (2):1–16.
Baker, Dennis, and Rainer Knopff. 2002. "Minority Retort: A Parliamentary
    Power to Resolve Judicial Disagreement in Close Cases." *Windsor Yearbook of*
    Access to Justice 21:347–59.
– 2014. "Daviault Dialogue: The Strange Journey of Canada's Intoxication
    Defence." *Review of Constitutional Studies* 19 (1): 35–58.
Bakvis, Herman, Gerald Baier, and Douglas Brown. 2009. *Contested Federalism:*
    Certainty and Ambiguity in the Canadian Federation. New York: Oxford
    University Press.

Banfield, Andrew C., and Rainer Knopff. 2009. "Legislative vs. Judicial Checks and Balances: Comparing Rights Policies Across Regimes." *Australian Journal of Political Science* 44 (1): 13–27. https://doi.org/10.1080/10361 140802654968.

Bateman, Thomas M.J. 1998. "Rights Application Doctrine and the Clash of Constitutionalisms in Canada." *Canadian Journal of Political Science* 31 (1): 3–29. https://doi.org/10.1017/S0008423900008660.

– 2000. "Charter Rights Application Doctrine and the Clash of Constitutionalisms in Canada." PhD diss., University of Alberta.

– 2015. "The Supreme Court of Canada as Moral Tutor: Religious Freedom, Civil Society, and Charter Values." In *Liberal Education, Civic Education, and the Canadian Regime: Past Principles and Present Challenges*, edited by David Livingstone. Montreal: McGill-Queen's University Press.

– 2018. "Liberal Versus Post-Liberal Constitutionalism: Applying the Charter to Civil Society (Updated)." In *Law, Politics and the Judicial Process in Canada*, edited by F. L. Morton and Dave Snow. 4th ed. Calgary: University of Calgary Press.

Bateman, Thomas M.J., Janet L. Hiebert, Rainer Knopff, and Peter H. Russell. 2008. *The Court and the Charter: Leading Cases.* Toronto: Edmond Montgomery.

Bateman, Thomas M.J., and Matthew LeBlanc. 2018. "Dialogue on Death: Parliament and the Courts on Medically-Assisted Dying." *Supreme Court Law Review* 85 (2): 387–434.

Baum, Lawrence. 2006. *Judges and Their Audiences: A Perspective on Judicial Behaviour.* Princeton, NJ: Princeton University Press.

Bellamy, Richard. 2007. *Political Constitutionalism: A Republican Defense of the Constitutionality of Democracy.* Cambridge: Cambridge University Press.

– 2011. "Political Constitutionalism and the Human Rights Act." *International Journal of Constitutional Law* 9 (1): 86–111. https://doi.org/10.1093/icon /mor024.

Bickel, Alexander M. 1986. *The Least Dangerous Branch: The Supreme Court at the Bar of Politics.* Indianapolis, IN: Bobbs-Merrill Educational.

Bronskill, Jim. 2018. "Jehovah's Witness Cannot Appeal Expulsion to a Judge, Supreme Court Rules." *CBC News*, 12 June 2019. https://www.cbc.ca/news /canada/calgary/jehovahs-witnesses-supreme-court-1.4685553.

Brudner, Alan. 2005. " 'Notwithstanding' Not Needed on Marriage." *Globe and Mail*, 1 February 2005, A1.

Butler, Andrew S. 2000. "Is This a Public Law Case?" *Victoria University of Wellington Law Review* 31 (4): 747–81. https://doi.org/10.26686/vuwlr .v31i4.5935.

Butler, Petra. 2014. "It Takes Two to Tango – Have They Learned Their Steps?" *Victoria University of Wellington Legal Research Paper* 136:1–53. https://dx.doi .org/10.2139/ssrn.2022681.

Cairns, Alan. 1992. "The Charter: A Political Science Perspective." *Osgoode Hall Law Journal* 30 (3): 615–25.

– 1995. "The Embedded State: State-Society Relations in Canada." In *Reconfigurations: Canadian Citizenship and Constitutional Change: Selected Essays*, edited by Douglas E. Williams. Toronto: McClelland and Stewart.

Cameron, Jamie. 2001. "Dialogue and Hierarchy in Charter Interpretation: A Comment on *R. v. Mills*." *Alberta Law Review* 38 (4): 1051–68. https://dx.doi.org/10.29173/alr1426.

Carter, Mark. 1995. "Non-Statutory Criminal Law and the Charter: The Application of the Swain Approach in *R. v. Daviault*." *Saskatchewan Law Review* 59:241–69.

– 2007. "Blackstoned Again: Common Law Liberties, the Canadian Constitution, and the Principles of Fundamental Justice." *Texas Wesleyan Law Review* 13 (2): 343–76.

Castiglione, Dario. 1996. "The Political Theory of the Constitution." *Political Studies* 44:417–35. https://doi.org/10.1111%2Fj.1467-9248.1996.tb00592.x.

Ceaser, James W. 1990. *Liberal Democracy and Political Science.* Baltimore: John Hopkins University Press.

– 2012. "Restoring the Constitution." *Claremont Review of Books: A Journal of Political Thought and Statesmanship* 12 (2): 32–7.

Choudhry, Sujit, et al. 2005. "Open Letter to the Hon. Stephen Harper from Law Professors Regarding Same-Sex Marriage." 1 September 2017. http://www.collectionscanada.gc.ca/eppp-archive/100/205/300/liberal-ef/06-01-22/www.liberal.ca/images/dir/PDFs/law_letter_to_harper_e.pdf.

Clinton, Robert Lowry. 1989. *Marbury v. Madison and Judicial Review.* Laurence: University of Kansas Press.

Debeljak, Julie. 2002. "Rights Protection without Judicial Supremacy: A Regime of the Canadian and British Models of Bills of Rights." *Melbourne Law Review* 26 (2): 285–324.

– 2017. "Rights Dialogue under the Victorian Charter: The Potential and the Pitfalls." *New Directions for Law in Australia: Essays in Contemporary Law Reform.* Acton: Australian National University Press.

Dicey, Albert Venn. (1885) 1962. *Introduction to the Study of the Law of the Constitution*, 10th ed. London: Macmillan.

Dixon, Rosalind. 2009. "The Supreme Court of Canada, Charter Dialogue, and Deference." *Osgoode Hall Law Journal* 47 (2): 235–86.

– 2015. "Partial Bills of Rights." *American Journal of Comparative Law* 63 (2): 403–37. https://doi.org/10.5131/AJCL.2015.0011.

– 2019. "Constitutional 'Dialogue' and Deference" In *Constitutional Dialogue: Rights, Democracy, and Institutions*, edited by Geoffrey Sigalet, Gregoire Webber, and Rosalind Dixon. Cambridge: Cambridge University Press.

Dodek, Adam M. 2007. "Canada as Constitutional Exporter: The Rise of the 'Canadian Model' of Constitutionalism." *Supreme Court Law Review* 36 (2): 309–36. https://ssrn.com/abstract=1062361.

– 2018. *The Charter Debates: The Special Joint Committee on the Constitution, 1980–81, and the Making of the Canadian Charter of Rights and Freedoms.* Toronto: University of Toronto Press.

Dworkin, Ronald. 1996. *Freedom's Law: The Moral Reading of the American Constitution.* Oxford: Oxford University Press.

Ekins, Richard, and Stephen Laws. 2019. "The Supreme Court Has Done Lasting Damage to Our Constitution." *Prospect Magazine, 14 December* 2020. https://www.prospectmagazine.co.uk/politics/the-supreme-court-has -done-lasting-damage-to-our-constitution-prorogation-law.

Elliott, Mark. 2011. "Interpretative Bills of Rights and the Mystery of the Unwritten Constitution." *New Zealand Law Review* 4:591–623.

– 2012. "Legal Constitutionalism, Political Constitutionalism and Prisoners' Right to Vote." *Public Law for Everyone* (blog), 2 June 2017. https:// publiclawforeveryone.com/2012/12/05/legal-constitutionalism-political -constitutionalism-and-prisoners-right-to-vote/.

– 2017. "Analysis/The Supreme Court's Judgment in *Miller.*" *Public Law for Everyone* (blog), 25 January 2017. https://publiclawforeveryone. com/2017/01/25/analysis-the-supreme-courts-judgment-in-miller/.

Epp, Charles R. 1998. *The Rights Revolution: Lawyers, Activists and Supreme Courts in a Comparative Perspective.* Chicago: University of Chicago Press.

Erdos, David. 2009. "Judicial Culture and the Politicolegal Opportunity Structure: Explaining Bills of Rights Legal Impact in New Zealand." *Law and Social Inquiry* 34 (1): 95–127. https://doi.org/10.1111/j.1747-4469.2009 .01140.x.

– 2010. *Delegating Rights Protection: The Rise of Bills of Rights in the Westminster World.* Oxford: Oxford University Press.

Finnis, John. 2016. "Terminating Treaty-Based UK Rights." UK Constitutional Law Association (blog), 2 September 2017. https://ukconstitutionallaw .org/2016/10/26/john-finnis-terminating-treaty-based-uk-rights/.

– 2019. *The Unconstitutionality of the Supreme Court's Prorogation Judgment.* London: Policy Exchange. https://policyexchange.org.uk/wp-content /uploads/2019/10/The-unconstitutionality-of-the-Supreme-Courts -prorogation-judgment.pdf.

Fish, Eric C. 2016. "Constitutional Avoidance as Interpretation and as a Remedy." *Michigan Law Review* 114:1276–1315.

Fisher, Louis. 1988. *Constitutional Dialogues: Interpretation as Political Process.* Princeton, NJ: Princeton University Press.

Flanagan, Thomas. 1997. "The Staying Power of the Legislative Status Quo: Collective Choice in Canada's Parliament after *Morgentaler.*" *Canadian*

Journal of Political Science 30 (1): 31–53. https://doi.org/10.1017 /S000842390001492X.

Foley, Michael. 1989. *The Silence of Constitutions: Gaps, "Abeyances" and the Political Temperament in the Maintenance of Government.* New York: Routledge.

Franks, Steven. 2004. "It Is the Court, Not Flag Burning, We Should Worry About." Stevenfranks.co.nz (blog), 14 December 2020. http://www.stephen franks.co.nz/it-is-the-court-not-flag-burning-we-should-worry-about/.

Gardbaum, Stephen. 2001. "The New Commonwealth Model of Constitutionalism." *American Journal of Comparative Law* 49:707–60. https:// doi.org/10.2307/841055.

– 2003. "The 'Horizontal Effect' of Constitutional Rights." *Michigan Law Review* 102:387–459. https://doi.org/10.2307/3595366.

– 2010. "Reassessing the New Commonwealth Model of Constitutionalism." *International Journal of Constitutional Law* 8 (2): 167–206. https://doi.org /10.1093/icon/moq007.

– 2013. *The New Commonwealth Model of Constitutionalism: Theory and Practice.* Cambridge: Cambridge University Press.

Geddis, Andrew. 2004. "The Horizontal Effects of the New Zealand Bill of Rights Act, as Applied in *Hosking v Runting.*" *New Zealand Law Review* 4:681–705.

Geddis, Andrew, and Bridget Fenton. 2008. " 'Which Is to Be Master?' – Rights-Friendly Statutory Interpretation in New Zealand and the United Kingdom." *Arizona Journal of International and Comparative Law* 25:733–78.

Gee, Graham, and Gregoire C.N. Webber. 2010. "What Is a Political Constitution?" *Oxford Journal of Legal Studies* 30 (2): 273–299. https://doi .org/10.1093/ojls/gqq013.

Geiringer, Claudia. 2007. "The Dead Hand of the Bill of Rights? Is the New Zealand Bill of Rights Act 1990 a Substantive Legal Constraint on Parliament's Power to Legislate?" *Otago Law Review* 11 (3): 389–415.

– 2008. "The Principle of Legality and the Bill of Rights Act: A Critical Examination of *R v. Hansen.*" *New Zealand Journal of Public and International Law* 6 (1): 59–93.

– 2013. "Sources of Resistance to Proportionality Review of Administration Power under the New Zealand Bill of Rights." *New Zealand Journal of Public and International Law* 11 (1): 123–59.

Glendon, Mary Ann. 1987. *Abortion and Divorce in Western Countries: American Failures, European Challenges.* Cambridge: Harvard University Press.

Goldsworthy, Jeffrey. 2008. "Unwritten Constitutional Principles." In *Expounding the Constitution: Essays in Constitutional Theory,* edited by Grant Huscroft. Cambridge: Cambridge University Press.

Hamilton, Alexander, James Madison, John Jay, and Gary Willis. (1788) 2003. *The Federalist: With Letters of Brutus*. Edited by Terence Ball. Cambridge: Cambridge University Press.

Harding, Mark S., and Rainer Knopff. 2013. "'Charter Values' vs. Charter Dialogue." *National Journal of Constitutional Law* 31 (2): 161–81.

Hausegger, Lori, Matthew Hennigar, and Troy Riddell. 2015. *Canadian Courts: Law, Politics, and Process*, 2nd ed. Don Mills. ON: Oxford University Press.

Haynes, C.E. 1965. *The Essentials of the British Constitution*. Oxford: Blackwell.

Hennigar, Matthew. 2004. "Expanding the 'Dialogue' Debate: Canadian Federal Responses to Lower Court Charter Decisions." *Canadian Journal of Political Science* 37 (1): 3–21. https://doi.org/10.1017/S00084239040 40041.

– 2009. "Reference Re Same-Sex Marriage: Making Sense of the Government's Litigation Strategy." In *Contested Constitutionalism: Reflections on the Canadian Charter of Rights and Freedoms*, edited by James B. Kelly and Christopher. P. Manfredi. Vancouver: University of British Columbia Press.

Hickford, Mark. 2013. "The Historical, Political Constitution – Some Reflections on Political Constitutionalism in New Zealand's History and its Possible Normative Value." *New Zealand Law Review* 4:585–623.

Hickman, Tom. 2007. "Proportionality: Comparative Law Lessons." *Judicial Review* 12 (1): 31–45. https://doi.org/10.1080/10854681.2007.11426507.

– 2010. *Public Law after the Human Rights Act*. Oxford: Hart.

Hiebert, Janet. 2002. *Charter Conflicts: What Is Parliament's Role?* Montreal: McGill-Queen's University Press.

– 2004. "New Constitutional Ideas: Can New Parliamentary Models Resist Judicial Dominance When Interpreting Rights?" *Texas Law Review* 82:1963–87.

– 2005. "Rights-Vetting in New Zealand and Canada: Similar Idea, Different Outcomes." *New Zealand Journal of Public and International Law* 3 (1): 63–103.

– 2006. "Parliamentary Bills of Rights: An Alternative Model?" *The Modern Law Review* 69:7–28. https://doi.org/10.1111/j.1468-2230.2006.00574.x.

– 2009. "Compromise and the Notwithstanding Clause: Why the Dominant Narrative Distorts Our Understanding." In *Contested Constitutionalism: Reflections on the Canadian Charter of Rights and Freedoms*, edited by Christopher P. Manfredi and J.B. Kelly. Vancouver: University of British Columbia Press.

Hiebert, Janet, and James Kelly. 2015. *Parliamentary Bills of Rights: The Experiences of New Zealand and the United Kingdom*. Cambridge: Cambridge University Press.

Hirschl, Ran. 2004. *Towards Juristocracy: The Origins and Consequences of New Constitutionalism*. Cambridge, MA: Harvard University Press.

– 2016. "Introduction: Politics and the Constitution – the Ties that Bind."
    Review of Constitutional Studies 21 (1): 3–11.
Hoffman, David, Gavin Phillipson, and Allison L. Young. 2011. "Introduction."
    In *The Impact of the UK Human Rights Act on Private Law,* edited by David
    Hoffman. Cambridge: Cambridge University Press.
Hogg, Peter W., and Allison A. Bushell. 1997. "The Charter Dialogue between
    Courts and Legislatures (Or Perhaps the Charter of Rights Isn't Such a Bad
    Thing after All)." *Osgoode Hall Law Journal* 35 (1): 75–124.
Hogg, Peter W., Allison A. Thornton, and W.K Wright. 2007. "Charter
    Dialogue Revisited – or Much Ado About Metaphors." *Osgoode Hall Law
    Journal* 45 (1): 1–65.
Howse, Robert. 1988. "*Dolphin Delivery*: The Supreme Court and the Public/
    Private Distinction in Canadian Constitutional Law." *University of Toronto
    Faculty of Law Review* 46:248–58.
Howse, Robert, and Alissa Malkin. 1997. "Canadians Are a Sovereign People:
    How the Supreme Court of Canada Should Approach the Reference on
    Quebec Secession." *Canadian Bar Review* 76 (1): 187–227.
Hughes, Patricia. 2003. "The Intersection of Public and Private under the
    Charter." *University of New Brunswick Law Journal* 52:201–14.
Hunt, Murray. 1999. "The Human Rights Act and Legal Culture: The
    Judiciary and the Legal Profession." *Journal of Law and Society* 26 (1):
    86–102. https://doi.org/10.1111/1467-6478.00117.
Hunter, Christopher. 2011. "Defining the 'Meaningful' – Collective
    Bargaining and Freedom of Association (Ontario (Attorney General)
    v. Fraser) Part I." TheCourt.ca, 15 September 2011. www.thecourt.ca
    /defining-the-meaningful-collective-bargaining-and-freedom-of
    -association-ontario-attorney-general-v-fraser-part-i/.
Huscroft, Grant. 2002. "Protecting Rights and Parliamentary Sovereignty:
    New Zealand's Experience with a Charter-Inspired Statutory Bill of Rights."
    Windsor Year Book Access of Justice 21:111–27.
– 2007. "Constitutionalism from the Top Down." *Osgoode Hall Law Journal*
    45 (1): 91–104.
– 2009. "Rationalizing Judicial Power: The Mischief of Dialogue Theory." In
    *Contested Constitutionalism: Reflections on the Canadian Charter of Rights and
    Freedoms,* edited by Christopher P. Manfredi and James B. Kelly. Vancouver:
    University of British Columbia Press.
Huscroft, Grant, and Paul Rishworth. 2009. " 'You Say You Want a Revolution':
    Bills of Rights in the Age of Human Rights." In *A Simple Common Law
    Lawyer: Essays in Honour of Michael Taggart,* edited by David Dyzenhays,
    Murray Hunt, and Grant Huscroft. Portland, OR: Hart.
Hutchinson, Allan C. 1995. *Waiting for Coraf: A Critique of Laws and Rights.*
    Toronto: University of Toronto Press.

– 2010. *Is Eating People Wrong? Great Legal Cases and How They Shaped the World.*
    Cambridge: Cambridge University Press.
Hutchinson, Allan C., and Andrew Petter. 1988. "Private Rights/Public
    Wrongs: The Liberal Lie of the Charter." *University of Toronto Law Journal*
    38 (3): 278–97.
Jackson, Sara. 2007. "Designing Human Rights Legislation: 'Dialogue,' the
    Commonwealth Model and the Role of Parliaments and Courts." *University
    of Auckland Law Review* 13:89–115.
Jacobsohn, Gary Jeffrey, 2010. *Constitutional Identity.* Cambridge, MA: Harvard
    University Press.
Jenkins, David. 2009. "Common Law Declarations of Unconstitutionality."
    International Journal of Constitutional Law 7 (2): 183–214. https://doi.org
    /10.1093/icon/mop004.
Joseph, Philip A. 2004. "Parliament, the Courts, and the Collaborative
    Enterprise." *King's College Law Journal* 15:321–45. https://doi.org/10.1080
    /09615768.2004.11427576.
Joseph, Rosara. 2013. *The War Prerogative: History, Reform, and Constitutional
    Design.* Oxford: Oxford University Press.
Kahana, Tsvi. 2001. "The Notwithstanding Mechanism and Public Discussion:
    Lessons from the Ignored Practice of Section 33 of the Charter." *Canadian
    Public Administration* 44 (3): 255–91. https://doi.org/10.1111/j.1754-7121
    .2001.tb00891.x.
Kavanagh, Aileen. 2009. *Constitutional Review under the UK Human Rights Act.*
    New York: Cambridge University Press.
Kelly, James B. 2005. *Governing with the Charter: Legislative and Judicial Activism
    and Framers' Intent.* Vancouver: University of British Columbia Press.
– 2009. "Legislative Activism and Parliamentary Bills of Rights: Institutional
    Lessons for Canada." In *Contested Constitutionalism: Reflections on the
    Canadian Charter of Rights and Freedoms*, edited by James B. Kelly and
    Christopher P. Manfredi. Vancouver: University of British Columbia Press.
– 2011. "Judicial and Political Review as Limited Insurance: The Functioning
    of the New Zealand Bill of Rights Act in 'Hard' Cases." *Commonwealth and
    Comparative Politics* 49 (3): 295–317. https://doi.org/10.1080/14662043
    .2011.582736.
Kelly, James B., and Matthew Hennigar. 2012. "The Charter of Rights and the
    Minister of Justice: Weak-Form Review within a Constitutional Charter of
    Rights." *International Journal of Constitutional Law* 10 (1): 35–68. https://doi
    .org/10.1093/icon/mor067.
Knopff, Rainer. 2003. "How Democratic Is the Charter? And Does It Matter?"
    Supreme Court Law Review 19:199–211.
Knopff, Rainer, Dennis Baker, and Sylvia LeRoy. 2009. "Courting Controversy:
    Strategic Judicial Decision Making." In *Contested Constitutionalism: Reflections*

on the Canadian Charter of Rights and Freedoms, edited by James B. Kelly and Christopher P. Manfredi. Vancouver: University of British Columbia Press.

Knopff, Rainer, and Andrew C. Banfield. 2009. " 'It's the Charter Stupid!' The Charter and the Courts in Federal Partisan Politics." In *The Canadian Charter of Rights and Freedoms after Twenty-Five Years*, edited by Joseph Eliot Magnet and Bernard Adell. Markham, ON: Butterworths.

Knopff, Rainer, Rhonda Evans, Dennis Baker, and Dave Snow. 2017. "Dialogue: Clarified and Reconsidered." *Osgoode Hall Law Journal* 54 (2): 609–44.

Kumm, Mattias. 2006. "Who Is Afraid of the Total Constitution? Constitutional Rights as Principles and the Constitutionalization of Private Law." *German Law Review* 7 (4): 341–69. https://doi.org/10.1017/S2071832 200004727.

LaSelva, Samuel V. 2018. *Canada and the Ethics of Constitutionalism: Identity, Destiny, and Constitutional faith*. Montreal: McGill-Queen's University Press.

Leane, G.W.G. 2004. "Enacting Bills of Rights: Canada and the Curious Case of New Zealand's 'Thin' Democracy." *Human Rights Quarterly* 26:152–88. DOI:10.1353/hrq.2004.0006.

Leckey, Robert. 2015. *Bills of Rights in the Common law*. Cambridge: Cambridge University Press.

Leclair, Jean. 2002. "Canada's Unfathomable Unwritten Constitutional Principles." *Queen's Law Journal* 27 (2): 389–443.

Lederman, W.R. 1991. "Charter Influences on Future Constitutional Reform." In *After Meech Lake: Lessons for the Future*, edited by David. E. Smith, Peter MacKinnon, and John C. Courtney. Saskatoon: Fifth House.

Leeson, Howard. 2001. "Section 33, the Notwithstanding Clause: A Paper Tiger?" In *Judicial Power and Canadian Democracy*, edited by Paul Howe and Peter Russell. Montreal: McGill-Queen's University Press.

Leigh, Ian. 1999. "Horizontal Rights: The Human Rights Act and Privacy: Lessons from the Commonwealth." *International and Comparative Law Quarterly* 48:57–87. https://doi.org/10.1017/S0020589300062886.

LeRoy, Sylvia. 2004. "Supreme Disabeyance: Law, Politics and the Secession Reference." MA thesis, University of Calgary.

Locke, John. (1690) 1999. *Second Treatise of Government*. Edited by C.B. Macpherson. Indianapolis, IN: Hackett.

Macfarlane, Emmett. 2012. "Conceptual Precision and Parliamentary Systems of Rights: Disambiguating 'Dialogue.' " *Review of Constitutional Studies* 17 (2): 73–100.

– 2013a. "Dialogue or Compliance? Measuring Legislatures' Policy Responses to Court Rulings on Rights." *International Political Science Review* 34 (1): 39–56. https://doi.org/10.1177%2F0192512111432565.

– 2013b. *Governing from the Bench: The Supreme Court of Canada and the Judicial Role.* Vancouver: University of British Columbia Press.

– 2017. "Dialogue, Remedies, and Positive Rights: *Carter v. Canada* as Microcosm for Past and Future Issues under the Charter of Rights and Freedoms." *Ottawa Law Review* 49 (1): 107–29.

– 2018. "Positive Rights and Section 15 of the Charter: Addressing a Dilemma." *National Journal of Constitutional Law* 38 (1): 147–68.

MacIvor, Heather. 2006. *Canadian Politics and Government in the Charter Era.* Toronto: Thomson Nelson.

Macklem, Timothy. 1999. "*Vriend v. Alberta*: Making the Private Public." *McGill Law Journal* 44:197–230.

Mahoney, James, and Kathleen Thelen. 2009. "A Theory of Gradual Institutional Change." In *Explaining Institutional Change: Ambiguity, Agency, and Power*, edited by Patrick Mahoney and Kathleen Thelen. Cambridge: Cambridge University Press.

Malcolmson, Patrick, Richard Myers, Thomas M.J. Bateman, and Gerald Baier. 2016. *The Canadian Regime: An Introduction to Parliamentary Government in Canada*, 6th ed. Toronto: University of Toronto Press.

Mancini, Mark, and Geoff Sigalet. 2020. "What Constitutes a Legitimate Use of the Notwithstanding Clause?" *Policy Options*, 20 January 2020. https:// policyoptions.irpp.org/magazines/january-2020/what-constitutes-the -legitimate-use-of-the-notwithstanding-clause/.

Manfredi, Christopher P. 1997. "Institutional Design and the Politics of Constitutional Modification: Understanding Amendment Failure in the United States and Canada." *Law and Society Review* 31 (1): 111–36. https:// doi.org/10.2307/3054096.

– 2001. *Judicial Power and the Charter: Canada and the Paradox of Liberal Constitutionalism*, 2nd ed. Oxford: Oxford University Press.

– 2002. "Strategic Judicial Behaviour and the Canadian Charter of Rights and Freedoms." In *Myth of the Sacred: The Charter, the Courts and the Politics of the Constitution in Canada*, edited by Patrick James, Donald E. Abelson, and Michael Lusztig. Montreal: McGill-Queen's University Press.

– 2007. "The Day the Dialogue Died: A Comment on Sauve v. Canada." *Osgoode Hall Law Journal* 45 (1): 105–23.

Manfredi, Christopher, and James Kelly. 1999. "Six Degrees of Dialogue: A Response to Hogg and Bushell." *Osgoode Hall Law Journal* 37 (3): 513–27.

Masterman, Roger. 2009. "Interpretations, Declarations and Dialogue: Rights Protection under the Human Rights Act and Victorian Charter of Human Rights and Responsibilities." *Public Law* 1:112–31.

Masterman, Roger, and Ian Leigh. 2013. *The United Kingdom's Statutory Bill of Rights: Constitutional and Comparative Perspectives.* Oxford: Oxford University Press.

McCormick, Peter, and Marc D. Zanoni. 2019. *By the Court: Anonymous Judgments at the Supreme Court of Canada.* Vancouver: University of British Columbia Press.

McGregor, Gaile. 2002. "Anti-claimant Bias in the Employment Insurance Appeals System: Causes, Consequences, and Public Law Remedies." *Canadian Journal of Administrative Law and Practice* 15:229–91.

McIlwain, Charles. 2005. *Constitutionalism, Ancient and Modern.* Clark, NJ: Lawbook Exchange.

McLachlin, Beverly. 2002. "Bills of Rights in Common Law Countries." *International and Comparative Law Quarterly* 51:197–203. https://doi.org /10.1093/iclq/51.2.197.

– 2006. "Unwritten Constitutional Principles: What Is Going On?" *New Zealand Journal of Public and International Law* 4 (2): 147–63.

McLean, Janet. 2001. "Legislative Invalidation, Human Rights Protection and s4 of the New Zealand Bill of Rights Act." *New Zealand Law Review* 4:421–48.

Mix-Ross, Derek B. 2009. "Exploring the Charter's Horizons: Universities, Free Speech, and the Role of Constitutional Rights in Private Legal Relations." MA thesis, University of Toronto.

Monahan, Patrick J. 2000. "The Public Policy of the Supreme Court of Canada in the *Secession Reference.*" *National Journal of Constitutional Law* 11:65–105.

Montesquieu, Charles de Secondat Baron de. (1748) 2002. *The Spirit of the Laws.* New York: Prometheus Books.

Montigny, Yves de. 1985. "Section 32 and Equality Rights." In *Equality Rights and the Canadian Charter of Rights and Freedoms,* edited by Anne Bayefsky and Mary Eberts. Toronto: Carswell.

Morton, F.L. 2001. "Dialogue or Monologue?" In *Judicial Power and Canadian Democracy,* edited by Paul Howe and Peter Russell. Montreal: McGill-Queen's University Press.

–, ed. 2002. *Law, Politics and the Judicial Process in Canada,* 3rd ed. Calgary: University of Calgary Press.

Newman, Dwight. 2015. "A Court Gone Astray on the Right to Strike." *National Post,* 26 February 2015. https://nationalpost.com/opinion/ed022715 -newman.

– 2019. "Canada's Notwithstanding Clause, Dialogue and Constitutional Identities." In *Constitutional Dialogue: Rights, Democracy, and Institutions,* edited by Geoffrey Sigalet, Gregoire Webber, and Rosalind Dixon. Cambridge: Cambridge University Press.

Nicol, Danny. 2004. "Statutory Interpretation and Human Rights After Anderson." *Public Law* (Summer): 274–82.

Nicolaides, Eleni, and Matthew Hennigar. 2018. "*Carter* Conflicts: The Supreme Court's Impact on Medical Assistance in Dying Policy." In *Policy*

Change, Courts, and the Canadian Constitution, edited by Emmett Macfarlane. Toronto: University of Toronto Press.

O'Brien, David M. 1986. *Storm Center: The Supreme Court in American Politics.* New York: W.W. Norton and Company.

Orr, Graeme. 2010. "A Fetishised Gift: The Legal Status of Flags." *Griffith Law Review* 19 (3): 504–26. https://doi.org/10.1080/10383441.2010.108 54686.

Ostberg, C.L., and Matthew E. Wetstein. 2007. *Attitudinal Decision Making in the Supreme Court of Canada.* Vancouver: University of British Columbia Press.

Palmer, Matthew. 2007. "New Zealand Constitutional Culture." *New Zealand Universities Law Review* 55:565–97.

Patenaude, Pierre. 2001. "The Provincial Judges Case and Extended Judicial Control." In *Judicial Power and Canadian Democracy,* edited by Paul Howe and Peter Russell. Kingston: McGill-Queen's University Press.

Peabody, Bruce. 1999. "Nonjudicial Constitutional Interpretation, Authoritative Settlement, and a New Agenda for Research." *Constitutional Commentary* 16 (1): 63–90.

Peacock, Anthony A. 2002. "Judicial Rationalism and the Therapeutic Constitution: The Supreme Court's Reconstruction of Equality and Democratic Process under the Charter of Rights and Freedoms." In *Myth of the Sacred: The Charter, the Courts, and the Politics of the Constitution in Canada,* edited by Patrick James, Donald. E. Abelson, and Michael Lusztig. Montreal: McGill-Queen's University Press.

Petter, Andrew. 2009. "Legalise This: The Chartering of Canadian Politics." In *Contested Constitutionalism: Reflections on the Canadian Charter of Rights and Freedoms,* edited by James B. Kelly and Christopher. P. Manfredi. Vancouver: University of British Columbia Press.

– 2010. *The Politics of the Charter: The Illusive Promise of Constitutional Rights.* Toronto: University of Toronto Press.

Phillipson, Gavin, 1999. "The Human Rights Act, 'Horizontal Effect' and the Common Law: A Bang or a Whimper?" *Modern Law Review* 62 (6): 824–49. https://doi.org/10.1111/1468-2230.00240.

– 2011. "Privacy." In *The Impact of the UK Human Rights Act on Private Law,* edited by David Hoffman. Cambridge: Cambridge University Press.

Phillipson, Gavin, and Alexander Williams. 2011. "Horizontal Effect and the Constitutional Constraint." *Modern Law Review* 74 (6): 878–910. https://doi .org/10.1111/j.1468-2230.2011.00876.x.

Poitras, Jacques. 2020. "MLAs Vote to Drop Notwithstanding Clause from Mandatory Vaccination Bill." *CBC News,* 16 June 2020. https://www.cbc.ca /news/canada/new-brunswick/mandatory-vaccination-bill-11-notwith standing-clause-1.5614659.

Poole, Thomas. 2003. "Back to the Future? Unearthing the Theory of Common Law Constitutionalism." *Oxford Journal of Legal Studies* 23 (3): 435–54. https://doi.org/10.1093/ojls/23.3.435.

– 2010. "United Kingdom: The Royal Prerogative." *International Journal of Constitutional Law* 8 (1): 146–55. https://doi.org/10.1093/icon/mop038.

Reichman, Amnon. 2002. "A Charter-Free Domain: In Defence of *Dolphin Delivery.*" *University of British Columbia Law Review* 35:329–92.

Rishworth, Paul. 2003. "When the Bill of Rights Applies." In *The New Zealand Bill of Rights*, edited by Paul Rishworth, Grant Huscroft, Scott Optican, and Richard Mahoney. New York: Oxford University Press.

– 2004. "The Inevitability of Judicial Review under 'Interpretive' Bills of Rights: Legacy to New Zealand and Commonwealth Constitutionalism?" In *Constitutionalism in the Charter Era*, edited by Grant Huscroft and Ian Brodie. Markham, ON: LexisNexis, Butterworths.

– 2007. "Taking Human Rights into the Private Sphere." In *Human Rights in the Private Sphere: A Comparative Study*, edited by Fedtke Jörg and Dawn Oliver. New York: Routledge-Cavendish.

Roach, Kent. 2001. "Constitutional and Common Law Dialogues between the Supreme Court and Canadian Legislatures." *Canadian Bar Review* 80 (1–2): 481–533.

– 2005. "Common Law Bills of Rights as Dialogue between Courts and Legislatures." *University of Toronto Law Journal* 55 (3): 733–66. https://doi.org/10.1353/tlj.2005.0027.

– 2007. "A Dialogue About Principle and a Principled Dialogue: Justice Iacobucci's Substantive Approach to Dialogue." *University of Toronto Law Journal* 57 (2): 449–77. https://doi.org/10.1353/tlj.2007.0019.

– 2016. *The Supreme Court on Trial: Judicial Activism or Democratic Dialogue.* Revised Edition. Toronto: Irwin Law.

– 2019. "Dialogue in Canada and the Dangers of Simplified Comparative Law and Populism." In *Constitutional Dialogue: Rights, Democracy, and Institutions*, edited by Geoffrey Sigalet, Gregoire Webber, and Rosalind Dixon. Cambridge: Cambridge University Press.

Robertson, David. 2010. *The Judge as Political Theorist: Contemporary Judicial Review.* Princeton, NJ: Princeton University Press.

Romanow, Roy J., John D. Whyte, and Howard A. Leeson. 1984. *Canada ... Notwithstanding: The Making of the Constitution, 1976–1982.* Toronto: Carswell/Methuen.

Ross, June. 1996. "The Common Law of Defamation Fails to Enter the Age of the Charter." *Alberta Law Review* 35:117–39. https://doi.org/10.29173/alr1065.

Rush, Mark E. 2002. "Judicial Supervision of the Political Process: Canadian and American Responses to Homosexual Rights." In *Myth of the Sacred:*

The Charter, the Courts, and the Politics of the Constitution in Canada, edited by Patrick James, Donald E. Abelson, and Michael Lusztig. Montreal: McGill-Queen's University Press.

Russell, Peter H. 1983a. "Bold Statecraft, Questionable Jurisprudence." In *And No One Cheered: Federalism, Democracy and the Constitution Act*, edited by Keith G. Banting and Richard Simeon. Toronto: Methuen.

– 1983b. "The Political Purposes of the Canadian Charter of Rights and Freedoms." *Canadian Bar Review* 61 (1): 30–54.

– 2004. *Constitutional Odyssey: Can Canadians Become a Sovereign People?* 3rd ed. Toronto: University of Toronto Press.

– 2007. "*The Notwithstanding Clause: The Charter's Homage to Parliamentary Democracy.*" *Policy Options* 28 (2): 65–68.

Russell, Peter H., Rainer Knopff, and Ted Morton. 1989. *Federalism and the Charter: Leading Constitutional Decisions*. Ottawa: Carleton University Press.

Russell, Peter H., and Lorne Sossin. 2009. *Parliamentary Democracy in Crisis*. Toronto: University of Toronto Press.

Schattschneider, Elmer Eric. 1960. *The Semisovereign People: A Realist's View of Democracy in America*. New York: Holt, Rinhart and Winston.

Schertzer, Robert. 2016. *The Judicial Role in a Diverse Federation: Lessons from the Supreme Court*. Toronto: University of Toronto Press.

Schochet, Gordon J. 1979. "Introduction: Constitutionalism, Liberalism, and the Study of Politics." In *Constitutionalism*, edited by J. Roland Pennock and John W. Chapman. New York: New York University Press.

Segal, Jeffrey A., and Harold J. Spaeth. 1993. *The Supreme Court and the Attitudinal Model*. Cambridge: Cambridge University Press.

Seidman, Louis Michael, and Mark Tushnet. 1996. *Remnants of Belief: Contemporary Constitutional Issues*. Oxford: Oxford University Press.

Sigalet, Geoffrey, Gregoire Webber, and Rosalind Dixon. 2019. "Introduction: The 'What' and 'Why' of Constitutional Dialogue" In *Constitutional Dialogue: Rights, Democracy, and Institutions*, edited by Geoffrey Sigalet, Gregoire Webber, and Rosalind Dixon. Cambridge: Cambridge University Press.

Sirota, Leonid. 2019. "Devaluing Section 33." *Double Aspect* (blog), 14 *December* 2020. https://doubleaspect.blog/2019/05/14/devaluing-section-33/.

Slattery, Brian. 1987. "The Charter's Relevance to Private Litigation: Does *Dolphin* Deliver?" *McGill Law Journal* 32:905–23.

Smillie, John. 1996. "Formalism, Fairness and Efficiency: Civil Adjudication in New Zealand." *New Zealand Law Review* 1 (2): 254–78.

– 2006. "Who Wants Juristocracy?" *Otago Law Review* 11 (2): 183–96.

Smith, Rogers M. 2008. "Historical Institutionalism and the Study of Law." In *The Oxford Handbook of Law and Politics*, edited by Keith Whittington, R. Daniel Kelemen, and Gregory A. Caldeira. Oxford: Oxford University Press.

Smithey, Shannon Ishiyama. 2002. "Cooperation and Conflict: Group Activity in *R. v. Keegstra.*" In *Myth of the Sacred: The Charter, the Courts, and the Politics of the Constitution in Canada,* edited by Patrick James, Donald. E. Abelson, and Michael Lusztig. Montreal: McGill-Queen's University Press.

Stemplewitz, Jan. 2006. "Horizontal Rights and Freedoms: The New Zealand Bill of Rights Act 1990 in Private Litigation." *New Zealand Journal of Public and International Law* 4 (2): 197–227.

Sullivan, Ruth. 2007. "Statutory Interpretation in Canada: The Legacy of Emer Driedger." In *Statutory Interpretation: Principles and Pragmatism for a New Age,* edited by Tom Gotsis. Sydney: Judicial Commission of New South Wales Agency.

Tarnopolsky, Walter S., and William F. Pentney. 2004. *Discrimination and the Law: Including Equality Rights under the Charter.* Scarborough, ON: Thomson Carswell Press.

Teles, Steven. 2012. *The Rise of the Conservative Legal Movement: The Battle for Control of the Law.* Princeton, NJ: Princeton University Press.

Tomkins, Adam. 2005. *Our Republican Constitution.* Portland, OR: Hart.

Tushnet, Mark. 1995. "Policy Distortion and Democratic Debilitation: Comparative Illumination of the Countermajoritarian Difficulty." *Michigan Law Review* 94:245–301. https://doi.org/10.2307/1289839.

– 2002. "Alternative Forms of Judicial Review." *Michigan Law Review* 101:2781–802. https://repository.law.umich.edu/mlr/vol101/iss8/9.

– 2003a. "Judicial Activism or Restraint in a Section 33 World." Review of *The Supreme Court on Trial,* by Kent Roach, *University of Toronto Law Journal* 53 (1): 89–100. https://doi.org/10.2307/3650888.

– 2003b. "New Forms of Judicial Review and the Perspectives of Rights-and Democracy-based Worries." *Wake Forest Lake Law Review* 38:813–38.

– 2008a. "Dialogic Judicial Review." *Arkansas Law Review* 61:205–16.

– 2008b. *Weak Courts, Strong Rights: Judicial Review and Social Welfare Rights in Comparative Constitutional Law.* Princeton, NJ: Princeton University Press.

– 2016. "Editorial." *International Journal of Constitutional Law* 14 (1): 1–5. https://doi.org/10.1093/icon/mow021.

Vipond, Robert Charles. 1991. *Liberty and Community: Canadian Federalism and the Failure of the Constitution.* Albany: State University of New York Press.

Waldron, Jeremy. 1999. *Law and Disagreement.* New York: Oxford University Press.

– 2016. *Political Political Theory: Essays on Institutions.* Cambridge, MA: Harvard University Press.

Walters, Mark D. 2008. "Written Constitutions and Unwritten Constitutionalism." In *Expounding the Constitution: Essays in Constitutional Theory,* edited by Grant Huscroft. Cambridge: Cambridge University Press.

Waluchow, Wilfrid J. 2007. *A Common Law Theory of Judicial Review: The Living Tree.* Cambridge: Cambridge University Press.

Webber, Gregoire C.N. 2009. "The Unfulfilled Potential of the Court and Legislative Dialogue." *Canadian Journal of Political Science* 42 (2): 443–65. https://doi.org/10.1017/S0008423909090362.

Webber, Gregoire C.N., Eric Mendelsohn, and Robert Leckey. 2019. "The Faulty Received Wisdom around the Notwithstanding Clause." *Policy Options*, 10 May 2019. https://policyoptions.irpp.org/magazines/may-2019/faulty-wisdom-notwithstanding-clause/.

Weiler, Paul. 1974. *In the Last Resort: A Critical Study of the Supreme Court of Canada.* Toronto: Carswell.

Whittington, Keith E. 2002. "Extrajudicial Constitutional Interpretation: Three Objections and Responses." *North Carolina Law Review* 80:773–851.

Wilberg, Hanna. 2015. "Resisting the Siren Song of the *Hansen* Sequence: The State of Supreme Court Authority on the Sections 5 and 6 Conundrum." *Public Law Review* 26 (1): 39–60. http://hdl.handle.net/2292/26038.

Woehrling, José. 1999. "The Quebec Secession Reference: Some Unexpected Consequences of Constitutional First Principles." In *The Quebec Decision: Perspectives on the Supreme Court Ruling on Secession,* edited by David Schneiderman. Toronto: James Lorimer and Company.

Young, Allison. 2017. *Democratic Dialogue and the Constitution.* Oxford: Oxford University Press.

– 2019. "Dialogue and Its Myths: 'Whatever People Say I Am, That's What I'm Not.' " In *Constitutional Dialogue: Rights, Democracy, and Institutions,* editor Geoffrey Sigalet, Gregoire Webber, and Rosalind Dixon. Cambridge: Cambridge University Press.

Cases Cited

Canada

Barbeau v. British Columbia (Attorney General), [2003] BCCA 406

Bell ExpressVu Limited Partnership v. Rex, [2002] 2 SCR 559

Canada (Prime Minister) v. Khadr, [2010] 1 SCR 44

Carter v. Canada (Attorney General), [2015] 1 SCR 331

City of Toronto et al. v. Ontario (Attorney General), [2018] ONSC 515

Conacher and Democracy Watch v. Canada (Prime Minister), [2010] 3 FCR 411

Daganais v. Canadian Broadcasting Corp., [1994] 3 SCR 835

Dunbar & Edge v. Yukon (Government of) & Canada (A.G.), [2004] YKSC 54

Fleming v. Atkinson, [1959] SCR 513

Good Spirit School Division No. 204 v. Christ the Teacher Roman Catholic Separate School Division No. 212, [2017] SKQB 109

Halpern v. Canada, [2003] OJ No. 2268

Harvard College v. Canada (Commissioner of Patents), [2002] 4 SCR 45

Health Services and Support – Facilities Subsector Bargaining Assn. v. British Columbia, [2007] 2 SCR 391

Hendricks and Leboeuf v. Quebec, [2004] RJQ 2506

Highwood Congregation of Jehovah's Witnesses (Judicial Committee) v. Wall, [2018] 1 SCR 750

Hill v. Church of Scientology of Toronto, [1995] 2 SCR 1130

Hills v. Canada (A.G.), [1988] 1 SCR 513

Law Society of British Columbia v. Trinity Western University, [2018] 2 SCR 293

McKinney v. University of Guelph, [1990] 3 SCR 229

Noble v. Calder, [1952] OR 577

Ontario (A.G.) v. Fraser, [2011] 2 SCR 3

Operation Dismantle v. The Queen, [1985] 1 SCR 441

PSAC v. Canada, [1987] 1 SCR 424

Reference Re Objection by Quebec to a Resolution to amend the Constitution, [1982] 2 SCR 793

Reference Re Public Service Employee Relations Act (Alta), [1987] 1 SCR 313

Reference Re Remuneration of Judges of the Provincial Court (PEI), [1997] 3 SCR 3

Reference Re Resolution to amend the Constitution, [1981] 1 SCR 753

Reference Re Same-Sex Marriage, [2004] 3 SCR 698

Reference Re Secession of Quebec, [1998] 2 SCR 217

Reference Re Supreme Court Act, ss. 5 and 6, [2014] 1 SCR 433

Retail, Wholesale and Department Store Union v. Dolphin Delivery Ltd. [1986] 2 SCR 573

R. v. Big M Drug Mart, [1985] 1 SCR 295

R. v. Butler, [1992] 1 SCR 452

R. v. Clayton, [2007] 2 SCR 725

R. v. Daviault, [1994] 3 SCR 63

R. v. Hall, [2002] 3 SCR 309

R. v. Leary, [1978] 1 SCR 29

R. v. Mills, [1999] 3 SCR 668

R. v. Morgentaler, [1988] 1 SCR 30

R. v. Oakes, [1986] 1 SCR 103

R. v. O'Connor, [1995] 4 SCR 411

R. v. Salituro, [1991] 3 SCR 654

R. v. Sharpe, [2001] 1 SCR 45

R. v. Swain, [1991] 1 SCR 933

RWDSU v. Saskatchewan, [1987] 1 SCR 460

Symes v. Canada, [1993] 4 SCR 695

Saskatchewan Federation of Labour v. Saskatchewan, [2015] 1 SCR 245

Toronto (City) v. Ontario (Attorney General), [2019] ONCA 732

Trial Lawyers Association of British Columbia v. British Columbia (Attorney General), [2014] 3 SCR 31

Vriend v. Alberta, [1998] 1 SCR 493

Working Families Ontario v. Ontario, [2021] ONSC 4076

New Zealand

Burt v. Governor-General, [1992] 3 NZLR 672

Curtis v. Ministry of Defence, [2002] 2 NZLR 744

Drew v. Attorney-General, [2002] 1 NZLR 58

Gisborne Herald Co Ltd. v. Solicitor General, [1995] 3 NZLR 563

Hopkinson v. Police, [2004] 3 NZLR 704 (HC)

Hosking v. Runting, [2004] 1 NZLR 1

Knight v. Commissioner of Inland Revenue, [1991] 2 NZLR 30

Lange v. Atkinson, [1998] 3 NZLR 424

Moonen v. Film and Literature Board of Review, [2000] 2 NZLR 9

Quilter v. Attorney-General, [1998] 1 NZLR 523

R. v. H., [1994] 2 NZLR 143

R. v. Hansen, [2007] 3 NZLR 1

R. v. Holford, [2001] 1 NZLR 385

R. v. N (No. 2), [1999] 5 NZLR 72

R. v. Phillips, [1991] 3 NZLR 175

R. v. Pora, [2001] 2 NZLR 37

R. v. Poumako, [2000] 2 NZLR 695

R. v. Rangi, [1992] 1 NZLR 385

Shaw v. Commissioner of Inland Revenue, [1999] 3 NZLR 154

Taylor v. Attorney-General, [2017] 3 NZLR 24

TVNZ v. Newsmonitor Services Ltd., [1994] 2 NZLR 91

United Kingdom

A. v. Secretary of State for the Home Department, [2004] UKHL 56

A.G. v. Jonathan Cape Ltd., [1976] QB 752

Campbell v. MGN Limited, [2003] UKHL 22

Ghaidan v. Godin-Mendoza, [2004] UKHL 30

Hyde v. Hyde and Woodmansee, [1866] LR 1 P&D 130

McDonald v. McDonald, [2016] UKSC 28

R. v. A., [2002] UKHL 25

R. v. Dudley and Stephens, [1884] 14 QBD 273

R. v. Lambert, [2002] UKHL 37

R. v. Secretary of State for Foreign and Commonwealth Affairs, ex p Bancoult (No 2), [2008] UKHL 61

R. (Daly) v. Secretary of State for the Home Department, [2001] UKHL 26

R. (on the application of Miller and another) (Respondents) v. Secretary of State for Exiting the European Union (Appellant), [2017] UKSC 5

R. (on the application of Miller) (Appellant) v. The Prime Minister (Respondent) Cherry and others (Respondents) v. Advocate General for Scotland (Appellant) (Scotland), [2019] UKSC 41

Searle v. Wallbank, [1947] AC 341

United States

Alden v. Maine, 527 US 706 (1999)

Brown v. Board of Education, 347 US 483 (1954)

Griswold v. Connecticut, 381 US 479 (1965)

Reynolds v. Sims, 377 US 533 (1964)

Roe v. Wade, 410 US 113 (1973)

www.ingramcontent.com/pod-product-compliance
Lightning Source LLC
Chambersburg PA
CBHW051725260326
41914CB00031B/1744/J

Index